Not So Dumb

The Life and Career of
Marie Wilson

BY CHARLES TRANBERG

NOT SO DUMB: THE LIFE AND CAREER OF MARIE WILSON
© 2006 Charles Tranberg

PUBLISHED IN THE USA BY:

BEARMANOR MEDIA
PO BOX 71426
ALBANY, GA 31708
WWW.BEARMANORMEDIA.COM

LIBRARY OF CONGRESS CATALOGING-IN-PUBLICATION DATA:

Tranberg, Charles.
  Not so dumb : the life and career of marie wilson / by Charles Tranberg.
    p. cm.
  Includes bibliographical references and index.
  ISBN-13: 978-1-59393-049-6
  1. Wilson, Marie, 1916-1972. 2. Actors--United States--Biography. I. Title.
  PN2287.W492T73 2006
  791.4302'8092--dc22
  [B]

                        2006024990

Printed in the United States.

Design and Layout by Valerie Thompson.

TABLE OF CONTENTS

INTRODUCTION

Marie Wilson is best remembered today as the daffy, not so bright, yet lovable Irma Petersen from the long running radio show *My Friend Irma*. Irma was constantly creating situations which got her friends, particularly her roommate Jane, into one mishap after another. Irma is the type of girl who would tell her boyfriend that she was spending the weekend with a war hero without telling him that the war hero is a canine. She is the type of girl who is told by her employer to deliver some plans to the Pentagon in Washington, and ends up going to the other Washington on the pacific coast. Irma is the type of girl who joins the WACS so she'll be closer to her boyfriend only to discover she had misunderstood and he wasn't drafted—he was drafty. Irma is the type of girl who thinks that flypaper is only used on airplanes.

Irma's stupidity is redeemed because she always means well and her heart is as big as her brain is small. Perhaps the best example of Irma's lovability is the classic Christmas episode of *My Friend Irma* where Irma plans a surprise Christmas Eve party for the gang—Jane, Jane's boyfriend Richard Rhinelander III, Irma's sharpie boyfriend Al, the neighbor Professor Kropotkin and the landlady, Mrs. O'Reilly—without realizing that they might have other plans. Irma is shattered when one by one her friends tell her that they can't make it to the party, and Irma has the realization that she is the one who will be all alone on Christmas Eve. Irma tries to get a ticket home to Minnesota and only has $11 and asks the train conductor how far that would get her? "Niagara Falls" is the reply, "Well, I'm not even getting married," Irma innocently says. While Irma is sadly walking the streets on Christmas Eve—feeling very alone—her friends one by one make the decision that they can't allow their friend Irma to be alone and make plans for a surprise party for her.

Marie Wilson was very adept at bringing out both sides of Irma's persona—the daffy, scatter-brained "dumb blonde" and the innocent, lovable waif who everybody looks out for. Perhaps it is because she had spent her entire professional career practically playing nothing but the "Dumb Dora" parts that she felt so comfortable in Irma's shoes? But one thing is for sure, Marie

Wilson was no scatter-brain in her real life. From the time Marie had been a little girl she dreamed of becoming an actress and she worked hard from an early age to make her dream come true. Marie, all on her own, realized she needed a gimmick which would differentiate her from the many other young, good-looking, busty blondes who were seeking Hollywood careers. She wrote a monologue which she would deliver at every audition—playing the part of a dumb blonde. It opened up doors, but it also typed her. Eventually she was signed by a major motion picture studio, and from that point on—with few exceptions—she was the character she herself had created.

Marie worked tirelessly for over twenty years and experienced the peaks and valleys of any major career. First she was signed by Warner Brothers and after a dozen or so "B" pictures she was finally given her big opportunity in a star-making role opposite James Cagney in an adaptation of the big stage success *Boy Meets Girl*. She won critical applause for her role as the sweet but uneducated Suzy, but within a year of that films release Marie was dumped from Warner Brothers because they didn't think she could ever escape her screen persona and become a true star. From there she went on the vaudeville circuit and appeared in a string of undistinguished films before being rescued by the cigar chomping comedian Ken Murray who cast Marie in his burlesque revue *Blackouts* and seven days per week for seven years Marie exhibited her sensational body in a mock striptease (always popular with the stream of servicemen visiting Hollywood during the war).

Then came Irma. Writer-producer Cy Howard had a vision of his Irma. She had to be very pretty and yet not sexy—and somebody suggested he try Marie. Howard was dubious because she was a knock-out—there wasn't anyway Marie Wilson couldn't be considered sexy, but he went to see her at the *Blackouts*. She was sexy, but her personality didn't allow her to take it seriously and so it wasn't offensive to the women in the audience—and besides, as Howard would later point out, it was all in her face—she had a wholesome, pretty face with deep blue eyes and an innocence about her. For seven years *Irma* was one of the hottest shows on radio and spanned two motion pictures which were both huge successes—except it is not Marie who is remembered for those films—but a hot new comedy team named Martin and Lewis. Finally Irma made it to television and enjoyed a two-and-a-half year run.

In the years after Irma Marie kept searching for that vehicle which would put her on top again, but she never found it, yet was content anyway. She was now happily married and had a son she doted on. She continued to work in nightclubs and occasional television and film appearances, but it didn't consume her. Besides times were changing and her persona was growing out of fashion by the mid 60's and into the early 70's when many women looked down on what they saw as the stereotypes of the Irma persona—the dumb, big busted blonde. Of course, Irma, like Marie herself, was always a career girl and it was Irma who worked and often supported her perpetually unemployed boyfriend Al. Marie in her "real life" from the age of sixteen was the main source of support to her large family. In short,

Marie was liberated when many of the feminists were in their diapers.

Marie was always philosophical about her decision to play "dumb blonde" parts. "I don't think I realized at first how completely I had sold myself down the river as a dumb blonde. I didn't care, and I still don't care as long as I have a chance to play comedy roles and learn the business of acting as I go along." She was often asked by reporters or fans if she was really dumb, and her stock reply was always, "Naturally, do you want me to lose my job?"

She didn't live long enough to see her comedy persona come back in fashion in the late 70's when the so-called "jiggle shows" came to television. One show in particular had a character who in almost everyway was *Irmaesque*. *Three's Company* was a television show about three roommates—two women and one man who platonically live together. The two female roommates were named Janet and Chrissy, but on closer examination (or even not so close) they were actually Jane and Irma. Like Jane, Janet was brunette, practical, pretty and considered the "smart one" while Suzanne Sommer's Chrissy Snow was blonde, sexy—yet in an innocent way, enormously sweet and dumb as a rock. The show became one of televisions biggest hits and the dumb blonde was back in fashion. Yet most of them lacked the good-natured humor, pathos and innocence which Marie's dumb blonde always possessed.

To be honest, I didn't know a whole lot about Marie Wilson when I agreed to take on this project. I knew she was a radio actress and she had been in the two *Irma* films, but those two films were only important to me because they launched Dean Martin and Jerry Lewis. I had no idea that Marie had made more than forty films—working with people like Laurel and Hardy, Bette Davis, Jane Wyman, Olivia de Havilland, Boris Karloff, Carole Lombard, James Cagney, Fred MacMurray, George Raft, Ann Sheridan, Groucho Marx, Rosalind Russell and Jimmy Stewart. I didn't realize she was a major pin-up girl during World War Two, rivaling Betty Grable and Rita Hayworth. It was news to me that she spent seven years as one of the headliners of Ken Murray's *Blackouts*—one of the biggest stage hits in Los Angeles history—and performed 2,332 consecutive performances without a day off! I didn't realize that she was one of the few people in show business who was successful in all four major mediums—stage, screen, radio and television. She may not have been the biggest star in all of those mediums (she was certainly one of the biggest for a time in radio), but she certainly was never out of work for over twenty years.

Her personal story was unique. She supported a family of nine from the age of sixteen and brought them all to Hollywood to live with her when she inherited $11,000. She was romantically involved with a director more than twenty years older than she for several years, and didn't have the heart to tell him when she married her first husband—keeping it a secret from him because she didn't want to hurt his feelings. Her energy level was extraordinary. There was a period of time when she was doing a stage show, a weekly radio show and shooting a motion picture all at the same time, yet in 1950 she nearly died due to blood poisoning and a case of phlebitis. She met her second husband while working with him in a play in which she starred with her first husband. She enjoyed a long and happy second marriage and adopted a son she was devoted to. She attempted to adopt a daughter a few years later, and was heartbroken when the birth mother changed her mind. She spent her final five years fighting cancer, but never gave up the optimism and generous spirit she always possessed. In fact, her generosity was legendary. One of her friends once said, "Marie will die the most beloved old lady in the poor house." She packed a lot of life and experiences in her all too short fifty-six years.

As always, writing a biography is not a solitary thing, and I have people I'm grateful to for their help. First, Elizabeth K. Miller, who spent hours poring through the scripts of the *My Friend Irma* radio shows which are held at the Thousand Oaks Library in California. She was able to come up with synopses to most of the *Irma* episodes broadcast, many never published before in either book or on the web. Elizabeth was later assisted by Caroline Mekhiel. This book would not be complete without their diligent assistance.

My friend Derek Tague, who so ably assisted me on my previous book, *I Love the Illusion: The Life and Career of Agnes Moorehead*, once again made copies of the vast clippings files at the Billy Rose Library of Lincoln Center. He sent me literally hundreds of clippings related to Marie's life and career from newspapers and magazines. I hope anytime I write a book, I'll have Derek's help because he is invaluable.

Charles Stumpf, a generous and kind man—as well as a fellow author, made available to me notes he had kept regarding Marie Wilson. He also provided some of the photographs which appear in this book. My thanks to Andrew Pepoy for allowing me to use his collection of Marie Wilson memorabilia including many photographs which are included in this book.

I want to thank the USC School of Cinema and Television for making available to me the Warner Brothers Legal files regarding Marie Wilson. Those files were a great asset in understanding the rules and regulations which Marie had to endure over the course of her five years at the studio as a contract player.

My thanks to the man who suggested this project, my publisher, Ben Ohmart. Ben also kindly provided me with his own files regarding Marie Wilson as well as the American Film Institute catalog of her films which were enormously helpful in providing some of the trivia which I was able to incorporate in the narrative regarding Marie's films. I'm very grateful to be associated with BearManor Media, a publishing house which insists that people like Marie Wilson not be forgotten.

Finally, my wholehearted Thanks to the people who helped make my first book, the biography of Agnes Moorehead, a big seller for BearManor Media and the kind words many of them have passed on to me. I truly appreciate it.

CHARLES TRANBERG
MADISON, WISCONSIN, NOVEMBER 10, 2005

CHAPTER ONE
DREAMS OF STARDOM
1916-1935

Katharine Elizabeth Wilson always wanted to be an actress ever since she was a little girl. She was born only forty miles from Hollywood in the then sleepy farming community of Anaheim, California on August 19, 1916. Today Anaheim is in the heart of huge Orange County and houses Disneyland among other popular southern California tourist attractions. Back in 1916 Anaheim housed more orange trees than people.

In her spare time Little Kathy liked to go to the cinema and see the movies of her favorite star, Mary Pickford. She later said that she saw Pickford in *Pollyanna* more than a dozen times and identified with the curly haired waif which Pickford portrayed on the screen. Like Pollyanna Kathy was always optimistic and cheerful and her enthusiasm was contagious. She didn't mind being a "goody two shoes," if it was good enough for her idol it was good enough for her. When she wasn't going to the cinema Kathy enjoyed reading the fan magazines, and cutting out articles on her favorite stars—particularly Pickford.

Kathy's father died when she was five. He'd been a successful enough middle-classed businessman to leave his family some savings and a nest-egg for Kathy, which stipulated that she could not inherit the money until she was sixteen years of age. Her father probably hoped that she would use the money to go to college, but he did not specify and by that time Kathy had other ideas of how his legacy would support her.

Within a couple of years her mother, Genevieve, remarried a man named Robert White who had several children. Kathy and her sister Marie now had two half-brothers and two half sisters living with them—as well as her grandfather on her mother's side who came to live with the family after his wife died. Kathy called her stepfather "Uncle Frank" even though his actual name was Robert—for some reason he reminded Kathy of a "Frank" more than a "Robert." Her stepfather was often in ill health and was partially deaf and Kathy would later recall that he spoke in a "stentorian voice and seldom heard any answers." He considered himself an inventor, and despite lots of interesting ideas was never able to patent one. Kathy later said that "I just had to work, My stepdaddy was the sweetest man in the whole world, but he didn't make a lot of money."

Kathy was developing into a very beautiful young woman. By age thirteen she had curly blonde hair, deep blue eyes, a slim waist, a blossoming bosom and very long legs which were tanned by the Southern California sun. She also had very long eye lashes which attracted much attention. According to Douglas Churchill, "she measured them carefully, and they hit the three-quarters of an inch mark on the ruler. Nature did it—no salves—and nature was crazily expansive. It got to be a bit of a bore, always having her friends tugging at those fringes to see if they were real, but maybe the exercise made them grow longer and longer!" She was already attracting boys and her protective "old fashioned" grandfather used to make it tough on the lads by backing them up against the fireplace mantel and "jabbing home his points by poking them in the vest."

At about this time she traveled by bus to Hollywood to compete in a contest sponsored by a movie theater to find the girl who would most likely become Jean Harlow's double. Her dream of becoming a movie star had not abetted. The publicity stunt did get her picture in the paper but didn't get her what she hoped it would—a Hollywood studio contract to be in motion pictures. In a Photoplay magazine profile from June, 1936, only a year after Kathy (then known as Marie Wilson) had been signed by the Warner Brothers studio as a contract player, writer Mitzi Cummings summed up Kathy's feelings at this period of her life, "Deep within the heart of this little girl, who today has the entire country predicting stardom for her, was a desire to go on the stage. A desire to be admired—to be famous—to be fussed over. One couldn't get much fussing in a house with several step-children, a sick father and an old grandpa and a busy mother, so Marie went her way, dreaming her own dreams." This house with nine family members was full of activity and noise and Kathy would recall few quiet times, "When Grandpa gets his paper and Uncle Frank gets a new idea for an invention and brother gets appendicitis or something, we have peace in the house."

The family had pretty much spent the legacy which had been left to Kathy's mother by her deceased father. Her stepfather, often ill, was not successful—it always seemed that there was another inventor just one step ahead of him. So while attending school Kathy tried to get experience in acting by appearing in school plays and talent shows. She wanted to take dancing lessons but the family didn't have enough money to pay for them. She had a friend who was taking lessons and through doing odd jobs Kathy managed to save $5.00 which she paid to her friend to teach her the routines which her friend learned in dancing class.

She also talked this friend into accompanying her on Monday nights to Loew's State Theater to see if they could land a dancing job. Her friend was not sure they would be successful, but Kathy was determined. One week they found themselves with another group of young hopefuls waiting to be discovered. Week after week Kathy and her friend would come to Loew's and week after week they were not called upon to audition. By the fourth Monday her friend finally had enough and dropped out, not wanting to waste anymore time, so Kathy talked her mother into taking her. Kathy looked physically older than her age; she was only thirteen but with makeup could pass for seventeen or more. On this particular Monday night she dressed herself in a black frilly costume which she had sewed herself. Kathy, with her mother at her side, waited patiently to be called upon to audition. Kathy was beginning to give up hope when she was finally called upon. She did a good job and the theatre was interested in her, but she had to admit to them that she was only thirteen years old—with her mother at her side she couldn't get away with telling a white lie, so she didn't get the job, since the theatre didn't employ children.

In August, 1932 Kathy finally got the inheritance left by her father—after taxes she received a lump sum of $11,000. She had been thinking long and hard about how she wanted to spend the money. She knew her mother wanted her to save it or use it for her education, but Kathy decided she wanted to use it in pursuit of her dreams of stardom. Her mother was very hesitant when Kathy told her, but it was her money and she decided that Kathy could use it as she saw fit. Kathy decided she wanted to move to Hollywood and make the rounds of casting offices to achieve her dream of being discovered and getting a Hollywood movie contract. But, being very family orientated, she wanted all of the family to live with her.

Kathy and her mother went to Hollywood where they found a house at the top of Gower Street that was large enough for the entire clan. Kathy immediately paid a years rent on it. Kathy then went grocery shopping and bought over $500 worth of canned goods—a considerable amount in those days. She bought a used car—a convertible—which she felt would attract attention. She bought clothes for the rest of the family and had their teeth fixed. She also paid off doctor bills which had been incurred by her stepfather. She felt when she went to auditions she needed to look the part of a successful aspiring actress so she bought herself a used $900 mink coat and several evening gowns. By the time she finished her $11,000 legacy had dwindled down to a $1.38 overdraft at the bank. She also discovered that while she had this mink coat and glamorous evening gowns to wear that she had completely forgotten to buy dress shoes to wear with them! Hollywood columnist Louella Parsons would later recall, "In the early days, she would apply for jobs wearing a mink coat and sneakers." She also felt that the name "Kathy White" wasn't flashy enough and wanted to take on a stage name. Her sister was named "Marie" a name which Kathy had always liked, so she took that as her first name. At first she thought she would call herself "Marie White" with her sister's first name and her stepfather's last name, but in the end believed that "Marie Wilson" had a nice ring to it. From that time forward Kathy Wilson was known professionally as Marie Wilson.

She moved the entire family to Hollywood to live with her in the house she had already paid the year's rent on. The other family members appreciated what

Marie was trying to do and in their own ways tried to help out. One of her half-brothers got a job working in a kitchen and her stepfather kept trying to come up with an invention which would strike them rich, "if General Motors hadn't beat him to the patent." Between auditions and occasional "extra" work Marie worked in a department store. One Christmas season she worked in the toy department in a downtown Los Angeles department store. The store was located in a working class area of town and it often frustrated and saddened Marie to see the little children come into the store and their eyes widen at the sight of the toys that their parents could not afford to buy for them. Thinking nothing more about it, the big-hearted Marie would mark seventy-five cent dolls down to ten cents, and sometimes when she was wrapping packages she would include some additional toy—at no charge. She was eventually fired, but not because her charity was discovered, but because she refused to sell a $25 toy to a drunk because she saw that the drunk couldn't really afford it.

Even though Marie and her family were struggling financially Marie felt it was important to create the illusion that she was well to do. "When I woke up to the fact that I was down to my last nickel, I didn't know where to turn, what to do or where to go," Marie later wrote, "I wasn't an inch closer to a screen career than I had been in Anaheim. I had my mink coat, the Packard car, and a closetful of beautiful clothes. I couldn't eat them, of course, and, since I was still determined to become a movie actress whether I starved or not, I decided to use them to keep up the front I still believed necessary for success. All my friends thought I was rich and I continued to let them think so even when the Wilson depression was at its worst. I made my family promise not to tell anyone how poor we were and we all agreed not to ask anyone for help—not even our friends in Anaheim."

For a time she attended Beverly Hills High, but eventually dropped out to devote her full energies towards landing a studio contract. She began going on auditions—one of her earliest was at Paramount pictures which in late 1932 was casting the film **Alice in Wonderland**. But she had little luck. She was determined that she needed some professional training so she began to take acting lessons. In a profile of Marie written just a few years later, writer Mitzi Cummings wrote of Marie's relationship with her acting teacher, Mrs. Saunders, "She, and only she recognized that Marie's naiveté, her whimsical, funny reactions, her baby face, her unconsciously awkward manner and conversation was money in he bank. Here, she said, is a natural comedienne. Marie was 'different'. Marie was also very pretty, with a glorious figure. There was nobody like her on the screen. So Mrs. Saudners, the teacher, went to work."

Mrs. Saunders spent a great deal of time working with Marie on her voice. When she first met her, it was very thin, so she worked with her on voice exercises and within a few months the pitch of Marie's voice had mellowed. Marie would later credit Mrs. Saunders for teaching her how to speak, "how to talk that is, like you're talking to somebody."

Marie was seventeen by this time, part woman and still part child. She would occasionally get restless and fidget during her sessions with Mrs. Saunders. She often would interrupt lessons to go get something to eat—often she asked for a chocolate bar, but Mrs. Saunders said that might cause her face to break out and better instead to have an apple. Over time Marie and Mrs. Saunders became very good friends and when a lesson was over she would often invite Mrs. Saunders to take a drive with her in her convertible. After a while Mrs. Saunders got leery of taking drives with Marie because Marie often let her gas tank get so low that they would run out of gas. But this never fazed the ever optimistic Marie who would tell Mrs. Saunders, "Somebody will come along and give us a hefty push to the gas station."

Interestingly it was running out of gas which led Marie to her first big break. There are two stories of how Marie came to meet director Nick Grinde, the man who would become her mentor and eventually her lover. Grinde happened to live next door to Marie on that hill up on Gower Street. One version goes that one day Grinde was terribly disturbed by honking outside his house. He went to investigate and discovered that Gower Street was backed up with cars honking and that directly in front of his house in her stalled car was Marie. Grinde went out and approached the car and was immediately enchanted by the young, good-looking bonde behind the wheel. He helped push her car out of the middle of the street and they introduced one another and learned that they were neighbors.

The other version is that Marie planned the whole thing—that she found out that the distinguished looking forty year old man who lived next door was then an Assistant Director at MGM, and could potentially help her career. Rather than simply go over and introduce herself, she plotted to stall her car directly in front of Grinde's house when she knew that he would be home. According to this story Grinde came over and looked under the hood and told Marie, "Carburetor's flooded." Marie knew this to be the case because she had been studying for days on how to flood her carburetor.

Whichever version is true, the point is that Marie did get to know Grinde very well. One account says that from that point forward "Marie got very neighborly. She was always paying visits which would consist of a recital of what she had done that day, or a solemn reading of her dramatic lesson, or she'd hop into the kitchen and cook him some delectable pork chops with tasty oyster dressing. Eventually (Grinde) got used to her." According to a 1936 article Grinde came to enjoy Marie's company very much especially, "her unconscious funniness, her vague, whimsical view points, her determination and courage in seeking a picture career, all these things became important to him. He found himself expressing faith in her eventual success. The faith began to get all mixed up with love."

Grinde wasn't the only man who bumped into Marie on the road who came away smitten by her charms. Another was a newspaper man named Douglas Churchill. Churchill literally bumped into Marie's fender while driving down

Hollywood Blvd. when Marie made an unexpected sudden stop. Churchill later recalled that the bump didn't amount to much but that he was determined to give the driver a piece of his mind. So he got out of his car and approached Marie—clad in her mink coat and sneakers, having just come from an audition. He was smitten by her youthful beauty and clear blue eyes smiling up at him. Churchill forgot that he was going to give her a piece of his mind and began sputtering that she "ought to be in pictures." He then took her into a nearby drug store where he got on a pay phone and called a friend who worked at RKO pictures and told him that he had just discovered "the most gorgeous blonde in Hollywood" and was bringing her to the studio to do a test.

Marie in an early glamour shot.
The Stumpf-Ohmart collection.

The result was a bit part as a ship passenger in a film called ***Down to Her Last Yatch***. She thought it would be her big break even though she is really nothing more than an extra. Marie would later recall that when she was signed for ***Down To Her Last Yatch*** that she and her family "had a celebration at home that night and instead of hamburger we had Swiss steak . . . it took six weeks to shoot the picture and I got $10 a day. I thought I was in the movies for good. I thought I was on Easy Street and that I'd never have to smell or eat hamburger again— but you can never tell in Hollywood. It was eight months before I got another part! And before I did my money was gone and we were back on our depression diet." Marie's memory of doing what she came to refer to as "that yatching picture" was spending two days in the hospital with a bad case of sunburn.

Marie continued to go out on auditions and did get regular work as an extra, but she took chances too. One day she got a tip that Paramount was looking for a blonde for the film ***The Pursuit of Happiness***. She somehow, perhaps through one of her connections, crashed the studio gate and managed to get into the office of the director of the film, Alexander Hall. She spoke quickly, interrupting the surprised and exasperated Hall, "How do you know I'm not an actress if you don't give me a chance?" she asked Hall, "Nobody would believe Elisabeth Bergner if they didn't know who she was." She then began reciting lines from the last lesson of some play she had memorized for her acting teacher. She was unintentionally very funny—and Hall couldn't help but laugh at the situation and admire Marie for her pluck. He decided to test her for the part of the servant girl. The test went well, but she was discarded because she was too blonde to be teamed with another very blonde actress (at the time), Joan Bennett, the star of the picture.

Marie would later refer to this time, remorsefully, as her "golddigger period." The family had a difficult time getting food on the table. Marie was doing occasional extra jobs but the $10 per day she was paid went almost as soon as it came in with the large family she was helping to support. Being an attractive young budding starlet in Hollywood Marie was constantly being asked out on dates. She used these dates as a way to get food for her family. "I will never forget the first time I tried it," Marie later explained. "I felt more nervous than on the day I took a screen test. I felt pretty much ashamed too, but we needed meat, and so—I would just happen to remember as we passed a market that I had promised my mother I would bring home some hamburger for the dog. I explained it was a very big dog, and when my escort drew up to the curb and hopped out to play errand boy I said again it was a very big dog, and ate as much as two pounds of meat at a meal . . . the family had hamburger for dinner the next day—the only taste of meat we'd had in a week . . . As a safeguard against getting caught in my deception I was very careful never to accept a date with the same boy twice."

It was tough sledding over these months for Marie and her family financially. In a move which demonstrated that she wasn't a dumb blonde in "real life," Marie came up with an idea which ultimately made it possible to keep the family fed—without relying on her male admirers for meat. About a block from where Marie and her family lived was a series of shops which were just getting by—just able to pay their bills—but without any real profits. The shops were on a busy street but the traffic wasn't stopping frequently enough at any of them. Marie guessed that the problem was that there was no stop sign. The shop owners recognized that this was one of their major problems and had even applied at City Hall for a stop sign but had been continually turned down.

"It occurred to me," Marie would later state. "That I might do something to help . . . I didn't know where the city hall was located, but I told them I did and that I knew a few important officials that might listen to me. First, though, before I did anything, they'd have to sign a paper agreeing to give me credit at their shops for whatever I wanted for as long as I wanted . . . I told the butcher, the baker, and the candlestick maker sorrowfully, and the only silver we'd have for the next few months would be what we could scrape up from the linings of the clouds the poets rave about. After a long look at my mink coat, my good clothes, and the big car, they finally decided I was worth the risk and each, in turn, signed the agreement I had written up."

The next day Marie located City Hall found the proper officials who administrated traffic stops and signs and went in. "There was a lot of hemming and haw-hawing after I finished," Marie recalled, "and I turned on my heel and made what I thought was a grand exit. I tried a different style of approach the next day with the same result, but I refused to quit. Finally after my sixth visit, they told me to stay home and give them a chance to catch up on their work. Two weeks later a crew of men came out and believe me, there was much rejoicing at the Wilson household when we saw the stop sign go up. I got all the store credit I needed, my family had proper food, and if we were short of actual money we didn't mind. I feel pretty proud of that accomplishment. I still do." When Marie finally did find stable work as an actress she paid back the store keepers for what they allowed her family on credit.

It was Marie's budding friendship with Nick Grinde that really paved the way for her first real break in Hollywood. Grinde was the co-writer and dialogue director on the Laurel and Hardy musical-comedy ***Babes in Toyland*** which was produced in June, 1934 at the Hal Roach Studios. The film was based on the popular Victor Herbert operetta and tells the story of Stannie Dum and Ollie Dee (Laurel and Hardy) who are almost banished from Bogeyland due to trumped up charges by the evil Silas Baraby. Only if Little Bo Peep will agree to marry him will he drop the charges against Stannie and Ollie. Bogeyland includes many inhabitants including Mother Goose, The Three Little Pigs, Tom-Tom, The Piper's Son, Little Boy Blue, The Big Bad Wolf, Santa Claus and Mary, Quite Contrary. The finale of the film is the appearance of 100 six foot tall toy soldiers to do battle against Barnaby and his Bogeymen. Grinde used his influence to have Marie cast in the small part of Mary, Quite Contrary.

This was Marie's first important film in that it was the first that offered her more than a passing glance on screen. Unfortunately it didn't lead to anymore projects and Marie was back hitting the pavement in search of any type of part she could get-usually, she would get some extra gigs. Marie's infatuated friend Douglas Churchill once wrote, "During the first three years she kept herself going with extra work . . . It is a pretty fair commentary on the seriousness with which studios look for new talent to record that she worked for virtually every big director in town without being discovered. Her personality blazed forth in fifty pictures but she was never seen." It has been calculated that Marie did extra work in around fifty films between 1932 and 1935.

Marie came to the conclusion that she was one of many young, attractive blondes who were competing for the same type of role and that she needed to find some kind of gimmick which would attract attention to her and give her an edge over the other girls. "The whole idea came to me like a flash one morning after I had spent weeks, even months trying to get through the front gates of seven or eight different studios," Marie later recalled, " . . . I was standing in front of the mirror in my room, curling my eyelashes and wondering what I could do to my face to get into the movies. 'Marie,' I said to myself, 'you should have an act or something that would attract attention. You ought to be different. When you ask for a job or a test for pictures, you look scared. Your hands won't stay still and your knees knock together. You look like a dumb blonde . . . Why don't you just be one? You might get further . . . ' So, when I finished curling the lashes, I sat down and wrote myself out an act to use if I ever did get a chance to make a test."

She got a chance to try out this act when she got wind that Universal Pictures was working on a production of *The Great Ziegfeld* in early 1935. For weeks she sat outside the front office of the man who was producing the picture, Anthony McGuire. She finally got the opportunity to come into McGuire's office because the producer had grown tired of seeing her sitting in his front office day after day with a pitiful look on her face, and so to get rid of her he decided to give her five minutes.

Marie stood in front of McGuire and said, "Let me show you how a dumb girl from the country would ask Ziegfeld for a job in the chorus." The performance convulsed McGuire, and he called in a member of his staff and had her repeat the monologue. While it went well and McGuire was impressed it didn't lead to Marie being signed by Universal. The studio decided to sell the project along with McGuire to MGM because Universal was already spending a fortune producing another lavish musical *Show Boat* and came to the conclusion that they couldn't afford to do another big-budget musical.

When McGuire got to MGM he didn't forget Marie and arranged for a screen test for her. He didn't think she was right for his movie, but he thought she had potential as a comedienne. Marie reworked the monologue and instead of being a dumb girl auditioning before the great Ziegfeld, she was a dumb girl auditioning before the Great Louis B. Mayer—the paternal and all-powerful head of MGM—about why she should be in his pictures. The test was seen by nearly every major executive at the studio and one major director, Clarence Brown (who had just completed filming *Anna Karenina* with Greta Garbo and was considered one of Metro's most dependable in-house directors) advocated signing Marie and went so far as to suggest that her test be expanded into a short film because he thought it was the funniest thing he had ever seen. In the end, Mayer decided that MGM wasn't the type of studio for Marie.

In three years Marie had a few scattered successes in her path towards becoming a star. She had gotten known at several studios and among their directors and executives, but she had not gotten the studio contract she coveted. But she felt she was finally on the right track with her "dumb" routine. It had gotten her noticed, by no less than Louis B. Mayer—even if it hadn't exactly led to being signed by the studio. The reputation of the screen test began to spread and by this time Nick Grinde was under contract at Warner Brothers and he had somehow gotten a copy of the test which he ran one day for some Warner Brother executives. Jack L. Warner, the powerful head of the studio which bared his name, heard uproarious laughter coming from the screening room and decided to check it out. If there was one thing J.L. Warner enjoyed it was a good laugh. It is said that his real ambition had been to be a stand up comedian, but unfortunately most of his jokes drew few guffaws. When the short test was completed and the lights came on, J.L. asked the surprised executives if the girl in the picture had been signed. When told that she had not, he barked out, "Put her under contract." Marie herself would remember it this way, "The test I made at Metro didn't get me a job or a contract there, but eventually it was useful in interesting Warner Brothers, who borrowed it, and liked it well enough to call me out there to make another."

Marie Wilson had finally gotten her big break—signed to a major Hollywood studio contract and would finally be given the opportunity to become a star.

Chapter Two
Warner Brothers Baby
1935-1939

On August 5, 1935 Marie, only nineteen years of age, signed a contract with one of the major motion picture studios in Hollywood—Warner Brothers. Her mother, Genevieve, had to co-sign since her daughter was still considered a minor until she was twenty-one years of age.

It was a customary stock player contract which guaranteed Marie thirteen weeks to prove herself and paid her $100 per week. If she didn't prove herself in that period of time the studio had the right to release her. The studio would assign her to roles which they felt she was right for and had the authority to control any and all other appearances Marie made even if it was on radio, stage or personal appearances. She couldn't work for any other studio unless Warner's agreed to lend her out, and if they did they would ask the other studio many times the $100 per week they were paying Marie and rather than pay Marie the difference the studio would pocket it themselves. Warner's would also have the "exclusive right" to use Marie's photograph or likeness in any way that they deemed fit and necessary and without her approval.

If the studio decided to keep Marie on it would be for an additional thirteen weeks and her weekly salary would be raised to $150 per week. The contract would be reviewed every thirteen weeks and if Warner's did keep Marie on she would receive a $50 raise each time it was renewed, so that by the end of that first year she would be making $300 per week—or $1200 per month, and $14,400 per year, very good money for that time, especially considering that the United States was still recovering from the Great Depression. But compared to the big studio names such as James Cagney ($5,000 per week) and Kay Francis ($8,000 per week) she was still a low man on the totem pole. After four years if she was still under contract to Warner's she would be making $750 per week. Of course if Marie caught on with the public, like fellow Warner's contractee Bette Davis did, she would then have the leverage to renegotiate her contract for substantially more compensation.

Within four days of signing her contract Marie was assigned to her first picture *The Broadway Hostess.* It was a 9 reel (approximately 65 minutes) programmer churned out by the studios "B" film unit which was supervised by Bryan Foy, the eldest son in the once popular vaudeville act of "The Seven Little Foys." In the years to come about two-thirds of Marie's films for Warner's would be produced by the "Foy unit" as it was referred to. According to Thomas Schatz in his book *The Genius of the System*, "The prestige pictures and other A-class features made up only half of Warner's output of sixty pictures per year. To supplement them and to keep the entire Warners system operating at full capacity, the studio relied on the newly formed Foy unit." In 1935, the same year that Marie was signed by Warner's; Foy was "the studio's B-movie specialist on a salary of $750 per week. In 1936 Warner's doubled his salary and put him in charge of all B-movie production, which totaled twenty-nine releases in 1936 and thirty in 1937." Marie's benefactor, Nicke Grinde, was one of the main directors assigned to the Foy Unit (and he would also do second unit work on "A" pictures when he got the opportunity). Unlike the major "A" productions Foy had considerable authority over his unit because, "few of the pictures were star vehicles or based on popular pre-sold properties. Jack Warner was rarely involved before the final cut. Wallis (Hal Wallis, the Warner production head, who would later produce the two *My Friend Irma* films in the late 40s) monitored each production, but the process was so mechanical that it required little real input." The shooting schedule for these programmers typically ran between fifteen to twenty-five days and the budgets were between $50-150,000. The films were then usually released as the lower half of a double bill. According to Schatz, "Warners had the most productive and efficient B-picture unit among the majors (studios)."

The idea was for a contract player to gain experience in front of the camera by working in a programmer and then to build them up with small parts in "A" pictures and then see if they catch on with the movie-going public. The Foy unit was used as a training ground for new, yet inexperienced talent. According to authors Joe Morella and Edward Z. Epstein in their biography of Jane Wyman (who was signed by Warner Brothers the year after Marie), "The Warner studio seemed to favor people who possessed personality and potential acting ability as opposed to rival studios MGM and Paramount, whose casting people looked first and foremost for players with extraordinary good looks." In many ways this is true because it's hard to imagine Bette Davis, Humphrey Bogart, James Cagney and Edward G. Robinson attaining the kind of success they did at any other studio than Warner Brothers.

Warner Brothers, like all the other major studios, had an acting school on the lot where many of the contract players could learn acting techniques. In the studio classroom they could learn diction, how to walk, how to walk downstairs without looking down at ones feet, and even such things as how to ride a horse and fence—if a picture called for it. Jane Wyman would later recall the studio as "a big family . . . James Cagney was a strict disciplinarian . . . Pat O'Brien was always teaching me the tricks of the business. Even Bette Davis was kind and encouraging to 'the kids' as we were called." Wyman would also recall that "the kids," people like Wyman, Ann Sheridan, Dick Foran, Wayne Morris, Ronald Reagan and Marie, often would have lunch together in the studio commissary.

Like all studios the contract players had to shmooze with various investors, businessmen and other prominent people who visited the studio—Marie was no exception. Stuart Jerome in his book *Those Crazy Days When We Ran Warner Brothers* recalls an incident when Marie met the head of an important Midwestern movie theater chain and when introduced to the elderly gentleman, "Wilson politely begged off accepting his outstretched hand on the grounds that she was suffering from 'a social disease' and didn't want to expose him to it. Shocked, the old man quickly excused himself and left. Upon hearing of her remark, Vice President Charlie Einfeld called her on the carpet. 'Don't you have better sense then to go around talking about your sex life?' She didn't know what he was talking about. He told her. 'Oh, that,' she said, brightening. 'Well, you know how you and the fellers in publicity are always telling me to watch what I say when I meet important people? I didn't want to tell him I caught a cold at a party.'" Marie went on to explain to Einfeld a cold caught at a party is a "social disease." It was stories like that which gave Marie a reputation for being somewhat dim in real life, but Jerome later wrote that Marie's dumb blonde casting, "wasn't completely true-to-life casting, it was close enough. Not that she was stupid, merely the most child-like innocent on the lot."

Broadway Hostess was set in a nightclub, and the leading roles were given to Lyle Talbot and Winifred Shaw in the story of a promoter who gets a girl singer an audition at a big nightclub, and then when she is successful uses his influence with her to gain more money and open up a gambling house. Marie has the small role of Dorothy Dubois, already perfecting her "dumb" persona as a less than bright showgirl. Variety dismissed the film when it was released that December, "Musical of program caliber which will prove adequate for family audience consumption, but will have to pull hard to get average grosses." due to the lack of star names in the cast.

Marie followed this up with a slightly higher caliber film—a "B+" if you will, *Stars over Broadway* which starred Pat O'Brien, who usually specialized in "cops" and priests. In this one O'Brien is cast as a failed theatrical manager, who giving up, decides to commit suicide until he hears a hotel porter sing and offers to help make him a star. The film was shot after *Broadway Hostess* but released before it, and was reviewed by *Variety* as a "satisfactory musical of moderate money possibilities." More importantly the review by the so-called "bible" of show business gives Marie her first major mention in films, "Frank McHugh, as a song plugger, has most of the comedy, and that puts him on top during much of the running time. Marie Wilson, a blondie, stooges for him." Marie was earning a reputation in these early films for "comedy relief."

Joan Blondell and Glenda Farrell were teamed in a series of comedy films at Warner's and Marie was cast in their next one, *Miss Pacific Fleet*, which went before the cameras in September, 1935. It's another hour long programmer, and

Blondell and Farrell are cast as two former showgirls who work in a booth at an amusement park—they go broke and come up with the idea of a "Miss Pacific Fleet" contest which Blondell enters and her major competition is a sweet, but not so bright beauty named Virgie (Marie, naturally). This is the biggest role for Marie, so far, and she makes the best of it. *Variety* in its review comments, "Blondell and Farrell team is spirited in this one, but the play is taken away from them. There's a new femme comic, Marie Wilson, whom something might be done with in a future film."

In December, 1935 Marie was cast in her fourth and biggest film to date at Warner Brothers, *Satan Met a Lady*, which was cast with two A level stars, Bette Davis and Warren William and directed by one of the studios most reliable directors, William Dieterle. It was the second screen adaptation of Dashill Hammett's *The Maltese Falcon* (The studio would produce the definitive version in 1941 with Humphrey Bogart and Mary Astor). The film isn't bad, but it's certainly not up to the level of the 1941 version, but Davis certainly didn't want to do it, "I was so distressed by the whole tone of the script and the vapidity of my part that I marched up to (Jack Warner's) office and demanded that I be given work that was commensurate with my proven ability."

The storyline is somewhat different than the later 1941 film, for instance, instead of a blackbird the private eye (Ted Shayne, not Sam Spade) is entrusted into finding it's a jewel-encrusted ram's horn. While there is certainly humor in the 1941 classic, this version is played more for laughs and Marie was brought in as one of the major facilitators of the comedy. Hollywood writer Lawrence J. Quick would later write, "Marie Wilson was given full rein in one of her standard comedy turns as Sam Spade's devoted and protected secretary," Miss Murgatroyd. *Variety* called the movie an "inferior remake" to the 1931 first screen version of *The Maltese Falcon*, and while not praising Marie's performance the review did give her encouragement, "Marie Wilson has a tendency to muff her best chances through over-stressing; although she shows enough to indicate she can do a good comedy job with the right handling." The *New York Times* critic Bosley Crowther found much to disdain in the film, "There is no story, merely a farrago of nonsense representing a series of practical studio compromises with an unworkable script."

Every twelve weeks Marie's contract option came up and in her first year at the studio she showed enough promise to be kept on with the added compensation of the $50 per week pay raise. While she was not yet offered any breakout role in a prestige film, she was acquiring a following. She had a wholesomeness behind her blonde sexiness which many people found appealing, and by early 1936 she was getting nearly 500 fan letters per week, certainly not in the league with Davis, Flynn, Dick Powell or Ruby Keeler, but for a relatively new actress, who had yet to have her big break it was heartening to her and intriguing to the studio. With the help of her mother she always insisted on answering every fan letter.

Marie's first release of 1936 came in March ***Colleen*** starring the popular team of Dick Powell and Ruby Keeler. The story had something to do with an eccentric businessman who buys a dress shop for a gold digger (Joan Blondell) and how the businessman's nephew (Powell) has to straighten out the mess this situation causes. Keeler is the stores book keeper, and of course Powell falls for her, but also has to contend with Blondell. Marie has little to do except provide a couple of scenes of comedy relief as a soda jerk. This is by far the weakest of the Powell-Keeler musicals and was destined to be their last.

For her next screen offering Marie was back at the Foy unit in a picture called ***King of Hockey***. The film starred Dick Purcell, who had been a hockey player for Forham University. Purcell plays a college hockey player who is recruited by the manager of a professional team and with his expertise takes the team directly to the top of the heap. Like any respectable "B" programmer there has to be a gangster who offers Purcell a bundle to throw the game. The second leads are Wayne Morris, as Purcell's teammate and best friend and Marie cast as Morris' girlfriend. ***Variety*** dismissed the picture as a "run of the mill" yarn, but praised Marie for providing "some invigorating humor."

Marie Wilson in a glamour pose, approximately, 1936. Author's Collection.

Marie worked with Pat O'Brien for the second time in **China Clipper** which also featured Humphrey Bogart in an early film performance. It's an aviation drama about an importer (O'Brien) who realizes that there is enormous potential for a commercial air service in Shanghai. He recruits a couple of war buddies (Ross Alexander and Bogart) to join him in this venture. The female lead is Beverly Roberts, who had a short lived film career at Warner Brothers before returning to the stage and later distinguished herself as the head of the Theatre Guild for 24 years. Marie is cast as Alexander's girlfriend. *Variety* viewed the picture itself as an action picture "without the usual thrills," but liked Bogart "in a sympathetic role," but pointed out that Marie was becoming increasingly typed and offered the Warner Brothers some advice, "Ross Alexander and Marie Wilson carry on a comedy love affair in which Miss Wilson is typed once more. It would be a good idea to give this promising comedienne a different part now and then."

This was Marie's second film with Ross Alexander, an exceedingly good looking 29 year old, who was getting increasingly frustrated with how Warner Brothers was using him. This film was indicative of his frustration. He was often cast as a second lead in films with Errol Flynn, Pat O'Brien and Dick Powell, but he didn't feel that the studio was doing enough to advance his career. The studio was also trying to keep Alexander's active homosexual lifestyle out of the papers and even arranged a marriage of convenience between Alexander and a young actress named Aleta Friele, which ended tragically when she took a shotgun and killed herself. He married actress Anne Nagel soon after, but continuing career frustrations and lingering guilt over the death of his first wife led Alexander to turn a rifle on himself, only months after this film was released.

After one of her most unforgettable programmers, **The Big Noise** (as a pants presser), Marie was cast in a romantic musical **Melody for Two**, unfortunately she wasn't one of the "two" in the title. Once again cast as one of the second leads, the bass playing girlfriend of a nightclub owner, Marie nevertheless runs away with the reviews, "Marie Wilson is the only comedy asset in the picture, but her role is only a sneezer (very quick) as a witless bull-fiddle bumper."

Marie was next cast as a stripper in a film directed by Nick Grinde **Public Wedding**, despite her relationship with Grinde, she was still cast in a supporting role with the lead going to Jane Wyman. **Public Wedding** is the story of a father and daughter who run an unsuccessful concession stand at an amusement park. To attract customers they decide to hold a public wedding in the mouth of the whale skeleton that is displayed at the park. The film does allow Marie several good moments including a scene where Marie (named Tessie in this one) is rescued from a police raid by dressing the stripper in a wedding dress. *Variety* dismissed the film as "slightly humorous at several scattered junctions, but seldom rises to the heights." The acting is dismissed as "blah" with Wyman having "plenty to do, but isn't overboard on acting." But, again, Marie is praised even when the picture is booed, "Marie Wilson, as a burley fan dancer, gives one of the most natural portrayals. She has the looks, vivacity and thespian ability. Based on her work here, she will probably be given meatier roles."

And that is what Marie wanted—meatier roles, but she had yet to have a leading role in any Warner Brothers film, even those produced by the Foy Unit. Yet here was a contemporary, Jane Wyman, signed a year after she was, being given a build up by the studio and even landing an occasional leading role. Marie liked Wyman, and didn't begrudge her success, but she also felt that Warner's wasn't utilizing her potential. She also believed that with the continued emphasize of using her as comedy relief in "dumb Dora" type of roles that she would be typed.

Shortly after completing her part in **Public Wedding** Marie was badly injured in a car accident. On March 5th Marie, her mother and Nick were driving in downtown Hollywood when her car collided with two others. It's not clear who was at fault or if Marie was driving, but neither Nick nor Marie's mother were injured. However, Marie was taken to the hospital where doctors discovered that a piece of metal had pierced her skull and according to the next days' edition of **The New York Daily Mirror** doctors were preparing a "delicate" operation to attempt and remove the metal. Marie had already completed two films for release in 1937, and would not go before the cameras again for several months—a long enough period for her to recover from her injuries.

When she was well enough to go before the cameras, Marie was given the opportunity to work in an "A" production with a top notch producer in Melvyn LeRoy and director in James Whale when she was cast in **The Great Garrick**.

Marie as she appeared in the 1937 film, **The Great Garrick**. Author's collection.

The leads were Brian Aherne and Olivia de Havilland, and even the supporting cast was distinguished—Edward Everett Horton, Melville Cooper, Lionel Atwill, Albert Deckker, Harry Davenport and a young Lana Turner in one of her earliest roles. Aherne is cast in the title role as an egotistical 18th Century actor whose is going to appear in a French comedy in Paris. The French actors decide to teach him a lesson and take over a roadside inn where they know he will be lodging. But Garrick instantly recognizes that the staff and guests of the inn are actors by their conventional gestures and decide to play along with them to see what will happen. Intruding on this supposed deception is a beautiful young woman (de Havilland) who isn't in on the ruse.

Marie was also put in another big studio picture, a rare comedy for Errol Flynn *The Perfect Specimen* and given another quality director in Michael Curtiz, but her part ended up on the cutting room floor. Marie felt that she was given bigger chances in 1937, but the next year, 1938 would be the highlight of her career at Warner Brothers as she would openly campaign for a part which she hoped, would lead to the stardom she had long sought.

II

The first picture that Marie had in release in 1938 came out shortly after the New Year, and was another programmer, but for once she was given the leading female role, and she wasn't even her typical "dumb blonde." The film was *The Invisible Menace* and Marie came into it by chance, given the part only after Jane Wyman dropped out—shuttled off to do another film. The lead role is played by Boris Karloff. The film is a mystery with a military backdrop. A soldier (Eddie Craven) smuggles his new wife Sally (Marie) onto an army base so that they will be able to have their honeymoon. Looking for a place to be alone they sneak into an explosives storage building and just as they are beginning to get frisky (by the standards of 1938 censorship) they find a dead body. Karloff plays the leading suspect in the murder. The film was reviewed by *Variety* as "undistinguised" and the reviewer points out, in less than charitable terms that Marie is not her usual scatterbrain, "Marie Wilson is removed from her familiar stamping rounds of doing stupid, silly girls and used as the romantic interest opposite Eddie Craven. She's the only femme in the piece and should have been injected into more scenes to relieve the monotony of seeing so much of army uniforms."

One of Marie's favorites of her Warner Brother's films would come next, directed by Melvyn LeRoy, considered one the industries outstanding directors, in what would be his final film for the studio before leaving for MGM (where he would produce *The Wizard of Oz*). The film was *Fools for Scandal* which starred the delectable Carole Lombard as an incognito American film star who meets a supposed impoverished local (Fernand Gravet) in Paris, and offers to show her the "real" Paris. It is a movie of deception because the Gravet character is actually wealthy. Marie is cast as Lombard's maid, Myrtle.

During one scene, Marie forgot her lines in the middle of a speech, and gave a helpless shrug, finally remembered what she was to say and resumed. LeRoy decided to do another take, which went perfectly. When he screened the two takes, LeRoy decided to use the first take with Marie's memory lapse. He felt it fit well with the character which Marie was playing—the not too bright maid— and Marie's shrugging it off and continuing the line, would provide a big laugh, which it did, and so it was kept in the picture.

During the making of the film Marie became friendly with Carole Lombard, an actress she very much admired and looked up to. Lombard didn't get pigeon-holed into any one part, and while blonde, she was anything but a dumb blonde in films. While she excelled at comedy parts, and indeed was considered one of the finest comedienne's in motion pictures she also was able to show her versatility by doing an occasional dramatic role. They were opposites in that Marie, off camera, was very lady like—wore white gloves and rarely used foul language; Lombard was known, off screen, for her often salty language. Fred MacMurray her co-star in several films during the 1930's would recall that Lombard, "swore like a sailor." But most people believed that she was one of the few actresses who could do this without losing her femininity. While Marie was much lower on the Hollywood social ladder than Lombard, she and Nick Grinde were often invited by Lombard and her soon to be husband Clark Gable to get-togethers at their ranch in the San Fernando Valley. Marie would recall that when *Fools for Scandal* was completed that Lombard took her aside to tell her that she would be on the look-out for another film for them to do together, ideally one which would cast Marie as Lombard's "kid sister." It was never to be, and Lombard would be dead within four years—her plane crashing while on a war bond drive.

By this time Marie had been under contract to Warner Brothers for three years and in that time had mostly appeared in the programmers, but even so, critics had noticed her, often citing her as the best or only redeeming thing in the picture. She had gained a following by this time with her fan mail up to 3,000 letters per month—more mail than any other Warner's contract player with the exceptions of mega stars Errol Flynn and Bette Davis. But she was wearying of playing dumb all the time. In her spare time she was taking acting classes at the studio school and she and the other lowly contract players put on a production of *Camille* with Marie in the lead role. It went well, a little too well for Warner executives apparently, "The studio heard I was ambitious and jumped on me with both feet," Marie would recall, "They said I was funny and that I mustn't be spoiled by dramatic training. Which is strange, because I'm not good enough to be spoiled." But many at the studio also understood that there was more depth behind Marie's "dumb" act than met the eye. William Dieterle, one of her better directors, said that Marie was "one of the cleverest actresses on the screen."

Marie was ambitious enough to be on the look out for good projects. When she heard that the studio had paid $100,000 to acquire the screen rights to the hit play **Boy Meets Girl** she campaigned hard for the leading female role of the unwed pregnant waitress Susie Seabrook. But Warner's had other ideas which didn't include Marie. This was a very prominent stage play and they felt that a bigger name should be cast as Susie and had their sights on Marion Davies. Davies, a talented comedienne, was also the mistress of the very powerful William Randolph Hearst, who controlling the Hearst press syndicate, was a very powerful voice in Hollywood. Hearst felt that Davies would be hurt by playing a woman pregnant out of wedlock, and told her not to take the part. Next the studio approached Joan Blondell, who also turned the part down.

Marie had read and memorized the stage script of **Boy Meets Girl** and went to Hal Wallis, the producer in charge of the production, and asked to be tested for the part. Marie did very well in her test. Susie was considered "honest, unselfish and grateful" and also considered herself dumb because she never completed high school and her biggest wish is to go back to high school and get her diploma. Marie brought out an innocent, naiveté to the part which was very appealing. But the issue still wasn't settled in her favor; Jack Warner was also considering other contract players such as Joan Blondell (too breezy), Ann Sheridan (too sexy), and Jane Wyman (almost, but not quite capturing the innocence that Susie must have).

Marie, who always had a good rapport with the Hollywood Press Corp because of her willingness to make herself available to them for interviews and photo shoots, called in some chips and soon the trades were running stories supporting her for the part. Reader polls were also conducted on Marie's behalf and the studio was deluged with letters from her fans demanding that Marie be cast as Susie. Given her good test, public support and her enthusiasm for the part, Jack Warner finally decided to roll the dice and cast Marie.

Boy Meets Girl is the story of two Hollywood screenwriters Robert Law (James Cagney) and J.C. Benson (Pat O'Brien), who are assigned to write the latest film of a cowboy star whose career is fading. Nothing they come up with pleases the pompous producer (hilariously played by Ralph Bellamy). Susie, an unwed waitress, arrives to deliver lunch. She announces that she will be leaving her job at the end of the week because she is expecting. She also says that she wants to name her baby "Happy" because she wants him to be happy all of his life. The writers use Susie's baby as the inspiration for the film they have to write for the fading cowboy star, with the cowboy finding a lone baby in a variation of the classic Hollywood story, "Boy Meets Girl, Boy Loses Girl, Boy Gets Girl." The producer loves the idea and they will use "Happy" as the actual infant in the movie. The film is made and "Happy" becomes the biggest movie sensation in the country—and Susie gets to go back to school and be educated and ends up marrying a English actor who turns out to be an English Lord, to boot.

This was to be Cagney's first film after being put on suspension by Warner's for demanding better and more varied roles. He was tiring of playing variations of his stock gangster persona—good as it was. This was Pat O'Brien's third film with Marie and both actors were supportive of Marie since they knew this film could be her big break. According to writer Douglas Churchill, "For a year Marie lived with Susie Seabrook; she knew the character's every emotion and motive...on the set an attempt was made to revise Marie's conception but Susie remained inviolate and supreme just as the Spewacks (the writers, Bella and Samuel Spewack) fashioned her. James Cagney and Pat O'Brien, stars of the piece appeared to be in complete sympathy with Marie's ideas and threw every possible scene to her."

Movie poster for *Boy Meets Girl*, Marie's biggest break at Warner's was appearing with James Cagney and Pat O'Brien in the 1938 comedy, *Boy Meets Girl*. The Stumpf-Ohmart Collection.

That Marie and Susie shared an innate innocence is punctuated by a story told by former studio messenger and later screenwriter Stuart Jerome in the book *Those Crazy Wonderful Years When We Ran Warner Brothers*, "It was during the filming of *Boy Meets Girl* that she (Marie) casually made a remark . . . In a scene with Jimmy Cagney in which she sat on his lap, he kept fluffing his two lines . . . It took a dozen takes before he got it right. Afterwards, Wilson said to her makeup woman, 'Sitting on Jimmy's lap was like being on top of a flagpole.' She honestly had no idea why the woman suddenly broke up." When Jerome and his fellow messenger boys heard this story Cagney "gained considerable personal stature in our eyes."

Cagney never saw the film when it was released theatrically, but writes in his memoirs that when he saw it years later on television, " . . . it was so much better in the TV version than it seemed to be when we did it that I can't quite understand it. It's the same film, but I sense that the years have done something for it—What I don't know. While we were making it, Pat and I were harassed by the producer's insistence on more speed . . . " Cagney, in his only film with Marie, recalled her in his autobiography, "Also in the cast was that very savvy gal, Marie Wilson, who was very adept at giving an impression of naiveté." He had nothing to say about the "flagpole" incident.

Marie as Susie in *Boy Meets Girl*, 1938.

The film went on to become a success at the box office, but not as big as Warner's would have hoped. It got some pleasing notices from the critics as well. *Variety* wrote, "With Cagney-O'Brien for the marquee and the ballyhoo attendant to Warner's new Marie Wilson in the dumb dora role of the mother of "Happy" the filmation of "Boy Meets Girl" will meet box office success . . . Marie Wilson, newcomer, (indicative that this film was viewed as Marie's first big opportunity that she is called a "newcomer" despite twenty other films) rates the most attention, trade and public, in her assignment as Susie, who has been given the benefit of clergy in her role as mammy of Happy." **Life Magazine** was quite

Marie and Cagney in *Boy Meets Girl*, 1938.

enthusiastic about Marie's performance, ". . . so appealing are her gasping voice, her baby stare and nervous fluttering hands, that she steals the picture . . . she definitely attains the stature of a Grad A comedienne and actress." In fact, most reviewers did single Marie's performance out as a high point of the film.

Marie could have expected that given the attention afforded to her with **Boy Meets Girl** that she would be up for bigger and better parts, and at first it seemed that it would actually happen. Warner Brothers announced that they planned to remake the George S. Kaufman and Marc Connelly comedy **Dulcy** which stage titan Lynn Fontanne had played to great success on Broadway in 1922. Fontanne's biographer described **Dulcy** as "pure Kaufman: the bumbler, the little person, the innocent." In short, perfect for Marie's established persona. But it didn't pan out and MGM acquired the screen rights.

About six weeks after finishing *Boy Meets Girl* Marie was assigned to *Broadway Musketeers*, a remake of a 1932 Warner Brothers film *Three on a Match* which helped to further the careers of Joan Blondell and Bette Davis. While Marie is one of the three leads she is billed below Margaret Lindsay and Ann Sheridan. The three women, the Musketeers of the title, grew up together in an orphanage. They reunite when the characters played by Lindsay and Marie both arrive at the city jail to bail out the third musketeer (Sheridan), who was arrested for doing a strip tease. Each has a sad tale to tell. The Lindsay character is married to a wealthy man and has a daughter, but she is unhappy with her life. Marie (in the role which Davis had played in the earlier film) is a stenographer who is in love with her boss and Sheridan is reduced to stripping. The film evolves into soap opera when the Lindsay character leaves her husband and marries a gambler and the Sheridan character ends up marrying Lindsay's ex-husband. The film ends with the Lindsay character dying trying to save her daughter when they are kidnapped when her new husband is unable to pay off a gambling debt. The Musketeers continue a tradition of meeting to celebrate their joint June birthdays with the daughter of the Lindsay character taking her place and becoming the new third Musketeer. For once Marie is not cast as the stripper, but in this film she would have been better off if she had been since Sheridan has a much more flashier and substantial role. When the film was released in October, 1938, *Variety* found it to be "a programmer of average distinction that has been well cast and ought to get by satisfactorily." As for herself, Marie summed up the film this way, "There are three girls. One of them commits suicide, one of them is a strip teaser and the other is just a secretary. I play the secretary—I just go along for the ride."

There is a funny story related to a scene in this film which included Marie and Dewey Robinson, a character actor who specialized in playing heavies. It is a scene near the end of the picture where Robinson roughs up Marie—slapping her hard across the face. At the initial preview the film had scored well with the audience, but in this particular scene which is supposed to be very tense and dramatic there were scattered titters and laughter. It was only a small portion of the audience, but it puzzled Bryan Foy and director John Farrow. The reaction cards were of no help—nobody mentioned a thing about why that particular scene should get any snickers. The picture was previewed a second time—and the same thing happened—again with only a tiny fraction of the audience. Foy was again nonplussed, "Whatever the hell is wrong with that scene, it's obviously such a little things that most of the audience doesn't spot it." He decided to run the scene again back at the studio.

The next morning Foy, Farrow, Editor Frank Magee and another producer, Bill Jacobs met in the projection room to dissect the scene. The scene was run and only one person burst out laughing—Jacobs, the only one who had not viewed the scene previously. Foy gave him a "Ok, what is it?" and Jacobs told the assembled group to run the scene again and keep their eyes on Robinson. The scene is run again and finally Foy and the others see it—when Robinson lunged towards Marie for a fraction of a second but still very visible his fly is open. Why hadn't they noticed it before wondered Foy. "Easy," replied Jacobs, "It's a helluva scene for Marie. It comes as a shock when he suddenly hits her and your audience blinks in reaction—which is exactly what you guys must've done every time you ran it." Needless to say the scene was a pivotal one in the film and had to be reshot—with Farrow even checking Robinson's zipper. According to Stuart Jerome this led to a memo from Foy to "All Directors and Script Clerks" in his unit, "I realize you normally have enough to do without having to concern yourself with this, but since we can't depend on actors to always do it, you're going to have to be responsible for each and every actor having his fly fully zipped up before shooting a scene. Remember, this is your responsibility."

In August, 1938, Marie and Nick Grinde announced their engagement—with the press making the erroneous conclusion that a romance between them had only begun the year before when Marie had been injured in the automobile accident which had also involved Nick. They announced that the wedding would take place on October 21st. It is quite possible that they were serious about getting married—afterall they had been involved for over four years. But Nick had a reputation for being a "man's man" and a man who enjoyed women. Marie was devoted to him for all he had done to help her, but its questionable if she really was "in-love" with him—in many ways he was a strong father figure for her. But for the moment they had decided to go ahead and make plans, but when the 21st of October rolled around, they did not marry and no explanation was ever given to the press—other than they were still engaged and expected to marry "one day."

Marie returned to comedy in her next film, and was the indisputable lead of another programmer *Sweepstakes Winner*. It's the story of a waitress (Marie), a race horse and a couple of race track touts who try to cheat the naive waitress out of her sweepstakes winnings. Marie's wardrobe design in this film was based on the results of a poll conducted by the studio, in which twenty-five waitresses in the Warner commissary were asked what types of clothes they would buy if they were sweepstakes winners. There was one funny, perhaps slightly embarrassing thing which happened during the filming of this picture. The character played by Allen Jenkins, Xerxes Bailey, one of the men trying to swindle Marie's character, was given a nickname "Tip" when Marie repeatedly kept pronouncing "Xerxes" as "Jerky". The studio probably should have left well enough alone because the unintentional goof may have provided some intentional humor in an otherwise weak film and still fit in nicely with Marie's persona. The film didn't fare well even with *Variety's* critics who found the film "a weakie" and Marie's performance "forced."

In January, 1939 *The New York Times* announced that Twentieth Century Fox had borrowed Marie "for one of the featured roles" in the Tyrone Power-Alice Faye musical *Rose of Washington Square* (which was based loosely on the life of Fanny Brice) which would be going before the cameras that Spring directed by

Gregory Ratoff, but the announcement turned out to be premature and Marie was not loaned out to Fox and instead in February of 1939, Marie was cast in a supporting role as comedy relief in *Waterfront* which starred Gloria Dickson and Dennis Morgan in a story of corruption and violence among longshoremen in New York City. It was as if *Boy Meets Girl* never happened, and the critic for *Variety* noticed, writing in his review that Marie was "wasted" in this film. In April, 1939 Marie was cast in the final film she would shoot at Warner Brothers under her contract—a football comedy *The Cowboy Quarterback* The film marked the first professional role of Bert Wheeler following the death of his partner Robert Woolsey. It told the story of a scout for the Chicago Packers (William Demarest, in the first of three pictures he would appear in with Marie) who hears about the legendary prowess of Harry Lynn (Wheeler) a player from Montana. The only problem is that Lynn won't leave Montana because he's afraid if he does his girlfriend Maizie (Marie) will marry another local boy named Handsome Sam.

It was around this time that Marie began hearing some unsettling gossip around town that Warner's might drop her option and release her from her contact. It couldn't have helped her morale when the studio loaned her out for the first time, but not to one of the major competitors of Warner's—MGM and Paramount, but to lowly Republic which specialized in "B" westerns and other programmers. The film was *Should Husbands Work?* and she found herself billed fifth. This domestic comedy was shot in 13 days in June, 1939. Marie was now under no illusions about her position at the studio. In the year since *Boy Meets Girl* she had made four films—each progressively worse than the last with the latest being fifth billed in a quickie at Republic.

The Republic film wrapped on June 15, 1939 and five days later Marie signed her release from Warner Brothers. She was given compensation of $1,266.67 and told it wasn't her fault—it was just that there were not enough quality roles for her type at the studio. Warner Brothers didn't specialize in comedy but in gritty melodramas and women's pictures with the likes of Bette Davis. Jack Warner, the studio head, had already gone on record as saying he felt that Marie's screen persona was too limiting for her to ever become a star. Despite tons of fan mail, respectable performances which caught both the attention of movie-goers and critics—Marie was let go. Warner Brothers also obviously felt that there were too many ingénue types at the studio already and they had bigger hopes for two of them in particular—Jane Wyman and Ann Sheridan—both were getting bigger buildups than Marie—Sheridan in particular.

Marie went a long way towards creating the character she became identified with—the dumb blonde. She had presented this character in her audition at MGM which was seen at Warner Brothers. Warner's picked up on this and signed her and gave her roles fashioned around the character she seemed most at ease at playing, yet, with very rare exception, they didn't attempt to try her in other parts—they even resisted casting her in *Boy Meets Girl* until they exhausted all other avenues. So it's bewildering to know what exactly the studio planned to do with Marie. The fact that she was getting 3,000 fan letters per month indicates she had a pretty strong following, yet the studio did little to exploit her fan base. In the long run, it could be that Warner Brothers was the wrong studio for Marie, but on the other hand it took Humphrey Bogart and Jane Wyman years to establish their stardom. Bogart was limited to mostly gangster parts for many years when finally Warner's found breakout roles for him in *High Sierra* and *The Maltese Falcon* which took his gangster persona and transformed him into the anti-hero. Jane Wyman continued at Warner's in mostly supporting roles which Marie could have filled just as well (it's worth recalling that Wyman had her hair dyed blonde for many of these years) achieving her breakthrough only when Warner Brothers leant her out to Paramount for *The Lost Weekend* in 1945! Whatever the reason, Marie wasn't about to give up on her lifelong dream to be a star, not after all she had been through and achieved—but she knew it would be harder now without a studio behind her.

CHAPTER THREE
THE BLACKOUTS

After leaving Warner Brothers Marie had no new film prospects and really didn't consider herself a radio actress—despite an occasional foray into that medium. She received an invitation from Anita Loos to do a summer stock tour of *Gentlemen Prefer Blondes* but for some reasons the venture never panned out, so her agent arranged for her to join a vaudeville tour—doing a stage version of her 'dumb Dora' routine. Given the reviews she received it must have been a very discouraging and sad several months for Marie.

On September 27, 1939 Marie appeared with straight man Bob Oakley at Loew's State theatre in New York City. *Variety* savaged her performance, "Blonde Marie Wilson . . . had built up a rep as Hollywood's dumbest Dora and that's the type of stage act she's doing, but now she probably can also lay claim to Hollywood's worst personal appearance. If her chassis can be considered an act, it's great. But unfortunately it's not wired for sound and her 10 minutes of fog-bound talk with Bob Oakley, who co-authored her act, is just so much of a stage wait. There's hardly a snicker in the silly questions and answers and the applause at this catching was very quiet. One thing she does display to best advantage is her physical attributes, a very short, tight-fitting dress adds oomph, and she throws around plenty in a conga encore with Oakley."

By October, the Wilson-Oakley act was appearing at the Palace in Cleveland, but the reviews hadn't improved, "Although Marie Wilson of films is the weakest act, an obvious disappointment to hefty-sized crowds she drew over the week-end, the Palace spots several show-saving vets around her so deftly that she can't hurt the bill." When the team got to Dayton in November, the act had improved to "so-so." By Christmas she was back in New York appearing in Brooklyn, "The actress is an okay looker, but even a Beatrice Lillie couldn't enliven those dire gags." Finally, mercifully the tour ended at the Lyric Theatre in Indianapolis at the end of January, 1940, "Marie Wilson flounders with poor material." She returned to Hollywood to make the audition rounds in an effort to land a part in pictures—discouraged but still determined.

It took Marie over a year after her contract with Warner Brothers was terminated to find her next screen role. She auditioned for and won the supporting part of Southern belle Connie Potter in Paramount's *Virginia* which starred Fred MacMurray and Madeleine Carroll. Carroll plays a member of a prominent Virginia family who returns home for the first time in years, having lived in New York City and comes to have a new appreciation for the Southern way of life—as well as finding love with MacMurray. The working title of the film was, "The Southerner" and the film marked the acting debut of Sterling Hayden who was cast as a rival of MacMurray's for the love of Carroll. In "real life" Carroll and Hayden would marry in 1942. Marie is, as usual, used mainly as comic relief—a southern version of her patented dumb Dora—she has a taste for southern moonshine. Much of the exteriors were shot on location near Charlottesville, VA, and the Technicolor outdoor scenes are the best thing about the picture. *The New York Times* felt the picture, "smacks too much of magnolias and moonshine to be convincing." However the *Hollywood Reporter* would call it one of the truly "fine" films of the year.

Between February 28th through Mid-March of 1941, Marie found work at Republic Studios. Republic was not considered one of the major studios in Hollywood—such as Warner Brothers, Paramount or MGM. Republic specialized in "B" pictures. These were bread and butter entertainments often put on a double bill with another bigger film. Though sometimes—especially on a Saturday afternoon, it would be the Republic "B" which was the big draw at the local theatre; especially if they were showing a Gene Autry or Roy Rogers western. Autry and Rogers were the two biggest stars on the Republic lot—along with another contractee named John Wayne (Though Wayne, by this time, was often loaned out to the major studios after his break-through role in John Ford's *Stagecoach)*.

The film that Marie found herself in was called *Rookies on Parade*. It is the story of two songwriters who have gambling debts and women problems. They hit the big time with a new big show to write, but just as they are about to become successful again the army drafts them. Marie is cast as Kitty Mulloy, a show girl in the USO, who falls in love with one of the songwriters. The two leads are played by Bob Crosby, the bandleader and brother of the much more famous Bing and Eddie Foy, Jr. one of the kids from the famous "Seven Little Foys" vaudeville and broadway act and the brother of Marie's old unit boss at Warner Brothers. Veteran character actor William Demarest (later Uncle Charley on *My Three Sons*) was signed to play the hard bitten sergeant who vows to break the two new recruits. Besides the dependable cast the film boasts some good Sammy Cahn and Saul Chapin songs (*You'll Never Get Rich, I Love You More*) as well as the work of Jule Styne (*Rookies on Parade*). The film became a perfectly entertaining way for audiences to spend about 70 minutes in a theatre when it was released just a month after it completed principle photography! For her work on this picture Marie was paid $400 per week—she wound up earning about $1200.

It was while shooting **Rookies on Parade** that Marie met the man who would become her first husband. Allan Nixon was a strapping six foot four, 24 years old, with a chiseled face and dark wavy hair. In the looks department Nixon was everything a matinee hero would want to be, And Allan wanted to be a movie star. However in **Rookies on Parade** Nixon has a relatively small role as one of the soldiers at the camp where the two leads are drafted into. One day during the shooting Nixon caught sight of Marie who was wearing a very tight WAC uniform, "I thought she was the cutest thing I'd ever seen," he would later recall. His good looks gave Allan great security and even though Marie had a much bigger part in the picture and indeed was a minor star in her own right— he could tell that she was very approachable. She mingled with everybody on the set. He decided to approach her.

Marie as she appeared in *Rookies on Parade.*
The Stumpf-Ohmart Collection.

Marie later recalled that it was she who made the first move, "On the Republic lot some of the players were gathered around a make-up table one day. A tall young fellow was sitting on a chair, tilted back. He was very tall—six feet four, to be exact, and was very good looking. But he seemed bashful, extremely bashful. I was wearing a slinky tight gown, and I thought maybe that was what was making him so shy. So I moved closer to him and gave him a nice smile and said sweetly, 'hello!' Next thing I knew the boy had fallen clear backwards to the floor—and there was an awful lot of him to fall. When he recovered he said, 'Well, may we get acquainted? Would you have lunch with me?'"

They went to the Republic commissary and Nixon would recall that Marie "mothered him" almost from the start. At lunch Marie told Allan that despite his good looks and beefy build he looked "terribly pale and probably was dangerously anemic, and he should really have some home cooked meals and get some rest." Nixon explained that it was difficult for him to get those home cooked meals since he lived in a room at the Knickerbocker hotel. The lunch went well but no plans had been made. The next morning, however, Nixon was called down to the front desk at the Knickerbocker—a package had been left for him by a very attractive young woman. Intrigued he ran down to the desk and found that Marie had left a package and a note. The box contained seven types of vitamin pills and the letter was instructions on their uses. Nixon correctly came to the conclusion that if she cared enough to get him some vitamins and leave them for him at his hotel that she must have some kind of feelings for him.

Certainly Marie did find Nixon attractive and appealing. But she was also considered engaged to Nick Ginde. When Allan saw Marie on the set later that day he thanked her for leaving the vitamins and that he already took some. "Good!" Marie exclaimed, "You look better already." Allan proceeded to ask Marie out dancing at Ciro's. She reluctantly told him that she couldn't due to her engagement, yet over the next several weeks with great persistence he continued to ask her out. Again and again Marie would tell him that she was engaged to Nick Grinde and she didn't want to hurt his feelings—to which Allan would ask, "but what about my feelings!?"

Finally Nixon came up with another approach he asked Marie if she would be interested in taking rumba lessons together at one of Hollywood's private schools. Rumba dancing was becoming the rage thanks to the explosion in Latin music created by Desi Arnaz and Xavier Cugat. Marie thought for a moment and said, "Hmm, maybe it wouldn't be such a bad thing to know how to dance the Rumba." But she told Nixon that she would have to ask permission of Grinde. She did ask and did get Grinde's permission, but it's doubtful that she told him that, "by the way, I would be taking lessons with a very persistent young man who constantly tells me he wants to marry me."

The sensual rhythm of the Latin beats along with the close proximity probably had an effect on Marie and within a short period of time she was dating Allan, but still trying to keep a lid on it from Grinde—who she still felt very loyal too for helping her when she was still a young starlet and had just arrived in Hollywood. After several months of seeing one another covertly—Allan finally told Marie that he loved her and he knew that she loved him. Marie didn't deny this. He told her he wanted to marry her. "But I still care for Nick!," she replied. "But do you love him?" She couldn't or wouldn't answer that question.

One weekend Nick left town with some of his cronies to do some deep sea fishing. Allen pinned Marie down and gave her an ultimatum—either you marry me right now or we call off our relationship. Marie agreed, but again she told Allan, that their marriage would have to be kept, at least temporarily, a secret until she could break the news to Grinde. Allan wasn't happy about it, but he was willing to accept it if it meant getting Marie to the altar and then dealing with the Grinde issue afterward.

Marie and Allan decided to go to Las Vegas. In her efforts to keep the whole thing a secret Marie went to Max Factor's and rented a black wig and wore sun glasses. They decided that rather than drive together from Los Angeles to Las Vegas that they would take a bus "so they would go unnoticed." Shortly after arriving in Las Vegas they hurried from the bus station to the registrar's office, where Marie signed the marriage license by her legal name of Katharine Elizabeth Wilson. Apparently she didn't fool the registrar, who giggled, "Aren't you Marie Wilson?" Marie made sure to ask the registrar not to tell Louella Parsons or Hedda Hopper. Rather than staying in Las Vegas and enjoying their honeymoon the couple almost immediately caught a bus back to Los Angeles.

Unbelievably this deception went on for several weeks. Marie told her family, who she still lived with and supported, that she and Allan were married, but that they had to keep it a secret and that Allan wouldn't be living with them. She still had to find a way of telling Nick without breaking his heart! Ultimately Nick did find out but it wasn't through Marie initially, but gossip about her being seen around town with a young handsome actor. Marie finally admitted it was true and that the young actor was her husband and had been for weeks. A friend would later ask Marie why she married Allen if she didn't want to upset Nick? "Oh, he was so lonesome and about to go into the service and all. He wanted somebody to write letters to, and I decided to marry him." This was true to a certain extent. By the time Allan and Marie did marry the United States was in World War Two and Allan had been drafted. But it's doubtful she married him only to be his pen pal.

How exactly Nick took all of this is not known. Later accounts say he was terribly disappointed and angered. But he had been with Marie for over eight years and during that time he had enjoyed her favors sexually. He told people around town that they were "engaged," but there really wasn't any formal engagement. The truth is that Nick was a much older man who enjoyed having a trophy girl friend—a beautiful and desirable woman who was half his age. As for Marie, she used Nick as much as he used her. She used him to get ahead initially in the industry and Nick's interventions and contacts certainly did help. He also helped support her monetarily when times got lean. She was genuinely fond of him and didn't want to break his heart, but by deceiving him the way she did—it probably made a bad situation much worse.

Nick didn't want to lose her. He told Marie that if she got an annulment he would gladly take her back. He went so far as to contact Allan and tell him that if he left Marie and went to New York he would have a "bright future" in show business. But it was over and nothing Nick did or said would make any difference. Marie was happy as Mrs. Allan Nixon—for the time being.

II

Over the next year Marie kept busy professionally by appearing in several supporting parts in B or A- pictures for several studios. She worked with Richard Arlen in an aviation picture at Paramount called *Flying Blind*. She joined former boxer Slapsie Maxie Rosenbloom in a collegic comedy for Columbia titled *Harvard, Here I Come*. This picture introduced Yvonne De Carlo to film audiences. Apparently some of the Harvard undergrads and their professors took offense to the film and how it depicted college life on their campus, causing Slapsie Maxie to respond, "if dat is a insult to dose gents at Harvard, let 'em sulk. I'm gettin' a thusan' a week and what are they gettin'?"

Marie followed that one up with an interesting gangster film/musical at Universal titled *Broadway*. It was based on a 1926 Broadway show produced by the legendary Jed Harris. The story is novel in that George Raft plays himself in the film which is told in flashback about Raft's days as a dancer at a New York nightclub called "The Paradise" and a murder which occurs there along with various gangsters who populate the New York nightclub scene. The cast is strong and in addition to Raft includes Pat O'Brien, Janet Blair, Broderick Crawford, and S.Z. Sakall. Marie plays Grace, yet another showgirl part. But the music in the film is excellent and includes such roaring 20's favorites as *Dinah, Sweet Georgia Brown, I'm Just Wild About Harry, Yes Sir, That's My Baby* and *Chicago. Broadway* did fairly well with the critics. *The New York Times* wrote, "If *Broadway* no longer has the impact of the original play, it still affords an interesting cook's tour of an unsavory decade—with Mr. Raft, of course, as the knowing guide" and *Variety* said the picture retains the "thrill, tension and dramatic suspense of the original play" Marie's part was not showy enough to rate much of any mention, good or bad, in the reviews. One good thing to come out of making *Broadway* on a personal level was meeting Gus Schilling, an ex-burlesque comedian who had a small part in the picture. One night Gus took Marie home to meet his wife and have dinner. Schilling's wife was Betty Rowland, who did a striptease act and was known as "The Ball of Fire." Marie and Betty became very good friends. Marie later said that she and Betty "look so much alike we could be sisters" even though Betty had red hair, green eyes and was 5'1. Later Gus had a operation to remove stomach ulcers. Marie visited him with a pie she baked herself and five pounds of salted nuts, "If I had a stomach," Schilling recalled, "it would have turned."

Marie's next picture was at Monogram—another step down. Monogram specialized in B (or C) pictures—second features and serials like the *Charlie Chan* series. This was to be a feature which would probably be billed with a better "A" picture. It's called *She's in the Army* and began production on March 27, 1942—not even four months after the United States entry into World War Two. It's a comedy-drama about a singer who plans to generate some good publicity for herself by enlisting into an Army volunteer group. Later she is bet $5,000 she

Marie with, left to right, Dorothy Moore, Anne Gwynne, Elaine Morey, and Iris Adrian as one of the showgirls of *Broadway*. Author's Collection.

couldn't last six weeks in WADCA (Women's Ambulance and Defense Corp of America) along with her friend Susan Slattery (played by Marie) she takes the bet. Still the film is professionally done for very little money and includes a cast of veterans such as Lucille Gleason, Lyle Talbot and Charlotte Henry and was directed by Jean Yarbrough, who would later direct several Abbott and Costello films. The writer was Sidney Sheldon, who would within five years win an Academy Award for his screenplay for the Cary Grant film *The Bachelor and the Bobbysoxer* and would create the television series *I Dream of Jeannie*.

The parts that Marie was playing—showgirls and best friend to the heroine in (usually) B pictures weren't enhancing her film career, but it was getting her by financially. In addition to these films she would do an occasional radio job, but she didn't really care for radio—it scared her. It had an immediacy which she didn't have in pictures. Many times the programs were done live before a studio audience and this flustered her. On a radio show the cast usually got their scripts only a short time before they went on and they read their lines. For some reason this didn't work very well for Marie, who was used to memorizing her lines. With a radio script in hand she often found she lost her place and if she did she sometimes had to ad-lib her way out of it.

Shortly after the country went to war—her husband, Allan Nixon did too.

With Allan away in the army and her picture career drying up—after the picture at Monogram she had no fresh offers—and having no love for radio, Marie decided she had to do something to keep the income rolling in. She was not only supporting herself, but also her family. Her grandfather and stepfather had both died, but she still felt responsible for her mother and for her several half brothers and sisters. She thought she would return to the stage with a nightclub act. She occasionally did a song or two when she appeared at the Hollywood Canteen. Her voice was ok, but no great shakes—but her blonde good looks and voluptuous body kept the men interested and she was able to amuse the crowd with her trademark "dumb blonde" asides. She began the process of putting an act together, but this was interrupted when she heard about a project that vaudeville and Broadway entertainer Ken Murray was putting together—a revue which would provide Marie with seven years of steady employment and income and would help resurrect her career.

III

In the spring of 1942 it wasn't only Marie's career which needed resurrecting but also Ken Murray's. Murray was in New York and, as he would later state, "I was not only between pictures, but there was no line-up waiting for my radio services." So, Murray informed his agent that he was ready to do personal appearances ("which was another way of saying I needed some eating money.") Murray got a booking as an MC at Loew's State Theatre in New York City. He was playing four and five shows per day between showings of MGM films. While he was appearing at Loew's a friend of his came back stage and asked him what he was doing "playing the last dregs of vaudeville?" Murray truthfully told his friend that his work had dried up and he needed to do something to make a living.

His friend told him that before he went back to California he needed to check out a Broadway show called *Priorities*. Murray went to see the show, "I went to the 46th Street Theatre expecting to see a new musical comedy, but it suddenly dawned on me that, instead, I was seeing the best variety show since the Palace had closed more than ten years before." And they were doing outstanding business. Murray was inspired, "This is my dish. I'll do a show like this in California. With the defense plants booming and the population growing every day, there ought to be plenty of people to patronize a show like this. Only I'll make mine different. I'll add a line of beautiful girls but I won't just let them stand there and look pretty—I'll work with them. I'll give them funny things to say. I'll make personalities out of them . . . There're always a lot of movie starlets available."

When Murray returned to California he raised $10,500 to raise the curtain on a show he called *Blackouts*. The title was apt. In the theatre *Blackouts* refers to a series of sketches one after another, or as Webster's Dictionary would describe it, "a skit forming a short acting number in a revue, so called because the lights are cut off immediately on the final word, to heighten the point." (Interestingly, the popular late 60's television series, *Laugh-In*, would often do blackout types of sketches). It was also apt in that the United States was at war and everybody knew that at night you had to keep your curtains drawn and lights low because of blackout conditions.

Ken Murray would do what he usually did on stage, act as an MC with his long stogie in hand and introduce the various acts. But he didn't leave it there because he would often "butt in on them. I had bits worked out to take care of that butting in. But it seemed spontaneous and people said, 'Oh boy—what an ad-libber." So Murray had comics, singers, dancers (The fabulous Nicholas Brothers were hired for the *Blackouts*), animal acts, acrobats (Once Burt Lancaster and his then partner Nick Cravet appeared in *Blackouts* doing their acrobat act), and of course chorus line of beautiful girls that he did patter with.

Murray wanted a girl to do a comic striptease, but she couldn't be an overtly sexual woman. He later explained it, "Some friends of mine in the business think I'm corny, but I've a theory about beautiful, sexy women. It's all in the face! On stage it's entirely different than on TV. There, face and figure count. But on television, all a woman's sex is in her face. I've always liked wholesome, beautiful girls with angel faces. As soon as a face gets a little lascivious, suggesting the gal knows she has a beautiful figure and sex appeal—all's lost." And she had to be sexy enough so that she would "make every man in the audience want to climb up on the stage." Writer Fredda Dudley Balling later would write that Murray was seeking, " . . . a foil to his own wise-cracking, cigar gnawing emcee characterization. He envisioned a blonde with the body of Aphrodite, the face of a happy child, the voice of a mountain spring and the mind of Charlie McCarthy." Enter Marie Wilson.

Marie got a tip from her agent about Ken Murray's show and went to the El Capitan Theatre on Hollywood and Vine (this theatre had a rich history as a vaudeville house and later serving Jerry Lewis—even renamed The Jerry Lewis Theatre—and Merv Griffin for their television programs) to audition for Murray. Murray liked what he saw. He hired her on the spot for the comic striptease bit and leading lady. He had worked with Marie previously on a radio show and would recall that he "had a ball working on the air with her."

The next day Marie came to the theatre ready to rehearse—the show had only eleven days before opening on June 24, 1942. The first day of rehearsal was a hot summer day, and the El Capitan had been built many years before without air conditioning. The doors were wide open and Murray would later write that people off the street would keep dropping in to see what was going on. The theatre was a "beehive" of activity and many acts were there ready to rehearse their bits. Murray would recall that on this first day he was down in front of the orchestra "trying to whip this pandemonium into something resembling a show" when Marie arrived "wearing a sexy black costume that one could see immediately was never intended for the streets." Murray would expand on this, "Now nature

"Just the right combination of innocence and sexiness," Marie at the *Blackouts*. Author's Collection.

had endowed Marie Wilson with charms (39-19-36) that call attention to her presence like brass gongs being struck, and the engineering skill of the seamstress who made that costume must have been considerable. The upper part of the gown was so brief that it seemed to contradict the laws of gravity by staying up at all."

Murray would later relate that on the first day of rehearsals Marie was very anxious to do her act for him but he had many other things on his mind regarding the show which took priority, but Marie was persistent. He was walking around bellowing out instructions, looking over costumes, watching this or that act rehearse on different parts of the stage—all with Marie following closely behind trying to get his attention, "Oh, Mr. Murray! You've got to listen; I have the most sensational act written for me." All the time she was following him—to different corners of the stage or up and down the aisles of the theatre she was reading the material which had been prepared for her:

Now I'm a rebel, who's got a cause,
I'm going to settle a score
Against those dress designers
Like Schiaparelli and Dior.
Yes, they make us change the outside look . . .
Never mind what's underneath—
Oh, how I envy Mother Eve,
She only changed a leaf

Then she says to Murray, "Now honey, this is where you turn to the audience and say, 'You know Adam's favorite line is "When Autumn leaves start to fall."' The writers say this will be a big laugh."

Still following Murray around, she continued with the routine:

This year they wear the jeweled belt,
They say it's in good taste.
But I've got hips—I need no belt,
It's merely going to waste.

At this point Marie takes the belt off and drops it. She indicates that Murray would then have another funny line here and then she continues with her routine:

Designers pad us here
And flatten us there
And lead us a merry waltz—
So I'll just have to prove to you
That there isn't anything false.

Murray would recall at this point Marie takes off her shirtwaist, "revealing a very fetching but skimpy bra that just barely covered the most attractive part of Marie, according to the opinions of thousands and thousands of GI's who had her picture pasted up in their barracks."

And so it goes on with Marie reciting more lines and then removing more clothing such as her skirt. Well by this time this is causing a commotion in the theatre. The other acts have stopped rehearsing, carpenters, electricians and stage hands have stopped to watch Marie—the crowd of on-lookers walking in from the open doors leading to the street has grown—and why not? Marie Wilson was down to her black bra and panties. At this point Murray tells her, "Look, Marie, put a robe on and I'll rehearse all this with you in a few minutes—just as soon as I get through here."

But Marie demurs and says, "You've got to hear the finish. It's so cute."

I'm told the flat look is here to stay,
It's not a fad or stunt;
But naturally when it comes to style,
I want to be out in front.

As Murray recalls it, at this point Marie stands there with her chest protruding. He emphasizes that even though the lines sound very daring that with Marie's feather brained delivery the lines don't come out of her mouth offensively. But she is standing there, chest protruding and says, "of course, I have a few things left." After a few seconds a voice comes out of the darkness of the theatre—one of the on-lookers, "You ain't kiddin, Lady!"

All of this was incorporated into a routine between Marie and Murray

IV

It was a risk for Marie to even go into ***Blackouts.*** It was distinctly a vaudeville show with touches of burlesque. Both were considered a part of show business which had either died out (burlesque) or was on life support (vaudeville). It was especially risky to appear in such a show in Hollywood. For Marie to do a striptease in vaudeville type of show would be an indication that she was desperate and may close other doors in the industry. But Marie was desperate. Her career was struggling and this was the best offer to come along and at $750 per week she wasn't going to turn her back on this gift horse.

Blackouts opened on June 24, 1942. Writer Don Hall would recall that the show opened with Murray "chewing on an unlit cigar doing his Bugs Bunny "What's up, Doc?" impersonation. After a few topical jokes of the day, he would "warn" us that he was about to introduce Marie Wilson, who would come out wearing a very low-cut strapless evening gown. And if she decides to take a bow,

Promotional brochure for *Blackouts of 1943*.
Author's Collection]

we were admonished; the first four rows of the theater would be immediately evacuated. He'd then beckon to her, and she'd prance out with a provocative jiggle that made the top of her gown appear to be in imminent danger of losing its grip. Before she could say anything, he'd tell her to go back and come out again. His eyes would then be fixed on the top of her dress as she again bounced her way towards center stage. "One more time," he insisted, but she shook her head No. "Darn!" he said as he turned back to the audience, "one more time and I'm sure we'd have had it!" And so it went. From there more gags, songs, acrobats, girls and plenty of Marie Wilson sprinkled in through out the show.

Murray would recall that the reviews the next morning "were only lukewarm, except the one in the *Hollywood Daily Variety*, which panned it unmercifully." And indeed like many new shows it was off to a slow start but it kept picking up speed—helped, without a doubt by the influx of servicemen who were visiting Hollywood while on liberty during the war—and word of mouth. Murray recalled that "The first week the *Blackouts* lost $700. The second week, $500. The third week we broke even, and from then on we never had a losing week until it closed, more than seven years later." Indeed the first year *Blackouts* grossed a staggering $750,000. Murray took some particular delight in the fact that the *Variety* office was directly across the street from the El Capitan Theatre and that the critic who had panned the show had to look at the long lines which waited to get into the theatre day after day, night after night (*Blackouts* played ten shows per week, one every night, two on Saturday and three on Sunday). But the reviews which meant the most to Murray came from service men who would come back time and again and from just folks who loved the burlesque aspects of the show. Mrs. Edward Brodie would write Murray, "My husband went to see 'Blackouts' and laughed so hard he ruptured his appendix and had to be rushed to a hospital for an operation. This has caused much expense and worry. My husband thinks you should either pay for the operation or send him Marie Wilson. All I can say is you sure keep him in stitches."

The notoriety which Marie attained through *Blackouts* with servicemen didn't go unnoticed by Allan, who became increasingly jealous that many of his buddies had his wife—Marie—as a pin-up along with their pin-ups of Betty Grable and Rita Hayworth. Marie would later say this was a time when Allan got "a little peeved." She recalled Allan telling her that "There are too many wolves around Hollywood." Marie explained to him, "That's so, but a girl who wants to, gets to know how to keep the wolves from her door." Marie later recalled meeting a show business figure backstage who she called "very influential," who asked her out to dinner, "And he had that look in his eye. 'I'd love to,' I said, 'but I'm married.'" "Well," he said, "you don't have to be married every day." I said as sweetly as I could, 'I'll tell you the truth. I'd really love to go out with you but I have the worst habit. I tell everything I do to my husband.' That must have got him, because he left." Her explanation must have mellowed Allan because he later seemed to take it in stride. One new recruit must not have realized that Allan was Marie's husband and Allan decided to play dumb when the new recruit put up a provocative picture of Marie on his bunk wall.

"Who's that?," asked Allan.

"My girl," answered the recruit.

Van Heflin, who had just spent three months in a marine boot camp, came back stage and found Marie looking very glum. "What's wrong, Marie?" Heflin asked, "I feel so sorry for all you poor boys," Marie replied, "My husband is having a terrible time too. He calls me up sometimes and is just miserable." "Where is he?," Heflin asked, "Oh Fort MacArthur", Marie replied, indicating a local induction center. "How long has he been there? Asked Heflin, "Since yesterday," Marie sorrowfully replied.

Another time Marie finished at the theatre around midnight and was driving home, "I didn't realize a car was following me until it suddenly dashed ahead and cut in sideways until I had to stop. A man stepped out of the car and though he was a nice-looking fellow he got pretty insistent naturally I refused to get out of my car. As he got more insistent, I used an old trick—started laughing. 'You look so silly,' I said, and laughed some more. By that time I thought he looked awful silly, and I got hysterical with laughter. He began to look embarrassed." Finally the stalker apologized and drove off. While Marie didn't come out and say it, this situation could have turned out much worse—she was lucky.

The *Blackouts* became an enormous hit and gradually Marie's salary began to climb. Within a few months she was making $1200 per week and she paid Ken Murray back in kind by not taking any time off—and eventually would hold a record for 2,332 consecutive performances—and this was working seven days straight. Blackouts began getting national attention and Marie benefited from this. New York's *PM* had an article when *Blackouts* began its third season in June, 1944, "Ken Murray's *Blackouts*, which is Hollywood's answer to whatever happened to vaudeville, is starting its third year with a lot of new acts. But the little gal who packs 'em in is still luscious Marie Wilson . . . she's beautiful and dumb before the footlights, but, according to Murray, she's the one who holds the show together." *PM* pointed out that the highlight for the males in the audience is when "she (Marie) does a patriotic strip tease. Off comes her wool skirt for Army uniforms, her silk blouse for parachutes and her shoes for Russian relief. This leaves Miss Wilson clad in nothing but sheer black chiffon lingerie. She doesn't linger long after that, but the effect is enough to make every soldier in the audience wish the Army could dream up some use for black chiffon."

Time magazine even did a story on *Blackouts* in its February 12, 1945 issue in an article titled, CALIFORNIA GOLD MINE:

"In Los Angeles this week a variety show with nine-plus lives and 21 acts was racing merrily towards its 1500th performance. As *Blackouts* of 1945 it was packing them into the El Capitan Theatre even more solidly than it did as *Blackouts* of 1942. Almost as many people (1,541,000) have paid admission to the show as live in Los Angeles. Many of them have seen it four or five times—one man has attended 125 Sunday matinees and invariably writes a note of apology when he cannot be present."

The story went on to say that one of the drawing cards (besides Marie) was the ability to get big name entertainers to appear on the *Blackouts* stage, "Murray's biggest card is his ability to get headliners in the audience to participate. Some of them, such as Bob Hope and Bing Crosby, chime in from down front. Others, such as W.C. Fields, Mickey Rooney, Victor Moore, Edgar Bergen,

Dick Powell, Rudy Vallee, take over the stage. Murray exploits his guest stars brilliantly—by not exploiting them at all. They are never given billing, are often not even introduced. As a result, the audience feels it is really getting something extra for its money."

Sometimes embarrassing moments did happen on the *Blackouts* stage. Marie was afraid that the audience would turn hostile one night when she couldn't slip out of her dress because the zipper was stuck—the ever obliging Murray came on stage to help her out of it before the riot took place. More embarrassing for Marie was the time she showed too much skin (luckily for Marie not seen by the audience):

"The boys around the theater always have stories to tell about me. One of their favorite tales concerns the time I was in *Blackouts*. Because I had to make so many costume changes, they put a portable dressing room on the stage. During intermission I used to pick up my clothes and go up to my permanent dressing-room. One intermission I was in a great hurry, so I snatched my dress, clutched it up to my neck to cover myself and ran upstairs. I didn't know why there was so much commotion on the stage until later. Then I discovered that while I was completely covered in front, I had forgotten about the back."

Then there was the time that a press agent talked Marie into appearing in a Los Angeles court room wearing a mink coat and very little else underneath it. This was during a period when the authorities were conducting a drive against burlesque houses and the immorality they represent. The press agent devised a little script for Marie to follow: "This is what the boys are fighting for. This is what they want to come home to." She then was to remove the mink coat and stand in all of her glory in a negligee. The judge was outraged, his face red with anger. Marie burst into tears. The Judge lectured her about making a mockery of his courtroom, and the newspapers reported the incident the next day—further embarrassing Marie—not that it hurt her career, the crowds just kept coming to *Blackouts*—especially the servicemen.

It was not only the grunts in the service that came to see Marie and *Blackouts* but also ranking officers—including Generals. One Two-Star General came backstage covered with all his medals and probably expecting to get a special audience with Marie. What the General didn't know was that another serviceman, a private, was already backstage visiting with her, A Private Gonzales. To Marie they were both equals—both on the same team, fighting for their country. But the General didn't approach the private and finally between acts Marie approached the General and asked what his first name was. "Tom," the General replied. "Tom," Marie said leading him by hand to the private, "Say hello to Salvador. I want you two to buddy up. I see you're in the same outfit."

Marie got to know many entertainers during the run of *Blackouts*—those who were in the show and those who came to watch and one of the closest friends she made during this time was that pint-sized (4'5 tall) wonder Bonnie Baker, better known as "Wee Bonnie Baker" who had made a national craze with the song "Oh, Johnny, Oh, Johnny, How You Can Love." Murray signed Wee Bonnie to the *Blackouts* and she and Marie became life-long friends and when Bonnie gave birth to her baby daughter Sharon, she asked Marie to be the baby's godmother, which Marie enthusiastically agreed to. Marie loved children. There was a couple who did an acrobatic act at the *Blackouts* who had a ten month old baby—and when they were on stage performing—Marie, always happily, babysat the baby.

Marie was back—and Murray had her, but soon she would be back in pictures again, not—usually—in leading roles, but in higher quality productions and better parts—and *Blackouts* helped make it possible. She would always stay loyal to Ken Murray for helping resurrect her career and for improving her performances, "He has helped me so much with my timing. I used to stammer and stutter around—it was impossible to be funny Ken taught me about the economy of words . . . how if you put in any extra words before you come to the punch line you're dead." She credited Murray for giving back her self confidence, "When I started in *Blackouts* I was scared to death. Now I am so sure of myself. Ken did that."

Marie in a *Blackouts* promotional photo. Author's collection.

The success of **Blackouts** along with praise for Marie's performance brought her back to the attention of the Hollywood studios again. During the war years Marie would appear in five major studio productions, most of which had a wartime setting. After sixteen months since her last picture Marie was invited back by none other than Warner Brothers to appear in a major period musical. It was not a leading role (again) but **Shine on Harvest Moon** was certainly a big step up from Monogram's **She's in the Army**.

The cast was led by the popular Warner Brothers contractees Ann Sheridan, Dennis Morgan and Jack Carson. The first rate supporting cast was led by S.Z. Sakall, known to most people as "cuddles" because of his huge cheeks which people felt an irrepressible urge to squeeze, much to Sakall's annoyance. Marie was cast as yet another ditzy showgirl—Margie. Warner assigned his new contract director, David Butler helm the film. Butler had just come off directing Hope and Crosby in **The Road to Morocco** at Paramount and would go on to helm many of Warner's best musicals of the 1940's and 1950's including many for Doris Day including **Calamity Jane**.

The film was based on the life of Nora Bayes who, according to the American Film Institute, was, "a popular entertainer and songwriter in vaudeville and on Broadway, was known for her deep voice and dramatic style She was the first person to sing George M. Cohan's 1917 song **Over There**. Among the shows she appeared in were the **Ziegfeld Follies of 1907, 1908,** and **1909; Little Miss Fix It** (1911); **Maid in America** (1915); **The Cohan Revue** (1917); and **Queen O'Hearts** (1922). Bayes was married five times. Her second husband was Jack Norworth (the character Dennis Morgan plays), with whom she formed a stage act. In a **New York Herald Tribune** article, Norworth remembers that he first met Bayes when she came into his publisher's office looking for new material. They were married two weeks later and began to perform as a team in vaudeville. Later they performed for two seasons in the Ziegfeld Follies before their marriage ended. Bayes died in 1928." This formed the outline of the story, but of course in the film Bayes and Norworth live, in typical Hollywood fashion, happily ever after. Among the songs included in the film are ***Time Waits for No One, I Go for You, Pretty Baby, Every Little Movement, Take Me Out to the Ballgame*** and, of course, the title song which was written by Norworth and Bayes—and became one of the biggest hits of the early part of the 20th Century.

As good as Sheridan and Morgan are it's the secondary leads Carson and Marie who steal the show. Carson plays a down on his luck Magician "The Great Georgetti" and Marie becomes his scatter-brained assistant, Margie. The two perform a funny, show-stopping number together, ***So Dumb but So Beautiful***, which capitalized on Marie's dumb blonde persona. The picture had a three month production schedule from mid June through Mid September, 1943, and Marie had a clause in her contract to make sure she made her nightly ***Blackouts*** appearance. When the film premiered nationally in April, 1944 (after opening in New York on March 10, 1944) it went on to become a big money-maker for the studio. Surprisingly, the reviews for the film were mixed. The ***New York Times*** hissed, "You will see at the Strand, however, a two-hour marathon in which all the familiar clichés of back stage romance are indulged . . . You will see Jack Carson and Marie Wilson as a recurring sleight of hand act, with jokes and funny sayings, most of which are not." ***Variety*** thought the script had clichés, but praised the performances especially the supporting ones lauding Carson and Marie for their "major support" and Director Butler for getting "plenty out of cast members despite script deficiencies."

Marie in *Shine on Harvest Moon*, 1944. The Stumpf-Ohmart Collection.

In the fall of 1943 Marie was invited to make another film for Paramount—another romantic musical-comedy *You Can't Ration Love* which unlike *Shine on Harvest Moon* was set in the present. Naturally Marie is cast as a not too bright showgirl, this time called "Bubbles."

Marie followed this up by going to MGM for another musical—*Music for Millions*. The film was produced by Joe Pasternak and directed by Henry Koster—the team which had been behind the very popular Deanna Durbin musicals at Universal of a few years earlier (and incidentally the working title of this film was *One Hundred Girls and a Man* which was supposed to evoke the earlier Durbin film *One Hundred Men and a Girl*). The star was little Margaret O'Brien who had began wowing war-time movie audiences in 1942's *Journey for Margaret*. Since that film she had appeared in a string of box office hits the most recent being *Meet Me in St. Louis* which Margaret had almost stolen from Judy Garland. The cast also included June Allyson, in one of her earliest parts and the veteran Jimmy Durante. Marie is cast as a clarinet player with the reasonable sounding name of "Marie" (as opposed to "Bubbles"). The story is a bit of froth dealing with little Margaret unexpectedly arriving in New York City to visit her big sister (Allyson) who is a bassist in a symphony orchestra. While MGM always had O'Brien (by then considered a major box office star) slated as the lead—Allyson got her part only after Susan Peters, who had been paralyzed after a hunting accident, and Donna Reed (a scheduling conflict) were eliminated. This film did get some decent reviews including one from the *New York Times*, "Much of the same tender feeling and melodic felicity which Joe Pasternak and Henry Koster got into their early Deanna Durbin films some years ago has been recaptured . . . only some of the old zing is missing."

Joe Pasternak liked Marie well enough to use her in another film shot the same year of 1945 for MGM, *No Leave, No Love* another romantic musical comedy with a wartime setting. Marie is again not cast as the leading lady. Metro used this film to introduce a British actress and singer named Pat Kirkwood (who has a resemblance to Merle Oberon). Van Johnson and Keenan Wynn were cast as army buddies in a story which is told in flashback about how the Johnson character meets and eventually marries the Kirkwood character. Marie has the secondary female role of Rosalind—the love interest for the Wynn character. Van Johnson was at the peak of his bobbysoxer box office appeal and one review of the day said of the film, "Don't take *No Leave, No Love* seriously, but go ahead and take it if your devotion to Van Johnson is deep enough." Bosley Crowther at the *New York Times* begged to differ, "Talk about escapist entertainment! Wait until you see "No Leave, No Love" at the Capitol. It is really an inducement to escape."

The fifth and final film that Marie shot during the war was not a musical or a comedy but a home front drama titled, *Young Widow*, which was produced by Hunt Stromberg for United Artists and had a storied production history. The

Jo Kelly
with Love
Marie Wilson

Glamour shot of Marie from the mid 40's. The Stumpf-Ohmart Collection.

film went through three directors and two leading ladies before Stromberg was able to negotiate the services of Jane Russell from Howard Hughes who had Russell under exclusive contract. In fact, this would be Russell's first film since the notoriety of **The Outlaw**. Ida Lupino began the film under the direction of William Dieterle in February, 1945. By late March Lupino was out and Stromberg tried to entice his contract player Joan Fontaine to take the leading role, but she took suspension instead of the part and finally production resumed in mid April with Russell cast as the widow whose husband was killed during the war and has to go back to work while being pursued by an attractive young lieutenant (played by Louis Hayward). Her grief at losing her husband will not allow her to get on with her life and so she rebukes him—but eventually falls in love with him. Marie plays MacAllister, a showgirl, who has recently returned from a USO tour with a flock of servicemen in tow. She shares an apartment with the Russell character and another girl played by Penny Singleton (the radio and movies *Blondie*).

Jane Russell, in her autobiography, recalls the succession of directors who were brought in, "Worst part of the movie was the fact that I had three directors who were all totally different. The first was William Dieterle, a dark moody European who had me weeping over flowers and kissing one in a particular way that sent Louis's (Hayward) eyes heavenward with an 'I say, isn't that a bit much.' Dieterle was off the picture. Next was André "Bunty" deToth, who was marvelous! But he hated the project as much as I did, so he finally managed to escape. He directed

Marie as she looked in the 1946 film, *Young Widow*. The Stumpf-Ohmart Collection.

most of it though . . . The third director drove me mad. He was one of those raving perfectionists who insisted that every jot and title of that terrible script was gospel." This final director was Edwin L. Marin, who got the screen credit for directing the picture. Russell though, did fall a bit in love with her leading man, "Louis Hayward, my co-star, was an absolute charmer and I was in love again."

The film did nothing to enhance anybody's reputation and didn't do very well at the box office. Many critics thought that Jane Russell had been miscast. The *New York Times* wrote, "but Miss Russell's expressions and her written lines add little to this . . . trite and flat role" and even *Variety* called Russell an "unfortunate choice." Of Penny Singleton and Marie the *Varitey* critic wrote that they perform "in their normal fashion."

II

Allan was discharged from the service in late, 1945 and anxious to re-establish his own career. He and Marie were also looking for a house to live in. They still were living in the house Marie owned and lived in with her mother and younger half brother. During the course of the war her grandfather and stepfather, both of whom had been in poor health had passed away. Her two step sisters had married but often visited. Marie knew that she and Allan needed a measure of privacy, but she (and Allan) were both devoted to her relatives, so they wanted privacy but also to be close enough to Marie's family.

Marie's mother agreed that the newlyweds deserved to have a home of their own without the rest of the family being ever present. She agreed to help Marie by going house hunting with her. One day they began covering the Hollywood Hills in search of a place to live. They were surprised and delighted when they found two little Normandy cottages joined by an archway facing a communal driveway and backyard. They were further shocked to discover that both houses were for sale. The two women immediately came to the same conclusion that Marie and Allan would live in one cottage while Mrs. Wilson and whatever other family members were around would live in the other. So, Marie and Allan would have their privacy, yet when craving family togetherness they only need walk next door. With Allan's consent they bought the twin cottages and made plans to redecorate.

The cottages were relatively small with the larger one going to Marie's mother since she would be housing more people either living with her or visiting. Marie's living room when she bought the cottage was dark, dull brown and small. There wasn't adequate closet space and throughout the house there was that same dull brown coloring. Before moving in Marie redecorated her cottage. The wall and ceilings were painted light blue and dark blue carpeting was put in running wall to wall through into the bedroom. To make the living room appear larger than it actually was they put a sheet of solid mirror behind the fireplace. Marie measured the walls in the small hallway which led to the bedroom and using those measurements they made ceiling high clothes closets, with mirrored doors. For his own privacy, Allan made one small upstairs bedroom into a den for himself. Marie would joke that with the 6'4 Allan occupying the den it was indeed private because it was so small and stuffed with personal effects that nobody else could fit into the room! Another small bedroom was made into a dressing room for Marie.

The house was drafty so Marie and Allan installed a heating system. They also tiled the bathrooms and kitchens of both houses. They laid a patio outback for their patio furniture. Marie would later say she bought the two houses for "a song" but then spent about $25,000 to remodel both of them.

Marie was making enough money that she could afford a maid for her mother and two for herself—one who came in the mornings to clean and the other who came in the afternoons to cook. One account of her relationship with her two black maids is that Marie felt "motherly" towards the women. She would later say she would have done the work herself except, "I hate to make beds, and I hate to squeeze orange juice and besides they have to work someplace."

Marie loved to have dinner parties and had to be creative when it came to seating her guests since the house was so small. "It's very simple," she told an interviewer, "I put an extra leaf in the tea table. I have the big armchairs moved into mother's house. Then we get out four card tables and set out two of them in this room, one in the kitchen and one in the bedroom. Of course some conventional souls might think it sort of strange to eat in the bedroom, but our gang doesn't seem to mind." At one such dinner party Marie and Allan entertained twenty-four guests serving pepper steaks, tossed salad and chocolate fudge cake. While the guests ate dinner in different areas of the house: living room, kitchen and down stairs master bedroom—they would all reconvene in the living room before a lighted fire and those without furniture to sit on would sit on the floor—Indian style—or on pillows which Marie provided. "All very cozy," Marie would contend. On beautiful California evenings they would move the dinner parties outside to the patio area.

Marie always maintained that she kept her luscious figure not through sensible eating and exercise, but simply by being active and working hard. Allan was a very athletic man who played football in school and enjoyed many different sports. Marie believed that a married couple should have things in common, so she was determined to take up tennis because it was a activity which Allan greatly enjoyed and was quite good at. Marie ended up taking a few lessons but could never master the sport. Her serve seldom made it over the net and her back hand was non-existent. So Allan plays his sports while Marie would often look on or be at the pool while Allan played tennis at the club.

Into this domestic scene came an addition in Allan's 1946 Christmas stocking—A five pound, fluffy gold and grey Yorkshire terrier which was named Mr. Hobbs. While Hobbs was a present for Allan he became totally devoted to Marie and she to him. Marie became known for taking Mr. Hobbs everywhere with her. When she worked at **Blackouts** the little dog was in her dressing room waiting for her to return from performing her routine. He would come to the studio when she was shooting a picture and even join Marie and Allan when they dined out for dinner or went to a nightclub. Later when Marie was doing the **My Friend Irma** radio series Hobbs was present but the little yorkie made the unforgivable mistake of barking while the show was on the air and producer-director Cy Howard had him banned from the set. Once when Marie and Allan were at a press photographer's costume ball, a burglar broke into their house and stole Marie's mink coat. A friend, assuming that Hobb's must have been home, sarcastically told Marie, "Fine watch dog you got!" Marie took great pleasure in telling her friend that Hobbs wasn't at home, "He was with us at the ball, of course."

There was also the time when Marie and Allan were visiting New York and staying at the Waldorf. They had been there one night already when Allan and Marie came in with Hobbs on a leash. The manager took Allan aside and explained that they had a policy of no pets. When Allan told this to Marie she told him, "Nonsense! I carried him right past the desk last night." Allan explained that they the previous night they thought that Hobbs had been a fur piece because Marie had carried him around her neck. The couple and Hobbs moved to the more pet friendly St. Regis.

But all wasn't idyllic with the couple. Allan was a hard drinking man and often got into public altercations with people in bars while under the influence. These encounters made their way into the gossip columns of Louella Parsons and Hedda Hopper and caused considerable embarrassment for Marie especially when she had to bail him out of jail. Also, the fact that Marie was constantly working—**Blackout's** every week night and five times over the weekend. She was working in films and doing occasional radio work while Allan was still struggling—ocassionally getting a "B" movie role such as in the campy **Prehistoric Girl**. Allan also got some summer stock roles including one opposite Helen Hayes. Reportedly Allan called Marie in despair telling her that Hayes was getting paid $2,000 per week while he was only getting $300. Marie didn't sympathize, telling him, "That's about right." Yet the early days of her marriage were on the whole quite happy for Marie and Allan. They talked eventually of having children, but for the time being their child would be Mr. Hobbs—who they both doted on.

In 1948 when Marie was working on **My Friend Irma** and was a huge success on radio with plans being made to make a movie version, Marie was constantly working and the focus of media attention. This took a toll on their marriage with the insecure Allan believing that a man should be the principle bread winner. The couple separated for about a week. Since Hobbs was officially Allan's dog—he went with Allan during that week—and moved into the Roosevelt Hotel. But Hobbs without Marie was despondent and refused to eat. After a week of separation, Allan got Marie back by having Hobbs appear at her front door with a note tied around his collar. Marie's heart melted when she read the note:

Dear Mother,
I can't eat or sleep. Even a tree holds no interest for me. My father nearly
cried when he told me that he couldn't keep me in the manner to which I
have become accustomed. I am lonesome and I want to come home. Please.
Hobbs

Marie took both Hobbs and Allan back. She would never let Hobbs go again which is more than can be said for Allan.

Marie, circa, 1947. The Stumpf-Ohmart Collection.

CHAPTER FIVE
MY FRIEND IRMA

In 1945 a young radio writer named Cy Howard arrived in Los Angeles to try his hand in Hollywood. He had been an actor in New York—without any notable success. He went on to write jokes for Danny Thomas and later Jack Benny. Howard was a brash 31-year old who some felt was full of himself, but he had an innate optimism which could be contagious—especially when he was describing one of his ideas. His friend and fellow writer Larry Gelbart (later the writer and producer of the *Mash* television series) would later recall that Howard, "was an original" in "a town full of carbon copies." John Crosby, the radio critic of the *New York Herald Tribune*, wrote that shortly after Howard arrived in Hollywood—he used his connections at CBS and "wormed" his way into the presence of William S. Paley, the chairman of the network. But he had an idea he wanted to sell to CBS—and he felt the network would be receptive since NBC had recently raided many of the networks stable of stars—and they needed new ideas and new blood. He had the idea for a new radio series based on the people he met while living in a rooming house in Brooklyn.

Howard's idea was built around the tried and true character of the All-American Dumb Blonde. Gracie Allen and scores of others had trailed this path long before on stage, films and radio. Jane Ace's dumb blonde was more or less the Norm Crosby of her day—the master of the malapropism (American Heritage Dictionary defines a malapropism as a "ludicrous misuse of a word.") For instance, "Time Heals all wounds" would come out of Ace's mouth as "Time wounds all heels" which if you think of it—has certain logic, but usually not in the context that Ace uses it. Another example would be, "you hit the nail on the head" which in Ace-speak would come out as "you hit the nail right on the thumb that time."

Gracie Allen though was the acknowledged master of the "dumb blonde" persona. In life Gracie was a highly intelligent (she proved her intelligence on the quiz show, *Information Please*, in 1939) and well-read woman who wasn't anything like her scatter-brained on-stage persona—which is usually the case with most "dumb blonde" actresses. But on stage with husband and partner

George Burns her dumb blonde often had a logic that if you seriously thought about it—made a great deal of sense. For instance, Gracie would speak of "the president of today is the postage stamp of tomorrow" or a painter would invite Gracie to the "hanging" of one of his pieces and Gracie would innocently reply, "Oh yes, you should come to Alcatraz—they're hanging one of my brothers." Radio historian John Dunning would keenly observe that most of Gracie's mutterings often just would come out of the blue with no rhyme or reason behind them.

Gracie was attractive and demure in a lady-like way. The character which Cy Howard had in mind for his show was, like Gracie, big-hearted and dumb but unlike Gracie his character would be a blonde bombshell—a wolf magnet, yet so innocent that she is unaware of her attraction to the opposite sex. She had to have a little-girl quality and basic good will about her character which would make her most ridiculous mutterings or actions forgivable. He needed to find the right actress to pull off this really rather complex characterization.

II

The scenario that Howard had envisioned concerned two single young women who share a Brooklyn apartment to make ends meet. Jane Stacy was brunette, pretty—but not overtly beautiful. Jane was level-headed, a bit wary of people—particularly men and their intentions and saw situations in a logical and intelligent way. Her roommate, Irma Peterson, was the complete opposite—blonde, sexy—yet innocent, naive, out-going, friendly and very dumb. For instance if Irma was asked about compulsory military service she would answer, "A girl shouldn't have to go out with a sailor if she doesn't want to." And she thought that fly paper was "stationary used on airplanes."

Yet, despite their differences, Jane and Irma become the best of friends. Indeed the theme song, Cole Porter's Friendship, pretty much summed up the plots of the show: "If you're ever in a jam—here I am." Irma would get herself and the others around her in a jam and often it is Jane who has to figure a way out. The episodes would be narrated by Jane who often introduced the show in this way, "Mother nature gave some girls brains, intelligence and cleverness. But with *My Friend Irma*, Mother Nature slipped her a mickey."

Indeed, the show would be titled *My Friend Irma*. The title made clear that Irma was the pivotal character, but the *My* in the title gives an almost equal prominence to the Jane Stacy character. For without Jane as the solid and reliable counter balance the Irma character could easily descend into burlesque. Jane, like George Burns to Gracie Allen or Dean Martin with Jerry Lewis, serves the very functional purpose of reining the idiocy in—and making the comics more human in the process, In effect, Jane is the straight man—or straight woman of this team.

Howard began to refer to **My Friend Irma** as a "soap opera with laughs." Howard saw his show as the original "show about nothing" forty years before **Seinfeld**. "In a situation comedy somebody puts his money in a drawer and they sell the table," Howard explained, "Irma is different. Irma buys a pair of nylon hose—and that's enough for a show." He saw the "Irma" character as universal, "Being a bachelor, all my women are frustrated. Everybody thinks they're Jane when in reality they're Irma. Irma is universal. The whole world is Irma, nice people who get panicky. Then years from now, Irma will be happy. She'll have five children . . . and be happy. Jane may not be so happy. She's too smart." When asked who he modeled Jane after, Howard matter of factly answered, "I'm Jane."

Cy Howard came to the conclusion that both the Irma and Jane characters had to have the right chemistry to work correctly. In fact, the Jane character was cast first. According to radio historian John Dunning in his essential book, **The Encyclopedia of Old Time Radio**, Howard believed that the casting "would make or break it." Finally Howard thought of Cathy Lewis for the part of Jane Stacy. Lewis was in her early 30's and was one of the busiest women working in radio at the time. She did it all—comedy, dramatic shows such as **Suspense** and even was a band singer with Kay Kyser. She was married to Elliott Lewis another busy radio actor who was also a writer, producer and director. When Howard finally approached Lewis she was on her way to one of her many radio gigs (which made her one of the highest paid people working in the medium) and she told Howard that he had "five minutes—that's all." She read the script in her usual no-nonsense manner and Howard was convinced that he had found his Jane—and immediately signed her.

Howard had these traits in mind for Irma, "She must be a pretty, wide-eyed little girl, kind and sweet—but not sexy. She must be able to look like a secretary and sound like a secretary. Gentle, naive, innocent." Marie certainly was pretty and had wide blue eyes—but there is no way she could not be considered sexy. After-all, she had done numerous pin-ups in revealing bathing suits and was wowing audiences nightly with Ken Murray's **Blackout**—often clad in a skimpy black negligee. But the thing about Marie was that she could make her sexiness non-threatening to other women. Her gentleness and kindliness were as much a part of her character as her physical development.

Somebody at CBS had suggested Marie after Howard had auditioned and dismissed yet another contender he found unsuitable for his Irma. Howard wasn't convinced about Marie and decided he would have to see her for himself. So one night he went to the **Blackouts** and watched her performance. She was pretty sexy of course, he would recall thinking, "the audience was going nuts about her—and she had such an angelic face and those big wide blue eyes—I still wasn't convinced until I went to meet her backstage and she was so sweet and cute—not a sexpot at all."

Howard asked her if she'd like to do a radio program. For years afterward,

Marie as she looked around the time she began *My Friend Irma*, 1947. The Stumpf-Ohmart Collection.

Howard would fondly recall and laugh at her reply, "Yes, but I can't read." At first Howard thought she meant that she was illiterate. Then he realized that in an Irmaesque way Marie was telling him that reading live on the air with a script was difficult for her. Howard reassured Marie that she could and that he would teach her the techniques of successfully reading and keeping place with a script on a live radio show. Marie was still unsure telling Howard, "Oh, Mr. Howard, it's so nice of you, but I couldn't really. You'll get fired, you know, and that would be terrible. I would feel so guilty."

Howard finally arranged for Marie and Cathy Lewis to do a reading together and knew he had what he wanted—he had the first string for ***My Friend Irma***. Marie, still somewhat apprehensive finally agreed to do the show.

Once Howard found his leads—putting together the supporting cast was a piece of cake. He found some extraordinary radio talents for the other pivotal roles. John Brown was cast as Al, a hustler always on the look for an easy mark. Al was also Irma's boyfriend—she could always see the good in him even when Jane tried to convince her otherwise. Al's weekly greeting to Irma became a national catch-phrase, "Hi-ya, Chicken." Originally Jane Morgan was cast as Mrs. O' Reilly, the owner and landlady of the rooming house where Irma and Jane lived, but Morgan didn't quite work out and Howard eventually cast veteran Gloria Gordon in a role described by John Dunning as "a fierce Irish battleaxe." Gordon was also the mother of another radio veteran—Gale Gordon, who would soon begin appearing with Lucille Ball in *My Favorite Husband* and Eve Arden in *Our Miss Brooks*, but would become best known on television's *The Lucy Show* as Mr. Mooney. Hans Conried was cast as Professor Kropotkin, a violinist at the Paradise Burlesque, who lived in the apartment right above Irma and Jane. Alan Reed (later the voice of Fred Flintstone) was cast as Irma's long suffering employer at the law office she worked at. And finally tall, handsome Leif Erickson was cast as wealthy Richard Rhinelander III, Jane's boss who she was in love with—even if he didn't seem to notice (Jane: "Wouldn't it be great if I wound up being Mrs. Richard Rhinelander the third?" Irma (innocently): "What good will that do if he's got two other wives?").

Marie, Cathy Lewis and John Brown looking over a *My Friend Irma* radio script. The Authors Collection.

CBS liked Howard's script and cast selections well enough that they decided to give it a chance—even though it would be non-sustaining—meaning without a sponsor when it debuted. But if it did well enough and audiences ate it up getting a sponsor would be no problem. Many radio programs had started this way. For instance, Orson Welles' *Mercury Theatre of the Air* debuted without a sponsor. After the famous *War of the Worlds* broadcast on Halloween 1938 which scared half the listening public on the Eastern seaboard half to death—it didn't take Welles long to get Campbell Soup as a prominent sponsor.

But the rehearsals for that first show were not without difficulties. Cy Howard was a tough task master. He could be very assertive with his actors and anybody who worked for him—and not always in a nice, gentle or nurturing way. He felt he got the best results when he kept things on a set a little tense. Marie was terrified of him and after the first day of rehearsals she had so many doubts about whether she could work with him along with mastering the techniques of reading a radio script live—that she quit. Howard, knowing that she was perfect for the part of Irma, coaxed her back and she developed a technique to deal with the abrasive Howard. She turns her back on the control room when she works—so she didn't have to face him—and his often exasperated reactions when mistakes took place. As for Marie's fear of reading a radio script live on the air—this was eased when the writers began to write her dialogue in capital letters—it helped her keep pace and track. Marie also adopted what would be described as "the Irma voice." The Irma voice was described as a "lilting, empty bird nest soprano" where her private voice was an octave below and where the Irma laugh was more of a chirp, her private laughter was described as "deep and soft."

Marie and Alan Reed in a typical *My Friend Irma* scene.

Howard finally came to the conclusion that he had to stop yelling at Marie—because it only evoked sympathy from everybody else towards her, "If I yelled at her everybody else would yell at me. John Brown would say it was all his fault. Cathy Lewis would insist it was all her fault. My secretary, Pat Burton, would jump in with a thousand excuses for Marie. If Marie makes a bloop the audience loves it, and I'm the heavy." Marie didn't get mad at Cy Howard when he blew his top, she would rationalize it this way, "He can't help it. He's so nervous. It's glandular." For his part Howard would candidly tell a reporter, "I'm an egomaniac. The cast hates me, but better they should hate me and give a good show than love me and we're off the air."

Cy Howard, standing with pipe, along with Marie and other members of the *My Friend Irma* cast including John Brown, standing over Marie and Gloria Gordon, seated on far right. The Author's collection.

The first episode of the series explained how Irma and Jane meet—on a New York City street and decide to share a small, run-down apartment. Also introduced is Al, who doesn't work a regular job and is always on the look out for a "easy mark." Jane invites her wealthy boss Richard Rhinelander III to the apartment for dinner and is soon embarrassed when Al drops by but it turns out that Richard likes Al and Irma because they come across as "real" people. The series debuted Friday April 11, 1947 over the CBS radio network at 10:30 PM.

By the end of the following week over 2,000 letters had been received by the network and CBS was sure they had a potential hit on their hands. The show soon moved towards the top of the Hooper ratings (the radio equivalent of the Nielsen television ratings) with a 20 share and situated as one of the top five radio shows in the nation. But interestingly it took a little time for **Irma** to acquire a sponsor—but after 20 weeks it did and it was a big one—Lever Brothers—a soap company which was, according to **Time** magazine, "one of the biggest spenders in radio." By the time the show returned for it's second season in September it had what was arguably the second best time slot in radio between the hugely popular **Lux Radio Theatre** and **Screen Guild Players** (The best time slot was NBC on Sunday nights between **Jack Benny** and **Charlie McCarthy**).

The reviews over time were on the whole quite positive. **Time** magazine would write, "**Irma's** characterizations are cut to the measure of the cast . . . Most astonishing of all is Irma herself. Cinema actress Marie Wilson, who has been playing the role of a dumb blonde for so long that she now lives the part." John Crosby radio critic for the **New York Herald Tribune** wrote, "**My Friend Irma**, one of the more fortunate properties of the Columbia Broadcasting System, has been constructed carefully out of reliable old chestnuts obviously with the intention of long-term service. The central idea, that of two young girl roommates, one bright, and the other almost intolerably innocent of all knowledge was taken almost intact from a very funny play called **My Sister Eileen.** The stupid but beautiful girl in the case is Irma; the bright one is known as Jane and her function is a sort of narrator and Greek chorus for the disasters Irma precipitates once a week. This sort of thing can go on close to forever. It has stood Gracie Allen in good stead for about fifteen years and it ought to keep Irma (Marie Wilson) pretty well heeled at least that long." **Variety** would sum up **Irma's** appeal, "Irma's success secret lies in its adroit mixture of humor and humanity. While basically a comedy show, this program doesn't attempt to snap the dialer's head off with a machine-gun fire of gags . . . "Irma" rolls up its gags effortlessly, letting them fall, however, with perfect timing. The quality of the laughs, moreover, is tempered in a framework of neighborly situations and characterizations."

Despite her apprehensions about radio and her rocky relationship with Cy Howard, Marie Wilson through **Irma** finally achieved true stardom. She began the series making $200 per week, but as the show became more and more popular her salary escalated to a reported $2,000 per week. Marie, perhaps best of all summed up the reasons for the shows success, "I never did make good on radio until Cy got hold of me. He not only created a great character, he created a great show. The whole show is alive. All the other characters are just as well written as Irma. Jane has her own viewpoint. Al has his. Everyone gets laughs, or drama, or something. Cy knew that a show can be pretty sad if only one character is great." For most people who knew her that statement summed up the Marie Wilson that they knew—not taking sole credit for the success of her show but giving credit to everybody involved. Marie better than anybody knew that *My Friend Irma* could only work well and successfully as an ensemble rather than a star piece.

The actors all had high regard for each other and their talents and all took to Marie's innate kindness and generosity. Cathy Lewis and Marie became particularly close and Lewis would recall that Marie had, "No camouflage to her make up and that's what makes Marie such a good friend. Loyalty, integrity and sincerity are the basic foundations for a very real character that endears itself to everyone who comes into contact with it." Hans Conried said, " . . . working with Marie is one of the most complete and satisfying things that can happen to anyone . . . She's first to help the other actor, last to criticize anyone—unless it's herself." Marie convinced everyone that she was indeed a lovable ditz, "playing a dumb blonde has a very definite effect on my personal life. It has helped me to make a lot of money, but more important, because people think I am dumb, they are nice to me and I have made many good friends this way. Some people even stop me in the street and ask me if I am really dumb. I always say, 'Yes,' and let it go at that. Why should I kill a good thing?"

Just after the show began its third season in 1948, Cathy Lewis, had a breakdown just hours before the show was to air and took a leave from the radio show which lasted through the entire season. For Marie it was like losing her right hand, and she let Cathy know that when she was ready she would be back on the show, a statement which Cy Howard backed up. But they had to have somebody very quickly. Joan Banks, a veteran radio performer, was at her doctor's office when an emergency call came from CBS. She was told that Cathy had collapsed during rehearsals, and they needed Joan to go on in her place. "I had to be there twenty minutes ago," Banks would later recall. On her way to the studio Banks ran out of gas, and arrived at the studio just as the show was to go on the air. Not only was Banks in a state of high anxiety, but so was the rest of the company—except for Marie, "She turned those fascinating eyes at me and calmly said, 'why are you worried Joan? you can do this.'" Marie's calm and friendly nature immediately put Banks at ease. Banks would also recall bringing her young five year old daughter to the *My Friend Irma* studio where Marie was wearing a salmon satin blouse and a light wool skirt with her blonde hair falling in waves to her shoulder—Banks' daughter tugged on her mother and said, "I know mommie, that fairy princesses are just pretend, but mommie, if there were fairy princesses they would look just like Marie."

Banks would recall that Marie had great generosity to her fellow players and all of those who worked in the studio. One day Banks admired a white sweater that Marie was wearing and then for Christmas that year she received its duplicate as a present from Marie. Hans Conried collected Japanese figurines and for his birthday one year Marie presented him with two rare Japanese figurines, which he was sure he could never have afforded himself. Conried had no idea that Marie was even aware of his hobby.

Marie as the lovable, wide-eyed and scatterbrained Irma Petersen. The Author's Collection.

III

In addition to the new radio show and her continuing daily performances in *Blackouts*, Marie had three films released in 1947. The first released in March had a long filming history—it began shooting at the Enterprise Studios lot from late April through late June of 1946 and then moved to RKO studios shooting from July 1st through early August. It is one of Marie's most interesting films *The Private Affairs of Bel Ami.* The film was written, co-produced and directed by Albert Lewin and based on the 1885 French novel *Bel Ami* by Guy de Maupassant.

George Sanders stars as Georges Duroy, a man who uses sex to gain social, economic and political power. How he gets the power is using his connections to an old army comrade to get a job on a newspaper and becoming a gossip columnist, and like the Burt Lancaster character in *Sweet Smell of Success* ten years later he uses his position to blackmail others—and they are only too willing to give in to him because of the dirt he acquires. He also uses his position to bed a variety of women. Ann Dvorak is cast as his wife Madeleine—the widow of the army friend (played by John Carradine) who Georges has been carrying on an affair with. Angela Lansbury is cast as Clotilde, Georges mistress and ultimately the one woman he is destined to truly love.

Marie is cast as Rachel, a Folies Bergere dancer who hopes to advance her career through the assistance of Georges—while he is really only interested in using her only for his own sexual gratification. For one of the very few times in her career, Marie isn't the typical "dumb blonde" character she made her trademark. Rachel is a woman who wants to be loved and is willing to put up with any indignity as long as she feels she has somebody who cares for her. The script at first, according to the censorship office of Joseph Breen, identified Rachel as a prostitute, and so her role was re-written to make her a Folies dancer, in much the same way that in a western a prostitute is re-made into a "dance-hall girl." In fact, the Breen office would later write that the original script had "too much emphasis on disrespect for marriage and infidelity." As usual in films of that period, the heavy, in this case the Sanders character, had to be punished at the end, and a duel was re-written which leads to the Sanders characters death. Unfortunately for Marie the film wasn't a hit at the box office and her role as *Irma* cemented her usual "dumb" persona.

The *New York Times* venerable Bosley Crowther didn't much like the film or any performance in it, " . . . everybody, from Mr. Sanders right on down through the whole list of love-laden ladies and fancifully costumed gents, acts as prosily and pompously as they are compelled to talk." *Variety* acknowledged that the screenplay had to be changed to get past the censors, "clean up process, which denatured most of the story's original flavor, results in a fair picture." Kudos also were thrown to the supporting ladies, "Ann Dvorak, Frances Dee, Susan Douglas, Katherine Emery and Marie Wilson all show well as the other women in his (Sanders) path."

Her next release was a silly comedy by Hal Roach about a talking dog titled *The Fabulous Joe*. Marie plays "Gorgeous Gilmore," an innocent by-stander in the marital difficulties of Milo and Emily Terkel. Through a series of misunderstandings Gorgeous is believed to be having an affair with Milo. There is slapstick galore in this typical Roach comedy which moves swiftly along in just under one hour. The film was produced by Roach to fill the bottom half of a double bill.

In the fall of 1947 Marie was cast in another comedy *Linda Be Good*. The film tells the story of a struggling writer, Linda Prentiss (played by Elyse Knox),

Marie's face was an asset in advertising *The Fabulous Joe.*
The Stumpf-Ohmart Collection.

who decides to gather life experiences for her writing. Linda meets a burlesque dancer named Margie LaVitte (Marie), who convinces Linda to go on tour with her also as a burlesque dancer. The result is a book titled, "I Was a Burlesque Queen," which was the original title of the film. The film is instructive in that Marie does a bit of a bump and grind routine that she did in *Blackouts*. Unlike star Knox, who accompanied the producer and director to two Los Angeles burlesque houses to watch several performances as research for her part, Marie knew what was expected of her through her work on *Blackouts*—which was based on burlesque.

As usual for Marie none of these films offered her a starring role. She was typically the second lead, but with the success of *My Friend Irma* on radio through 1947 and 1948, producer Hal Wallis, who produced many of Warner Brothers best films including *Casablanca*, *The Maltese Falcon* and *Now Voyager*, and also produced Marie's best film at the studio, *Boy Meets Girl* was interested in filming a movie version of *Irma* for Paramount pictures—where he now had a unit. But it turned out that Marie wasn't automatically thought of as a big enough movie box office name to recreate her part in the film—despite having appeared in well over thirty motion pictures. Wallis had just made the film version of the well known suspense play *Sorry, Wrong Number* and cast Barbara Stanwyck in a role which Agnes Moorehead had made a tremendous success of on radio. The major reason that Moorehead, who desperately wanted the part, didn't get it was because Wallis didn't feel she had a big enough box office name to carry the film. This was his thinking as well with Marie and the part of Irma. But Marie had a secret weapon at her disposal in the fight to get the part. Her good relationship with the Hollywood press paid its dues. Frank Daugherty later wrote in the **Christian Science Monitor**, "Marie Wilson seems to have been the only possible choice for Irma. She created the role on the air, and she has identified herself with it to such an extent that pre-production clamor in the newspapers for her to have the part was almost overwhelming. Half a dozen well-known actresses were tested, but in the end it was Miss Wilson who got the assignment."

A top choice of Paramount was Judy Holliday, who was creating a sensation on Broadway in the stage version of **Born Yesterday** (the movie version of this play was in the works at Columbia). Holliday's character in **Born Yesterday**, Billie Dawn, was also considered a "dumb blonde." Holliday was later to say, "When Hal Wallis was casting **My Friend Irma**, . . . I said 'What about Marie Wilson, she created it on radio.' Finally he tested her and she got the part." Infact, Marie ended up doing three tests for a role she was so well known for—and only after Holliday firmly turned it down was Marie finally chosen (it was decided that Holliday's screen debut should be in a prize supporting part opposite screen titans Spencer Tracy and Katharine Hepburn, who were championing her, in George Cukor's film of **Adam's Rib**—which was written by Ruth Gordon and her husband Garson Kanin, who had written **Born Yesterday**).

Recreating their parts from the radio show would be Gloria Gordon as landlady Mrs. O' Reilly and Hans Conried as Professor Kropotkin. Not so fortunate was Cathy Lewis who was not considered photogetic enough for Jane. Instead former child actress Diana Lynn was cast in the part. John Brown was discarded as Al in favor of Paramount contractee John Lund. Leif Erickson was also not asked to recreate the part of Richard in the movie version. Part of the reason being that he was too good looking. In the film version, Richard's character actually loses Jane to a good looking singer who operates a orange juice stand! So Don DeFore was cast as Richard (Defore was cast when Jack Carson, who worked with Marie in **Shine On, Harvest Moon** proved unavailable).

In reality the radio characters are not the focal point of the film version of **My Friend Irma**. Wallis used the film to introduce a new hugely popular nightclub act he had put under exclusive contract, Dean Martin and Jerry Lewis. They were breaking records at nightclubs all across the country. It was a cinch that Martin, who had a smoothly romantic singing style, would be cast as a love interest—and so the part of Richard was demoted to make way for the character of Steve Laird—Jane's romantic interest. More difficult to cast was Martin's partner, Jerry Lewis, whose spastic slapstick style didn't really fit any character on the radio show—in fact, Lewis' stage persona was unique.

Lewis' biographer, Shawn Levy, later wrote that ". . . for Jerry's talents there was no such obvious use. The radio series did have another male lead—Irma's con-artist boyfriend, Al—and Jerry got it into his head that he could fill the role." Lewis ended up begging Wallis to cast him as Al—a part which was totally against his established stage persona, a kind of a simple minded, chaos causing kid brother to Martin. Wallis eventually did have the director, the veteran George Marshall, test Jerry for Al. "There were more tests—nine, by one account," wrote Levy, "and acting lessons, all to no avail. Wallis remained sure that he wanted Martin and Lewis to debut in the film together, but he was equally sure that he'd have to cast a different Al. He asked Cy Howard to create a new character, a sidekick for Dean with plenty of physical business and verbal foolishness cut from the cloth of Lewis's stage persona. In a backhanded gesture, Howard named the character Seymour—his own given name, a name he loathed." Lewis apparently put an ultimatum to Wallis—he plays Al or else he wouldn't do the film. Wallis didn't take the bait and told Lewis that Dean would make his film debut and Jerry wouldn't. Given this choice, according to Levy, Jerry backed off.

Lewis recalls it differently in his 2005 memoir, **Dean and Me: A Love Story**. He recalls that the role of Al was being forced on him by Wallis even though Lewis understood that Al had nothing in common with his stage persona. He also felt that the ten year age difference between himself and Marie made it seem even more ridiculous. But they did a screen test, "Marie and I did the scene," Lewis writes, "She was cute, she was bubbly—but she was 32 years old to my 22, ten years that really made a difference. And I, having never acted before, was trying hard to pretend to be someone I profoundly was not."

As it turned out the film of **My Friend Irma** more or less took the focus off of Irma, Jane and the other radio characters and put it firmly on building up Martin and Lewis, who Wallis had plans to make into a bankable box office team like Abbott and Costello had been in the early to mid 1940's. Irma and Al are pretty much as they are in the radio show with Marie described in one review as "an absolute moron, but lovely" and Al still presented as a sharpie who doesn't want to do any heavy lifting. But with the new Jane comes a new attitude. This Jane wants to marry a millionaire and wants to marry her boss, Richard, just as the radio version does, but this Jane doesn't love Richard like the radio version does. The reason for this is Dean Martin. The plot twist has Jane falling in love with a orange juice vendor "with a voice like Crosby." The orange juice vendor has a sidekick named Seymour (Lewis) who is almost as big of a dumbbell as Irma. Al has a scheme to make the Martin character into a star and moves the boys into Irma and Jane's apartment to plan their future. At first Jane resents this but it doesn't take long before she falls in love with the Martin character. The importance of Martin and Lewis to the picture is probably best underscored by the fact that ten percent of the films entire budget went towards their salary.

The film went into production on February 22, 1949—less than two years after the radio show premiered. Marie rose at five AM so she could be at the studio and in make-up by six AM and on the set by eight and then worked until six PM. She got on well with the veteran director, George Marshall, who told the press that Marie is "one of those healthy, easy-going dames." When she was dismissed from the set she would go home and have a quick bite to eat. Then it was on to perform in the **Blackouts**. On Mondays, she also had the radio program. This back-breaking schedule went on for eight weeks until early April. If the attention given to Martin and Lewis bothered her, Marie didn't let on. "Jerry Lewis is such a nice guy," Marie told a columnist. "He won't steal a scene behind your back. Steals it right in front of you. But I love the boy. I hope they (Martin and Lewis) make lots more pictures without me!" In actuality Marie and much of the cast found Lewis brash and annoying. According to Shawn Levy, "He would pour water on people, props, and sets, cut colleagues' neckties or ignite their handkerchiefs, destroy journalists' notes and clothing, acting even off camera like the schlemiel from the Martin and Lewis stage act." Martin was more laid-back and generally better liked. They often operated as "good cop" (Dean) and "bad cop" (Jerry) with Dino more than willing to play it cool and let his younger and more passionate partner do his bidding—especially when it came with dealing with management. Both were married and enjoying the fruits of their success. Martin was carrying on an affair with June Allyson while Lewis was involved with Allyson's friend Gloria DeHaven. Lewis was also fascinated by the filmmaking process and was constantly shadowing director George Marshall.

The film was released that fall and to publicize it Marie went on a cross country tour. By this time she had finally ended her association with Ken Murray's *Blackouts*. She had given Murray a one-year notice. With the success of *Irma* on radio and now with the motion picture and her contractual obligation to publicize the movie she really had no choice. She couldn't be in Las Vegas, Denver, Minneapolis, Cleveland, Philadelphia, Boston and New York publicizing the film and still perform in the nightly *Blackouts*. Also after eight years in Hollywood, Murray himself felt it was time for a change and wanted to bring *Blackouts* East to New York and open on Broadway. Murray would later write, "In 1942 I gave her a seven-year contract and she played out every minute of it One night after the show in 1948 she did come to me and say, 'Ken, I'm in 'Irma' now on the radio and in pictures, and it's so much work I think I'll have to leave. I thought she meant immediately, and when she saw the disturbed look on my face she said, 'Oh, Honey, I don't mean now; I mean next year when my contract expires.' So I guess I'm the only person ever to receive a year's notice, and Marie's the only one who ever gave one—in a variety show, for sure." Marie's final *Blackouts* was on August 29, 1949 after some 2,300 performances. Incidentally, the *Blackouts* which opened on Broadway died a very quick death—only 51 performances. Later, Marie and Ken Murray would reunite and bring *Blackouts* back in a comeback bid for both.

The film version of *My Friend Irma* was every bit as successful as Hal Wallis hoped for with over $4 million in tickets selling in the United States alone. However, the reviews for the film were mainly negative except for the breakout stars—Martin and Lewis. Infact, the film does come alive only when Martin and Lewis are on screen. But this is pretty much as Wallis wanted it. He didn't have any real plans for Marie despite signing her to a contract for at least two more films (plans were to take *Irma* west and then to Europe in sequels). Despite Jerry Lewis threatening to leave the film he literally stole the movie in the opinions of most reviewers with his performance as Seymour. The *New York Times* critic Bosley Crowther wrote, "Jerry Lewis . . . who is the funniest thing in it. Indeed, he's the only thing in it that we can expressly propose for seeing the picture." Crowther dismissed Marie, "Playing the role of Irma, Marie Wilson does little more than offer a dismal reminder of Penny Singleton in the *Blondie* films." The *Los Angeles Herald Examiner* would write, "Frankenstein-faced Lewis all but steals win, place and show money in this comedy sweepstakes." *Variety*, would write, "The most notable value of 'Irma' is the introduction of two nitery comics." *Variety* was also much kinder to the film than many other reviews, "The fun is piled on lavishly and the pace is furious . . . Thanks to George Marshall the picture has a knowing comedy hand who can build a broad situation into yocks." Even Marie was praised, "Title role is in the exacting hands of Marie Wilson and she belts it over for a solid click. The camera could have been kinder but Miss Wilson's talents for portraying the very acme of dumb blondeness has no peer and needs no gauze treatment, even though better lensing of her pulchritude would have been an asset."

Ads appearing in newspapers advertising the first *My Friend Irma* film.
The Stumpf-Ohmart Collection.

Despite critics and audiences alike being mad about Martin and Lewis, and Marie being mostly left behind, Marie was more optimistic about her film career than she had been at any time since *Boy Meets Girl*. She felt sure that the success of the film would lead to more film roles—particularly one she coveted most of all—the film version of *Born Yesterday*. Her optimism flowed over in interviews she gave at the time in which she said, "Usually I'm put in a picture just for laughs; this time I was the cake instead of the frosting."

III

The success of the first *My Friend Irma* movie led to a sequel which began filming about a year after the original film had been shot. This one was titled, *My Friend Irma Goes West*. The plot was something about Irma and friends (Jane, Al, Steve and Seymour) heading west with nothing more than a promise from a phony movie producer (who turns out to be certifiably crazy) that Steve could become a huge star in pictures. On the train ride they meet French leading lady Corinne Calvet who helps them by getting Steve a job in a Las Vegas nightclub and later bringing him to Hollywood to be her leading man. Oh yeah, the plot also includes a bunch of Indians.

The film could easily have been titled "Steve and Seymour Go West" since the story centers even more than in the original film on Martin and Lewis. The cast of the radio show are pushed even further into the background. The film would go on to earn about $4 million at the box office and, as could be expected, the reviews favored Martin and Lewis, Jerry in particular, if they favored anybody, "Jerry Lewis, the slight, abject, elastic young man and his straight man accomplice with the velvety baritone singing voice, Dean Martin, are responsible for 99.9% of the fun," wrote the *New York Times* in its review, "Marie Wilson, John Lund and Diana Lynn work hard at carrying the other one-tenth of the picture." *Variety* pointed out the obvious, "There's considerable less emphasize on Marie Wilson's "Irma" and the other characters."

Paramount announced plans for a third Irma picture based on the box office success of the first two. This one was going to be set in Europe. One press release stated, "Now Irma is going to make the Grand tour. Hal Wallis will film the next "Irma" comedy in Europe. It will be titled, "My Friend Irma Goes Abroad." The third of the fun-films about the hectic adventures of the scatterbrained heroine calls for shooting in London, Paris, Rome, and possibly one of the Scandinavian countries." Marie was excited about the prospects and commented, "It's gay Paree for me! And the nicest thing about my vacation dream is that it's going to come true—at the studio's expense! We go on location in France for the next of the 'My Friend Irma' series. Of course, my husband, Allen Nixon, is already planning each precious day we spend there. When I arrive in Paris I want to swing from the Eiffel Tower, see all the Cartier's blinkers, sniff all the Coty perfumes, and get fitted and fitted and fitted in at least 100 Parisian gowns! Neither lack of money nor time will stop me in Paris!"

Newspaper advertisement for the second *Irma* film—note that Marie is billed last—even below Martin and Lewis. The Stumpf-Ohmart Collection.

But it wasn't to be and Paramount cancelled plans for the film—if Marie and Allen wanted to swing from the Eiffel Tower they would have to do it on their dime. Hal Wallis became convinced that Martin and Lewis didn't need the *Irma* formula to be a success on their own and began to star Dean and Jerry in a string of films which firmly established the team as one of the biggest box office draws of the 1950's. Unfortunately for Marie, Paramount wasn't interested in any more *Irma* pictures if they didn't include Dean and Jerry.

Marie, however, felt emboldened by the success of the two *Irma* films and began to actively campaign to get the lead role in Columbia's film version of the hit Broadway play *Born Yesterday*. *Born Yesterday* tells the story of a wealthy junk dealer and his mistress, Billie Dawn. In the script of the play Billie is described as "Stunningly beautiful and stunningly stupid." Billie and her boyfriend visit Washington, DC, where she meets a reporter who tries to educate her by showing her many of the historic sites around the city and they end up falling in love. By the end of this Pygmalion story Billie proves she is brighter than many people think. Judy Holliday made a huge success playing Billie on stage, but she hadn't really proved herself in motion pictures.

According to Holliday's biographer Gary Carey in his book *Judy Holliday*, "Cohn brought "Born Yesterday" for Rita Hayworth and Humphrey Bogart. Bogart owed Columbia a commitment, but he passed on this property." Hayworth also passed when she left Hollywood (temporarily) and married Aly Khan.

Marie felt the part was perfect for her established persona. Billie is "Irma" with an edge to her. She also felt that she had proved herself in motion pictures with nearly forty films to her credit and certainly knew a thing or two about performing in front of the cameras. She also had to her credit two very successful box office hits with the *Irma* films, regardless of who was credited for the success of those films. But she was also very affected by Holliday's performance. She would later relate how she cried all the way home after seeing *Born Yesterday* on Broadway, "she was so wonderful," she said of Judy Holliday. But that didn't stop Marie from writing a letter to writer-director Garson Kanin, "I have just seen Billie (sic) Holliday in "Born Yesterday" and she's so great. She's so great. But maybe she doesn't want to be in pictures, and maybe if she does she wants nine million dollars and Mr. Kanin if you make "Born Yesterday" into a picture I will play the part for nothing."

Marie wasn't the only actress who was interested in playing Billie Dawn. Among other interested parties was Jean Arthur (who the role of Billie Dawn had been written for by author Garson Kanin, but who backed out of the play due to ill health—or her own legendary nerves, take your pick). Arthur was a personal favorite of Columbia head Harry Cohn since she had made many successful films such as *Mr. Deeds Goes to Town, Mr. Smith Goes to Washington* and *The More the Merrier* at the studio. Also in the running was Lucille Ball who was finally given the opportunity to demonstrate her comedic talents and was also under contract to Cohn. Then there were the two

Maries—Wilson and Marie (the body) McDonald.

What worked against all of these other actresses was that Garson Kanin and the films director George Cukor favored Holliday to reprise her role in the film. As a matter of fact they used the movie **Adam's Rib** with Spencer Tracy and Katharine Hepburn as a sort of screen test to convince Cohn that Holliday could handle the demands of making a motion picture. Up to this time Cohn had referred derisively to Holliday as "that fat Jew." But Holliday's performance in **Adam's Rib** was enough to convince Cohn and he green lighted her and she went on to win the Academy Award for her performance. The nail which may have sealed Marie's fate according to Gary Carey was Marie's "lackluster performances in films during the 30's." Of course Marie hadn't been lackluster in those films— she was often considered the best thing in them—it was the films themselves which had been lackluster. But Marie would have another explanation, she had once done a test for a picture at Columbia called "Tillie the Toiler," which Marie believed was "awful . . . I wore a black wig, and tried to talk fast and oh, dear." She felt that Cohn also recalled that terrible test and held it against her.

Losing Billie Dawn was one of the biggest blows of Marie's career. She later said, "I felt I could have given the role justice, but all the major players were in Judy's corner." For her part Holliday was understandably somewhat bitter about Marie campaigning for what she considered "her" part, "When Irma was being cast and I was being considered for that part I said to Hal Wallis, 'Why not Marie Wilson, she played it on radio and then the next thing I hear is that the only part that Marie is dying to play is Billie Dawn!'"

Marie did at times attempt to get away from the "Irma" stereotype. She would occasionally appear at the small Circle Theatre in Hollywood in a play—usually picking projects which were different from the Irma role. One such role was as Lady Teazle, "a witty and frolicsome noblewoman of 18th Century England," in a production of **The School for Scandal**. The Circle was a type of theatre in the round which seated 135 and had a very intimate atmosphere. According to a **Life** magazine article on this production, "Marie makes a handsome Lady Teazle as she gets involved with a crowd of male and female scandalmongers, avoids seduction by her husband's friend and finally keeps both her husband and her reputation. Only rarely does the shrill giggle of "My Friend Irma" break into the speeches of Lady Teazle. Audiences have been distracted sometimes by loud bursts of laughter, evidently coming from Marie off in the wings when she heard something which struck her as particular amusing being said on stage." There was even more distraction when Charlie Chaplin appeared in the audience for one performance.

While Lady Teazle managed to keep her husband, in her next appearance at the Circle Theatre, in a play co-starring her husband, Allan Nixon, Marie would become attracted to another actor in the cast—the man who would go on to become her second husband—and the love of her life.

CHAPTER SIX
SECOND CHANCE GIRL
1950-1954

Marie and Allan's marriage was on thin ice when they agreed to appear together in the Los Angeles Circle Theatre production of *Three out of Four*. Marie had grown tired of Allan's public escapades spurred by his thirst for alcohol. More than once she had to bail him out of jail for drunk driving or initiating fights when under the influence. There was unwanted publicity earlier in the year when Nixon was held as drunk in a 3-car crash. "Sure I was driving— what's all the fuss," was his response when questioned by police. Louella Parsons noted in her column, "On several occasions, she and Allan have separated, but he has always managed to talk her out of a divorce." Marie was willing to give it one more chance—hoping that appearing together in a play would sober Allan up and bring them closer together. As it turned out the play would be the climax in the inevitable tail spin of their marriage.

In addition to Allan *Three out of Four* cast another tall, dark and muscular actor to support Marie, thirty-five year old Robert Fallon and the attraction between the two was instant and mutual. Fallon was very much a man's man. The take charge type Marie was always attracted to. He was known around town— very much like Allan—as being cat nip to other women and had more than his fair share of conquests. It is possible that a ladies' man like Bob Fallon was looking at Marie initially as his next conquest especially since it was common knowledge in Hollywood that Marie and Allan's marriage was teetering at the brink. Fallon was very much a man who appraised a situation and took advantage of any favorable odds he was dealt—not only in matters of business but in matters of sex. Needless to say at a time when Marie was very vulnerable and her marriage was on the rocks—Bob Fallon was there to pick up the pieces.

As it turned out Marie and Allan didn't appear in any of the four one-act plays together. Marie appeared in two of the one-act plays, and her leading man in one of them was Robert Fallon. But the play which got the most praise featured Marie with a young up and coming actor named William Schallert (who would become known for his many "father" roles on television including *The Patty Duke Show*) in an adaptation of Chekhov's *The Bear*. According to the Los

Angeles Mirror, ". . . the two best performances of the evening were in "The Bear." This was Chekhov by the remotest of control, but it was fun. Miss Wilson and Schallert never hesitated to pull the audience into their gags. At one point Marie even passed out fruit to people in the second row. To a man who couldn't decide what he wanted, she handed a banana, 'Here, this is what you had your eye on,' she said. I think she should have given him a grapefruit."

The play didn't do much to repair Marie and Allan's relationship. It is possible that Allan sensed that there was some kind of special chemistry between his wife and Fallon. He may have even confronted them about it. But the bottom line is that his drinking and brushes with the law didn't end and he and Marie drifted even further apart. Marie was determined to end the marriage. And soon after the play ended she filed for divorce. The columnists in Hollywood had long been expecting it—not so much because they knew—but kept quiet—about Marie's affair with Fallon, but for years Nixon had been a source of adverse publicity for Marie with his drunken escapades. Even though Marie was involved with Fallon she was seen as the victim in the divorce proceedings with Allan. For too many years she had stood by him and supported him only to see him continue on his destructive path. Years later Allan would be involved in a domestic dispute with his second wife—who would stab him—wounding him with a knife.

When she filed for divorce (she hired prominent Hollywood attorney Jerry Rosenthal and filed for divorce the day after *Three out of Four* closed) she and Fallon began to be seen around town together—no more secrecy. Fallon was an actor, but like Allan—an unsuccessful one. He was at heart a showman, a sort of junior league Mike Todd. He wanted to be a producer and he wanted to take charge of Marie's career. Debbie Reynolds, who later, after Marie's death, would have a serious romantic relationship with Fallon, recalls him as "Show Bizz. He had bravado about him. He stepped out from the norm, in my eyes. Nothing surprised him. He was willing to take chances. He was very different and I liked that." Despite her marriages to singer Eddie Fisher and Shoe store mogul Harry Karl, Debbie would also recall that Fallon "was the first man who ever really made love to me. Not Harry, Not Eddie, but Bob taught me what it was like to feel a true climax of lovemaking. I had never had that. He was a very experienced and unselfish lover." It was soon after filing for divorce and going public with Bob Fallon, who she would refer to in the press as "my new beau," that an event took place which almost put an end to all of her dreams—in fact, it almost ended her life.

Marie was used to hard work. She had been doing it for many years not only to support herself but also to support her family. In the last year she had worked weekly on the radio show and made the motion picture *My Friend Irma Goes West*. She had undertaken an exhausting promotional tour for the picture and she had done several weeks of stage appearances with *Three out of Four*. Add to this the emotional impact of her divorce from Allan and the deepening bonds between she and Fallon—Marie had had an exhausting and rollercoaster year.

One day Marie went to the doctor to get a vitamin shot because she was feeling under the weather. Before she left she also let the doctor look at a swelling which had developed just above her left knee. The doctor was startled and immediately diagnosed phlebitis—a traveling blood clot in an important vein—which if it's dislodged could go to the heart or the lung and possibly kill her. The doctor recommended that she go home immediately and go to bed for several weeks.

Marie, professional that she was, had a radio show to do that night. She would honor that obligation. When she arrived at the studio she felt very strange or as she later said, "extra dizzy—even for me." She was waiting for the rest of the cast to arrive so that they could go over the script. She slumped into a chair. She tried to put on a professional face, but the pain got to be too much for her and she finally broke down in tears. She finally told the director, "Please call Bob Fallon and ask him to drive me home."

Fallon arrived and took her home. He was concerned enough that he stayed with her (he often stayed at Marie's house, but since they were not yet married they still had separate residences). The swelling on her knee was getting worse and she was obviously running a temperature and experiencing chills. Marie didn't have a thermometer except for one that was used to take a dogs temperature. She asked Fallon, "Do you think that a dog's thermometer works the same for girls?" Fallon decided to try it and it registered 106 degrees.

That was enough to frighten Fallon into calling a doctor, who came and took one look at Marie—took her temperature—and called an ambulance which rushed her to the hospital. Marie would recall that "everyone spoke in hushed tones—making me realize that I was desperately ill." It was found that the clot in her leg had broken off and was lodged in her lung. She was in critical condition. They gave her a blood transfusion and began her on anti-biotics. Complicating the problem was that she was also suffering from blood poisoning. An electro-cardiogram showed that her heart was "dangerously weakened." Her breathing was becoming labored and she was put in an oxygen tent. Her doctor, Irving Ress, pronounced her condition as critical to the press corp. which had assembled and issued a statement saying, "She will remain in the oxygen tent for many days yet and it will be at least two weeks before she is able to go home." Yet the doctors weren't even sure she would ever go home, so critical was her condition.

Marie had never felt so lonely in her life. She was inside an oxygen tent. She wasn't permitted visitors. Even her mother wasn't allowed to see her except to come once per day and wave at her from the open door leading to her room. Because they were not yet married, Bob Fallon wasn't allowed in the room, but he was at the hospital constantly—though Marie was apparently not aware of it. Marie would later recall this period as she lay inside her oxygen tent and drifted in and out of consciousness, "I had never felt so alone or lonely in my life . . . it seemed the end. To my career, my world, my family . . . in my more lucid moments I wondered what Bob might be doing. Wherever he was, would he be thinking of me? I hoped so." She later learned that Bob was at the hospital daily—often pacing the floors.

Absolutely forbidden to see Marie, Fallon sent messages. But the messages had been intercepted at the desk. The reason later given was that Marie was "too ill to be disturbed." He, along with scores of other friends and fans also sent flowers, but they were not permitted in her room due to flowers absorbing oxygen and Marie needing all the oxygen she could get couldn't afford that.

On more than one occasion Marie asked a nurse for a phone so that she could call Fallon. She was denied even this, being told by the nurses, "Be patient. Not Yet." She was unaware of the thousands of messages being delivered to the hospital and thought that nobody cared about her—this would cause her severe crying spells. One night the tears seemed to affect a nurse who was in Marie's care. Marie would later recall the nurse telling her, "No, honey, you really have to relax and get some sleep. Everybody's pulling for you. We've had hundreds of messages. Everybody wants you to get well quick."

Marie took the chance and asked this nurse for a phone—she just needed to call Bob. The nurse went out of the room and brought back in a plug-in phone and Marie dialed Bob's apartment—even though it was around four o'clock in the morning. Fallon was startled awake by the ringing phone in the middle of the night. He feared the worst—phone calls in the middle of the night often meant bad news. He answered and heard Marie's voice—weakened as it was and exclaimed, "Baby, you're all right!"

It probably turned out to be the best medicine that Marie received. After the phone call, Marie reassured that Bob had not only been thinking of her, but had spent parts of each day at the hospital went promptly asleep—the best sleep she had in several days and when she awoke her fever had broken. Marie now had a new determination. She was sure that Bob was more than a passing fancy. On occasion she would look up from her oxygen tent to see Fallon gazing into her hospital room from a half cracked open door. When their eyes met he would blow her a kiss.

As she got better the doctors allowed her to receive some of the many messages from friends and fans and allowed people to come to see her. She still wasn't allowed to have the oxygen hungry flowers in her room, but now the nurses would step in carrying the flowers which arrived and let her see them and then take them out and distribute to other patients. She began to read many of the messages which arrived from people she didn't even know but knew her only as the ditzy but lovable Irma and they were praying for her recovery. Many of the messages were addressed not to Marie Wilson, but to Irma Petersen.

It was also during this near death experience that Marie began to think more seriously about religion. She had always considered herself a Christian, but with her busy career she never was a consistent churchgoer. But with all the people praying for her recovery and her own thoughts turning to God and prayer she resolved that in the future she would be a better and more active Christian. Marie would later say, "I held on to my thought that God has his own way and his own time. I had absolute faith in God's goodness and unlimited power. I remembered back in Sunday school the words, The prayer that reforms the sinner and heals the sick is an absolute faith that all things are possible to God—a spiritual understanding of him—an unselfed love."

With her fever broken and her breathing becoming easier, Marie was taken out of the oxygen tent. She felt free for the first time in over a week. Her leg was getting back to normal and her condition was upgraded to fair. After a few more days in the hospital Marie was allowed to return home but cautioned that she must not rush back to work and should have several more weeks of bed rest.

The experience brought Marie and Bob closer together. There was no doubt by either of them that once the divorce from Allan Nixon became final that they would marry. Marie had finally, she felt, found a man who would take care of her—he proved it by his constant attention during this illness. For his part, Bob found that he cared for her more than he had initially realized. His attraction for Marie went beyond the sexual—which for him was quite a revelation. He had seen her looking very ill—her face red and blotchy and eyes swollen and in no means looking like the blonde, bosomy bombshell he was initially attracted to— and he was not scared off—infact, there was something in her very helplessness which attracted him even more.

Marie went to Las Vegas to establish residence for her divorce from Nixon, and she brought her mother with her for company. Marie hoped to get some rest while staying the requisite number of weeks. While in Las Vegas she called Cathy Lewis, "Cathy, I'm a wreck. I can't get any rest." Lewis questioned how this happened since Marie had been so adamant that she was going to do nothing but relax and sleep. Marie's answer convulsed Lewis, "Mother! Mother came home at all hours, and I had to sit up waiting for her—and worrying."

Marie would sum it up well when she later told a reporter, "Call me a second chance girl. I've had second chances in all departments. Second chances at my career, in marriage, and of course even a second chance to live." Friends would recall that Marie was more happy and at peace with her life than they had ever seen her. The last few years with Nixon had taken a toll, and she seemed to have complete and utter serenity with Fallon. Shortly before Marie and Fallon married, Marie's mother held a shower for her. With the exception of Cathy Lewis, the guest list only included Marie's family and Fallon's parents from St. Louis. Lewis would recall that Marie was "radiant" at the shower, "She wore a lovely organdy and pink dress. And because Marie loves to cook (and she's a wonderful cook) she also wore an apron. The apron was fluffy organdy and pink too. With or without the apron, Marie was the picture of loveliness. There was only one slightly incongruous note. Marie was wearing leopard skin bedroom slippers." Marie explained to Lewis that her feet hurt.

Shortly after her divorce from Allan Nixon became final, Marie and Bob married in Santa Barbara, California at the Santa Barbara Unitarian Church on

December 14, 1951. The **NY Daily News** reported that Marie wore a low-cut pink lace dress, and Lillian Russell's garter. The newlyweds bought a three story home (Marie and Bob lived on two stories, and Marie's mother occupied a floor of her own which was converted into her own apartment with her own furniture) in the Hollywood Hills near the home of Eve Arden and her husband, actor Brooks West. The Fallon's and the West's became close friends with both Eve and Marie working at CBS (Eve was the star of **Our Miss Brooks** on radio—and soon would bring that series to television) and they would occasionally go out as a foursome to a nightclub or enjoy each others backyards with a barbecue and swim.

Shortly before her marriage to Fallon, Marie was window shopping and saw a beautiful antique table she wanted in a decorator's window on Beverly Drive. She arrived on the **Irma** set and went into great detail about the table and how much she wanted it. Cy Howard decided to buy it for her as a wedding present. Howard had it delivered to Marie and Bob's new home and she was ecstatic about it, but after placing it in her living room, she looked around the room and her eyes opened wide as she groaned, "Oh!" The table was the outstanding piece of furniture in the room. It was a big table and distinctly out of place with the other more used furniture which populated the room. Marie would describe it as "a thoroughbred great Dane surrounded by a pack of half breeds." The other furniture included many pieces that Marie had collected over the years as well as some leather couches from Bob's bachelor days.

Marie called up the decorator's store where Howard had purchased the table and they sent a girl out. She, Bob and Marie looked at the table, the blank walls and the other furniture and the girl said, "That table doesn't fit. It really should go back to the shop." Marie argued that it was a wedding gift and "has sentimental value." The girl replied, "Well, it either has to go—or the other stuff should." Marie decided that the other stuff would go, and so all the other furniture was piled into the den and Marie put the girl from the antique store in charge of redecorating the living room to fit the table which Cy Howard had bought as a wedding gift. The new living room now sported mirrored walls, rose and blue drapes, rose carpeting and fine patterned pink flowered furniture—a very feminine touch which prompted Bob to later quip, "Walk through it (the living room) and you'll see in a minute what a powerful influence I was in the furnishings." It was a story which Bob would tell for years to come about how Cy Howard's wedding present had cost Bob $7,000 to redecorate the living room.

Marie was a very generous person to others, but she also enjoyed certain grandeur in her personal life. One day Marie went to Sak's in Beverly Hills where two women noticed this very extravagantly dressed woman holding a calfskin purse. One of the women said, "She looks a little like Jean Harlow!" the other said, "I think its Marie Wilson." The friend scoffed at that, "Marie Wilson! you mean 'My Friend Irma' with buttons and bows . . . it couldn't be." One afternoon

Marie and another friend decided to take a friend's children on a picnic to a nearby park. They divided up responsibilities with Marie bringing the dishes and cutlery, plus a salad and dessert. The friend believed it would be a nice, simple picnic with paper napkins and paper plates, and simple, but good food. Instead, Marie took out of her picnic hamper embroidered linen napkins, china plates, sterling silver forks, knives and spoons. The salad was crab and the dessert was French pastries. Her friend laughed and asked, "What! No pheasant or iced champagne?" The friend remembers that the question threw Marie into a fit of laughter.

Cathy Lewis was one of Marie's best friends as well as her trusted sidekick on the radio show. Cathy even had a pet name for Marie, "Cookie" or "Cook" for short and loved Marie's sense of humor. Lewis would recall one time she and Marie were posing for some publicity stills. Lewis was told to dress conservatively just like Jane Stacy would. Marie was asked to wear a black negligee. "While the cameraman adjusted his lenses," Lewis recalled, "Marie looked me and my demure little ensemble up and down. 'When my relatives see this picture, you know what they'll say? . . . they'll say, 'Now look at Cathy. She's a nice girl.'"

Marie and Bob Fallon relaxing in Las Vegas, 1952. The Author's Collection.

Even though Marie and Lewis were close they welcomed the chance to have a vacation from one another when the radio show went on hiatus because they spent so much time together the rest of the year. Lewis recalls the two "welcoming the idea of getting out of each other's hair for a while." Lewis and her husband Elliott went off to Las Vegas where they registered at the Desert Inn. She and her husband quickly found out that Bob and Marie were also in town, but staying at the Flamingo. "The first day in Las Vegas, to give some meaning to our vacation," recalled Lewis, "Marie and I deliberately went to those places where we felt certain the other would not be. This worked beautifully until midnight. At that time, I'm afraid neither of us could stand it any longer. It wasn't by prearrangement, but when I went to the Frontier at midnight, I just knew I would meet Marie there, and I'm equally sure she knew I'd be there. We both laughed uproariously . . . and since Marie and I appreciated the inevitability of our rendezvous, we howled." And for the rest of the vacation the two couples were practically inseparable.

II

The box office success of the first two *Irma* films did seem to resurrect Marie's film career. Marie signed a contract with RKO to appear in three films—one per year—between 1951 and 1953, and it is in these three films that Marie did her best film work since *Boy Meets Girl*. In the first film she joined Groucho Marx and William Bendix in *A Girl in Every Port*. The film was shot in about five weeks between June 11 and mid July of 1951 and produced by Irwin Allen, who would go on to produce many "disaster" films of the 70's such as *The Swarm*. It is a thin story dealing with two conniving sailors (Groucho and Bendix) who get involved with a race horse which is owned by a drive-in carhop played by Marie. The film did respectfully at the box office and RKO even announced plans to do a sequel called *A Guy in Every Port* which would focus on Marie's character and co-star her with Margaret Sheridan, but it never panned out. The reviews were mixed. The *New York Times* wrote, "The parlay of Groucho Marx, Marie Wilson and William Bendix to say nothing of a horse racing mix-up, the US Navy and sabotage should have paid off in plenty of laughs . . . but *A Girl in Every Port* which breezed into the Paramount yesterday . . . is merely an involved mélange of obvious antics and gags, only one or two are likely to generate chuckles . . . Marie Wilson, whose physical charms are not hidden, is properly lame-brained as the waitress." On the other side of the ledger *Variety* wrote that the film was a "zany comedy with chuckles . . . Miss Wilson less of the dumb Dora than usual is shown to advantage." At a studio luncheon which helped launch the picture, Bob Fallon mentioned Marie's legendary generosity and how she was known to "give the shirt off her back." That was the perfect cue for Groucho who piped up, "She'd look good without it."

Newspaper ad for the 1951 film *A Girl in Every Port*. The Stumpf-Ohmart Collection.

The best of the films came in 1952 and starred Rosalind Russell titled ***Never Wave at a Wac*** which was produced by Russell and her husband Freddie Brisson. The film was distributed by RKO but shot at the Walt Disney Studios (the first time an outside film production was produced at Disney) in the summer of 1952. Russell actually made her television debut in 1951 in an adaptation of the same story under the same title so that she could "determine audience reaction, before sinking a hefty budget into its filmation." It is the story of a divorced socialite played by Russell who joins the army in hopes that it will allow her to spend more time with her boyfriend, who is a Lt. Colonel being transferred to Paris to do work on behalf of SHAPE. She is in for a big surprise when she finds out that her ex-husband (played by Paul Douglas) is also working with the army and requests his ex-wife to disrupt any romantic plans she may have because he is (naturally) still in love with her. Marie is at her best playing Clara Schneiderman, who is a USO girl, who works under the stage name of Danger O'Dowd and follows Roz into the service because she admires how sophisticated she is, and hopes some of it will rub off on her. Leif Erickson, who was Jane's boyfriend Richard for several years on *My Friend Irma* is cast as Marie's love interest in this film (they share a very funny scene where Marie tricks him into proposing to her). Exteriors of the film were shot at Fort Lee, Virginia, a WAC training camp.

Marie enjoyed making this film and especially admired Russell, "When I think of how hard Rosalind Russell always worked when we made *Never Wave at a Wac*, I just couldn't complain," she recalled. "Rosalind was marvelous. We worked at Camp Lee, the base camp for WACS, and the temperature was round 98 almost every day. Furthermore, the humidity seemed to be about 105. We all cried about the weather—except Roz. She is a great gal, believe me. She has had the great star treatment from MGM—and there's nothing like it to swell an actor's ego. But she never once uttered a complaint at the hardships we went through during that hot, humid summer."

The *New York Times* gave the picture a good review, "Life in the army in these perilous times could be grim, but Rosalind Russell and a covey of cuties, to say nothing of a small posse of pursuing males, are fairly successful in proving that WACS can be wacky . . . Miss Russell and her happy crew are having a good natured go at a mild and obvious tale . . . with a generous consignment of laughs." Marie was praised for more than her performance, "Marie Wilson is given ample opportunity to display her charms—the army's severe styling does nothing to hide them—as well as her penchant for malapropisms. She is undoubtedly the least likely candidate for the intelligence branch of the army ever to hit the WACS." *Variety* also liked the picture, "Shapes up as fine escapist entertainment . . . box office prospects will be further fortified via marquee values of Rosalind Russell, Paul Douglas and Marie Wilson . . . Miss Wilson undeniably is well cast as a one-time burlesque queen."

Next up was another picture distributed by RKO, but filmed at Motion Picture Center, which also shot the *I Love Lucy* television series, titled *Marry Me Again*. Marie and Bob had a piece of this picture which was co-produced by Fallon along with Alex Gottlieb. Gottlieb approached Frank Tashlin to write the picture, and Tashlin agreed to do the screenplay in two to three weeks, on condition that he also be allowed to direct it. Tashlin had just come off a huge box office and critical hit at Paramount directing the Bob Hope comedy *Son of Paleface* so this request was easily accepted. The film was shot in sixteen days in June, 1953 and released by October. A visitor to the set would recall that "whether she is working in TV or motion pictures, Marie comes on the set prepared for the days shooting. She is a quick study and never forgets her lines, until late in the day when she droops with weariness. Very much a morning glory, she is full of vigor early in the day, gradually grows quiet and more quiet as the sun sinks." Tashlin would later attribute his ability to shoot the film so quickly to the fact that both Marie and Cummings had television backgrounds and were used to quick-paced shooting schedules. The film recalls the screwball comedies of the 1930's. Marie finds out she is about to inherit a fortune just before she is to marry a gas station attendant (played by Robert Cummings). She tries to keep the news from him because she knows he has a great deal of pride, but it leaks out on their wedding day and he leaves her at the alter because he doesn't want people to think that he is only marrying Marie for her money.

Marie with Robert Cummings in the 1953 comedy, *Marry Me Again*.
The Author's collection.

Variety liked the film, "A succession of chuckles, even a guffaw or two, is tossed off in this wacky slapstick romp . . . Frank Tashlin's direction and script . . . stir up enough free-wheeling comedy frenetics to keep both the young in age and young in spirit giggling . . . Miss Wilson's character is just dumb enough to fit the comedy pattern and there is some heart underlying her left at the alter role."

This is one of Tashlin's least known films. He was an animator at Warner Brothers and when he made the transition to live action films he utilized many of the techniques used in animated films—adapting them to humans. He was particularly successful in doing this with Jerry Lewis, whom Tashlin would direct in nine films. He was also well known for a certain leering suggestiveness towards the female anatomy. As he would later do memorably with Jayne Mansfield in *The Girl Can't Help It* and *Will Success Spoil Rock Hunter?* As well as a bevy of other voluptuous ladies—his cameras do emphasize Marie's well-endowed chest.

In October, 1951 *I Love Lucy* premiered on CBS and quickly became the biggest hit on television up to that time. The powers that be at CBS believed that *Irma* could also perform well in the ratings thanks to its continued success on radio and how well it had performed at the movies. By the fall of 1951 CBS made Cy Howard an offer he couldn't refuse, and Cy didn't. It was too late to premier the show in the fall, so plans were made to rewrite some radio scripts and premier the show in the winter of 1952.

Marie had made her television debut in 1950 on an episode of *The Ed Wynn Show*, and she was a realist about the medium. When she appeared as a guest star on the *Bob and Ray* radio show in 1949 she was asked her opinion regarding the future of television. "It's like Sex," Marie responded, "here to stay!"

My Friend Irma debuted on CBS television on January 8, 1952 only three weeks after Marie and Bob had married, and was sponsored by R.J Reynolds to promote its Cavalier Cigarettes. Most of the original cast from the radio show made the transition to television—Marie, Cathy Lewis, who wasn't deemed photogenic enough for the big screen, was green lighted for the small screen. Gloria Gordon and Sid Tomack (who had replaced John Brown in the radio version of *Irma* as well) also recreated their roles as Mrs. O' Reilly and Al respectively. Hans Conried decided not to make the transition to television and Sid Arno was cast as Professor Kropotkin. For the role of Jane's boyfriend, Richard Rhinelander III, Brooks West, Eve Arden's husband, was cast. Also appearing occasionally is actress Margaret Dumont, the Marx Brothers favorite matronly socialite, as Richard's socialite mother. Selected to direct the series was Richard Whorf, known to his friends as "Dickie." Former actor Whorf was once a member of the stock company of stage legends Alfred Lunt and Lynn Fontanne Even though Hans Conried was not on the television show (and he also quit the radio show), he sent a telegram to Marie on the night the show premiered which only said, DONT FORGET YOUR GLOVES! Wearing white gloves had long been a Marie Wilson trademark.

The television version of *My Friend Irma* was also the first show to be telecast from the huge muti-million dollar CBS Television City facility located at 7800 West Beverly Boulevard at the corner of Beverly and Fairfax in Hollywood. It was built on a former racetrack and next to the Farmer's Market where the cast and crew would occasionally go for lunch. The new facility was necessitated due to the increasing demands of television and the CBS facility on Columbia Square was deemed hopelessly outdated—too small and cramped. *My Friend Irma* was telecast from Studio 33, which later housed the long running *The Carol Burnett Show* from 1967–1978, among other shows.

The reviews for the new program were mixed. Jack Gould, the television critic of the *New York Times*, found the show "very labored and contrived." He dismissed most of the cast except for Cathy Lewis, "hers was the unenviable assignment of carrying the whole show. Her skill and craftsmanship gave the work what little pace and substance it enjoyed; without her *My Friend Irma* would have been in a very bad way." Gould ended his review with some hope for the new series, "*My Friend Irma* has the makings of a good farce for television, but it must be careful not to succumb to one of the older TV pitfalls. It can't take a free ride on its radio reputation." Gould wrote his review after only viewing the first episode. His competitor at the *Herald Tribune*, John Crosby, wrote a decidedly more upbeat review after three viewings, "The transition of *My Friend Irma*, a highly successful radio show, to television has been done with meticulous care . . . *My Friend Irma* is frankly a very funny and thoroughly professional show . . . Its stars, Miss Wilson and Miss Lewis, are appealing enough to be welcome once a week without being so overpoweringly possessed of personality that you tire of them." On the other coast, *Variety* found the show, "sock—a faithful video reincarnation of likeable, familiar characterizations, aided and abetted by some slick direction and production, with particularly sparkling performances by Miss Wilson and the long-suffering Miss Lewis as her roommate, and the sort of glib, light scripting that's been one of the basic assets of *Irma* in its radio career."

As always when doing the television series Marie kept on an even keel. Cathy Lewis would recall that they did a television show she wasn't very happy about and, "Marie and I exchanged knowing glances, but I managed to summon enough self control not to say anything about my misgivings." After the show, Marie and Lewis walked together back stage to their dressing rooms when Lewis couldn't help herself and uttered, "Really not good at all, Cookie, huh?" To which Marie conceded, "yes, but Cathy, we must never say that at all before the show." Because it might throw them off.

Despite the move to television, the show continued as a weekly radio series (and indeed the radio show would outlast the television show by two months), due to the radio shows still solid ratings. The show remained faithful to the radio series for the first two seasons, and then as the show began its third—and final—season in the fall of 1953, some important changes took place. First, Cathy Lewis overworked and tiring of the role of Jane quit both the radio and television show. It is explained in the first episode of the season that Jane has moved to Panama with her millionaire husband, Richard Rhinelander III. It necessitated a new roommate/best friend for Irma. Enter radio actress Mary Shipp, who is introduced as Kay Foster who moves in with her 7-year old nephew Bobby,

Marie Wilson says

"I think it's perfectly wonderful about the Sylvania Service man. I mean, it's wonderful how he keeps my radio and television sets in such perfectly wonderful condition."

Marie appeared in several newspaper and magazine advertisements during the *Irma* years including those for
1) Sylvania Television
2) A foot massager and
3) Pepsodent Toothpaste.

played by Richard Eyer. Shipp performed the same function as Lewis did, straight woman to Irma's wild antics.

Shipp, who considered Marie, "a really fine talent who is just now beginning to be appreciated" was a close friend of many years, but Marie didn't use her pull to get Shipp her job. Shipp would later tell the story of her audition for the Kay Foster role, "Marie is so honest it's downright painful. She wouldn't tell a soul she knew me. When the director introduced us, she played it perfectly straight and called me Miss Shipp, and then fled for fear she would give herself away. She avoided me like the plague for two solid days."

With a new roommate and a young child added to give the show some domestically, other changes were made. The biggest one was bringing in a new love interest for Irma. Part of the reason for this change was the exasperation of the audience of Irma continuing to put up with a never-do-well like Al and so enter Hal March, who was younger and more handsome and whose character, Joe Vance, had more promise than the hapless Al. Also added to the cast was veteran movie actor John Carradine who basically replaces the Professor Kropotkin character. Carradine plays a unsuccessful Shakespearian actor named Mr. Corday.

The television series ended up running two and a half years (January 8, 1952–June 25, 1954), and the show never achieved the anticipated huge ratings. It did well enough, starting off on Tuesday nights during season one, but then it moved to Fridays at ten pm, and had a gradual falling off of its audience. There was talk of a new format where Irma would be married off and new characters being brought in and calling the new show "My Wife Irma" thus turning the show into a domestic comedy more in line with *I Love Lucy*. But in the end the network decided that Irma's magic was fading they cancelled the show all together. And by the end of the summer of 1954, *Irma* the radio show was gone too. After seven years the ratings were falling off and the show had begun to repeat itself once too often (many scripts were recycled from earlier shows). It was a bittersweet moment for Marie when the final broadcast was aired, "we all had tears in our eyes," Marie would later recall, "but I knew it was time to move on—it was a good seven year run and we did all we could do with the character."

CBS asked Marie to stay with them—that they would find another project for her to star in, but little would Marie know that despite CBS's promises the best years of her career were now behind her.

Marie with Roy Rogers at the Indianapolis 500 in 1954.
The Author's collection.

CHAPTER SEVEN
TWILIGHT
1955-1972

In 1955, Marie was without steady work for the first time in thirteen years. From 1942–1949 she had worked seven days per week on **Blackouts** with **Irma** overlapping for part of that time, and running from 1947–1954 as a highly successful radio series, two spectacularly successful motion pictures and then a two-and-a half year run on television. She had also gone through, in her personal life, a divorce, a major health crisis and now was in a happy remarriage. She felt maybe it was time for a break. Not that she was going to retire—she was only 38, but she had also been working in Hollywood for over twenty years and perhaps it was time to slow down and start putting her personal life front and center over her professional career. She and Bob very much wanted children and an opportunity to bring a new baby into their life was just around the corner.

While on a trip to Oak Ridge, Tennessee to entertain employees of the Atomic Energy Commission in October, 1955, Marie took a side trip a Memphis hospital to entertain patients. While on this trip the couple saw a baby that Marie later described as "the most healthy, beautiful baby you ever saw." The baby had been given up for adoption and Bob and Marie decided they wanted the little boy. The process was begun and six weeks later, in late November, just after Thanksgiving, Bob flew back to Memphis and completed the paperwork and along with a nurse he brought the baby to Hollywood. The four month old weighted sixteen pounds and had dark blue eyes and "what hair he has is blonde." They named the boy Gregson, after Bob's close friend Hollywood attorney Gregson Bautzer. Bautzer had one of the busiest law firms in Hollywood and a reputation as a playboy with well publicized affairs with Lana Turner, Dorothy Lamour, Jane Wyman and Joan Crawford. In Christina Crawford's book **Mommy Dearest** Bautzer is referred to as "Uncle Greg." The Fallon's kept young Gregson (or Greg) as their foster child for the next year and a half as the adoption didn't become official until the spring of 1957. By all counts Marie was a warm and loving mother who doted on her young son. Marie was so excited that she called all of her friends in Hollywood about her new little baby and her good friend Cathy Lewis threw her a baby shower.

It was shortly after officially adopting Gregson that Marie and Bob attempted to adopt another baby—a little girl they would call Christy, to add to their family and give Greg a little sister. In July, 1957 they took home a newborn that had been born out of wedlock to a twenty-one year old UCLA student. The young mother had consented during her pregnancy and the Fallon's agreed to pay for her maternity and delivery expenses. Bob and Marie had the little girl in their home and grew much attached to her when the mother decided she wanted the baby after all. California law allowed the birth mother up to six months to take back her child after giving them up and the birth mother decided to exercise this right. Marie was prepared to challenge the law, "My husband and I will fight for her," she told reporters who gathered at her home. With tears in her eyes Marie said, "Once you have a baby, they shouldn't be able to take it away from you . . . to tear out your heart. The law must be wrong."

The young mother also commented publicly telling reporters who gathered at the home of her parents, "I tried to prepare myself to give up the baby. But, in truth, I could not do it. I knew I had to have my child back." Marie followed this up by saying that she was "as much that baby's mother as she is. We've taken this child into our home and she's in our hearts, and always will be. She is like our own child now; we'll do the best we can to keep her."

But the law was clear and on October 15th Marie and Bob were served with a writ to produce the child before Superior Court Judge Burdette J. Daniels. Reluctantly the Fallon's decided to surrender the child. "It is with great reluctance and a heavy heart that we have decided to return Chris to her natural mother," Marie and Bob said in a prepared statement handed out to reporters, "We both believe that further airing of this incident in court would only make a legal football out of an innocent baby and cause further grief to every one concerned. As any parents, our only thoughts have been for the welfare of Chris. We have always thought that Chris' place is in our home, but we sincerely hope now that her natural mother will give her all the love and affection that we had planned for her. We have instructed our attorney to make legal arrangements for return of Chris to her natural mother some time today."

When all was said and done, Marie would exhibit no bitterness, "It's nobody's fault. It's just the adoption laws." But the process took a lot out of her and she never again tried to adopt another baby.

II

Marie, nor Bob had forgotten totally about her career. She was doing nightclub appearances—including Las Vegas, in a revue type of act with songs and plenty of Irmaesque stories. She also did summer stock. In 1953 she appeared in the *The Little Hut* in theatres on Cape Cod. The production she appeared in was directed by Lee Falk, who was better known for creating such comic strips as *The Phantom* and *Mandrake the Magician*. *The Little Hut* was a comedy written by Andre

Roussin and about a husband and wife stranded on a deserted island with another man. The husband takes his wife for granted and she appears to respond to the attention given to her by the other man. When asked at a press conference why she was appearing in summer stock, Marie responded with candor, "I can always learn something." Then during the summer of 1955 she made a tour of east coast theatres in the comedy *For Love or Money*. One audience member during this tour was writer Charles Stumpf who would recall that the nearly 40 year old Marie still possessed an attention-getting body and in one scene even did a mock striptease which brought on a standing ovation.

Postcard advertising Marie's appearance in *The Little Hut*.
The Stumpf-Ohmart Collection.

Her name was in the news in other ways too. She allowed the March of Dimes to bid her out for a day as a secretary to raise money. The winning bid was made by a Fort Worth, Texas firm for $5000. She was chosen "Police Force Sweetheart" by the Los Angeles Police and pledged to help sell tickets for the annual Police Show to benefit widows and orphans. In 1956 she was selected for the first award given by "The Cheesecake Hall of Fame" due to her legendary cheesecake poses. She fought against Proposition C on the California ballot which would allow vivisection (the act of cutting into or dissecting a living animal). She appeared at several rallies and leant her name to newspaper ads—her message always consistent, "I think vivisection itself is all wrong. It just doesn't make sense that God could mean for one living thing to benefit through cruelty performed on another living thing."

She also did occasional television guest shots, mainly on variety shows, and she was also trying to find a new television series. From 1957 through 1959 she appeared in pilots for three prospective series. The first was produced by she and Bob for their own production company and titled *Miss Pepperdine*. This character and all the others would be variations on Irma—maybe not quite as dumb. Of course this didn't bother Marie in the least since she had been playing the Irma character even before there was an Irma since the beginning of her career she had specialized in the dumb blonde. Though in *Miss Pepperdine* she claimed she wasn't her regulation dumb blonde, "For the first time in my career I'm not a completely dumb blonde. At long last I can prove I have something else besides a body." This was a curious statement for Marie which would seem to indicate that below the surface she had at least some resentment of being typed as a feather brain with a sexy body.

In the new series Marie plays a receptionist in a fashionable New York dress house whose overwhelming desire is to be a fashion model. This would provide the comic impetus with Miss Pepperdine always trying to get into the act much the same way that Lucy Ricardo kept trying to get into Ricky's nightclub act. She would have a boss, who like Ricky, would always be trying to rein her in—usually without success. And like Lucy, Miss Pepperdine would plot out outrageous schemes which usually backfired. The show would also allow Marie to wear fashionable designer's gowns, unlike the plain dresses she wore as working girl Irma Petersen.

The Fallon's indeed were trying to emulate the successful husband and wife team of Lucille Ball and Desi Arnaz with Marie being the up front talent and Bob the brains in the background. With their own production company producing *Miss Pepperdine* they were also developing a movie which would star Marie, who had been off the big screen for four years since the disappointing returns of *Marry Me Again*. The film was to be called "One's A Crowd" about a girl who is hired by a gang of kidnappers to be a baby sitter for a child they intend to kidnap. Unfortunately neither the pilot nor the movie sold.

Marie around the time of *Miss Pepperdine*. The Stumpf-Ohmart Collection.

But Marie was back on the big screen in 1957 as part of the all-star cast of the Irwin Allen production of *The Story of Mankind*. The plot had to do with a council of elders deliberating on whether or not mankind was not to be allowed to survive or be destroyed—through use of the A-Bomb. Vincent Price plays the devil (an inspired choice) and Ronald Coleman, with his equally smooth and cultured voice is perfectly cast as "the spirit of man" who argues that mankind should be allowed to live. The gimmick of the film is that various famous stars would appear as historical characters that the devil and the spirit of man use to back up their arguments to the council. Among those appearing are The Marx Brothers (who don't appear together in any scenes), Hedy Lamarr as Joan of Arc, Agnes Moorehead as Queen Elizabeth, Virginia Mayo as Cleopatra, Peter Lorre as Nero, and a young Dennis Hopper as Napoleon. This gimmick of packing a film with stars in small roles had been done to great advantage the previous year in *Around the World in 80 Days* with even bigger names. Marie was cast as Marie Antoinette complete with a huge blonde wig atop her head and plays Antoinette much like Irma set in the French revolution. The film failed at the box office, but is of some interest today due to its theme, camp value and especially for being the last screen appearance of the Marx Brothers, even though they don't share any scenes together.

In 1958, Marie got another chance at episodic television with *The Marie Wilson Show* which was produced by George Burns. Burns' wife and long time partner Gracie Allen had just retired and Burns had the idea of replacing her dumb blonde with Marie's in a series of her own. Marie was cast as a wacky heiress, but this too was passed over by CBS. In 1959 Marie went over to Desilu for a third pilot that she recalled as "a fun one, too" called *Ernestine*. Marie plays Ernestine McDougall who works in a loan office run by her father (the great character actor Charlie Ruggles). Ernestine has a big heart and yes, a simple mind. But she always looks out for the underdog and makes bad loans—yet, somehow by the end it seems like the right thing to have done. Desi Arnaz decided to hold back on televising it because the TV market was saturated by westerns. "Desi said we'd be wise to wait until later," recalled Marie, "The westerns and the giveaways maybe will lose their fire by that time and TV will be given back to the comedians." But this pilot was passed over too. Ultimately it was shown, but not until 1961 as an episode of a summer replacement series for *The Red Skelton Show* which showed discarded pilots.

Marie took these rejections in stride, but her annoyance was evident nonetheless, "Stay with us," she recalled CBS executives telling her after *Irma* left the air in 1954, "I guess CBS didn't try too hard to sell one or the other, but they were nice to me. Paid me my full salary all the time I was off." In 1960 in an interview with columnist Marie Torre of the *New York Herald Tribune*, Marie was asked what she thought went wrong—why didn't any of her pilots sell? "Gee, I don't know. Maybe they weren't buying situation comedies. Maybe I got too far away from the *Irma* character in those pilot films. Well, in the next pilot I'll be more like

Irma." And indeed a fourth pilot was in the works at Paramount. Marie joked that if this one failed she would make nine more and sell each of them as a thirteen week anthology series! It didn't sell, but she also was through with television. She would never make another pilot and she would never have another television series. What she decided to do was return to the stage—and she did in a very big way and with a familiar partner.

III

In the late 1950's Marie's old friend Ken Murray became an executive at NBC, it turned out to be an unhappy and unproductive association and Murray left after only a year. He ran into Marie, who was having problems getting reestablished with a television series and they both reminisced about the old days with the **Blackouts** and how hardly a day went by when somebody wouldn't approach them on the streets to ask, "so when are you going to open **Blackouts** again?" They talked it over and as Murray later wrote, "I guess the ham in both of us just couldn't help coming out when we were urged by my new manager, Pierre Cossette, to accept an offer to revive **Blackouts** in Los Angeles for a limited engagement." Murray and Marie were excited, but before opening in the city of Angels they decided to take a limited run of **Blackouts** to Las Vegas to test it at the Frontier Hotel and were emboldened by the enthusiastic reception it received.

After Las Vegas they came back to Los Angeles and it was like old times except that instead of appearing at the El Capitan Theatre they would open the show on Christmas Eve, 1958 at the Ritz Theatre. Other than that it was almost like nine years hadn't passed. Murray was his familiar wise-cracking and cigar chomping master of ceremonies and Marie was her usual ditzy but sexy and endearing leading lady—and at age 42 still had the body to do the comic striptease she was known for. Without a doubt it would be Ken and Marie who would be the big draws, but they had plenty of other acts to back them up: show girls, burlesque styled comics, singers, dancers, acrobats and animal acts (including a chimp which did an Elvis Presley imitation!).

The theatre had a capacity of 1,330 seats and Murray would recall with pleasure that the place was filled to capacity, "It was like a reunion of long-separated relatives. As I peered through the spotlight there were, of course, many faces I recognized. The rest of the audience was so enthusiastic and eagerly anticipatory that I felt a little ashamed I didn't know their first names too." Marie was as loved as she was a decade earlier, "By the time I stepped into the audience to moderate Marie's combination mind reading act and strip tease," Murray would recall, "the crowd was ready for the ovation that followed."

The reviews were everything that the original shows opening reviews sixteen years earlier were not: ecstatic. **The Los Angeles Herald and Express** wrote, "The latest number **Blackouts of 1959** last night raucously slam-banged into the Ritz

Variety Advertisement for *Blackouts of 1956* with Ken Murray and Marie, then appearing in Las Vegas. The Stumpf-Ohmart Collection.

Theatre with the old master puffing a cigar and Marie Wilson looking her delectable best . . . the packed house got what it came for, and plenty of new material as well." Hazel Flynn in the **Beverly Hills Citizen** gushed, " . . . but mainly it was Ken himself and Marie Wilson, his blonde costar, reunited after years of separation and TV, that people apparently came to see, and they saw lots of them. The couple work together as closely as an eggbeater and an egg. Marie displays her epidermis and plays dumb, but manages to top the ebullient Ken now and then, to everyone's delight. It still is one of the greatest acts in the business, and you'll never see it on TV for obvious reasons." Though Ken and Marie did take a portion of the act—a kind of Burns and Allen routine—to **The Ed Sullivan Show** in 1960.

The original run of **The Blackouts of 1959** at the Ritz was supposed to be two-and-a-half weeks, but due to the public appetite for the show it was extended to over seventeen weeks. There New Year's Eve shows set an all-time record, grossing $16,500, with a ticket price which topped out at $7.00. The show finally closed at the end of April, 1959, but the Murray-Wilson combo wasn't done yet. They would continue to revive the show in Las Vegas, Lake Tahoe and New York City through out the year and return to Hollywood in December, 1960 for the new **Blackouts of 1960** to usher in the New Year at the Cocoanut Grove which was situated at the Ambassador Hotel—as always to sold out crowds.

On February 22, 1959 Marie did her final major dramatic radio appearance. It was on an episode of **Suspense** and titled "Star over Hong Kong." **Suspense** was one of the last of the great radio series, and the show was built around Marie's established dumb blonde persona. She plays a movie actress who almost causes an international incident. While the episode had some suspense—it was basically played for laughs. It was a fun swan song to the medium for which she was most successful.

Marie got her next chance to appear in a major motion picture in 1961 when Producer Jerry Wald and Director Henry Koster approached her to play a funny supporting role in Twentieth Century Fox's domestic comedy **Mr. Hobbs Takes a Vacation**. James Stewart and Maureen O'Hara are cast as Mr. and Mrs. Hobbs who along with their three children try to enjoy a peaceful and restful vacation in an old beachfront house, but with two teenagers who find love and a pre-teen who is always up to mischief as well as unwelcome houseguests like Mr. and Mrs. Turner (Marie and John McGiver) it is hardly a vacation for the Hobbs'. Backstage was hardly serene as well, according to Maureen O'Hara who in her autobiography **Tis Herself** recalls a cold Mr. Stewart who wanted to replace her after one day of filming because he felt that she was trying to upstage him. Somehow O'Hara survived but the atmosphere continued to be frosty. O'Hara would recall that on a Jimmy Stewart picture the only thing that mattered to Jimmy Stewart was Jimmy Stewart.

Marie, however, didn't get involved in the problems of the films stars and her scenes were shot in a few weeks under the careful eye of her old friend Henry

Koster who directed her twice before. Marie would have no idea that *Mr. Hobbs Takes a Vacation* would be her movie swansong after 28 years and 41 films. She would go out in style as the film became one Fox's biggest box office hits of 1962 and she even won some good reviews. Even Bosley Crowther, still the grouchy critic of the *New York Times* threw her a bouquet, "In addition to Mr. Stewart and Miss O' Hara, the cast includes John McGiver, Marie Wison and Reginald Gardiner in reasonably adult and amusing roles." Coming from Crowther, who usually berated Marie and her films this was a rave. *Variety's* review was even better, after calling the picture, "amiable, but often misguided" the reviewer wrote, "Best support comes from Marie Wilson and John McGiver as a pair of wild house guests."

With motion picture roles drying up and television parts becoming sparse, Marie in her mid 40's continued to dote on Greg, who by the mid 60's was only 10 years old and she and Bob were seen frequently at social and charitable events in Los Angeles. The Fallon's also invested wisely in real estate, which allowed them to maintain a lucrative lifestyle even as Marie's career options were drying up.

Marie continued to tour and often appeared in summer stock or dinner theatre in productions of *Born Yesterday* and *Gentlemen Prefer Blondes*. Both roles were suitable for her ditzy persona and the middle aged and elderly patrons lined up to see her when she played venues such as Cincinnati's Summer Playhouse, The Dallas Summer Musical Theatre and the Meadowbrook Dinner Theatre in Newark, NJ. In July, 1961 she played the Meadowbrook in a production of *Gentlemen Prefer Blondes* and according to the headline of July 12, 1961 which appeared in *The Newark Evening News*: MARIE WILSON IS A HIT. The review by Tom Mackin gives a glimpse as to how Marie compensated for a less than stellar vocal range:

"Marie Wilson, one of the most remarkably constructed women in show business, unveiled her charms last night at the Meadowbrook Theater at the Meadowbrook Dinner Theater. The vehicle was "Gentlemen Prefer Blondes," but there probably were few in the packed house that cared. It was enough that Miss Wilson was in view. The blonde star of televisions "My Friend Irma," is not abundantly endowed with vocal talent. Or perhaps it was just that musical director Donald Yap persisted in playing in the wrong key. This may be one of those intramural disputes that will never be settled. But the star of the evening had her way of diverting the customers' attention from such minor matters as key, pitch, timbre, intonation or what have you. Her simple device was a wardrobe of the most startling gowns this side of a Cecil B. DeMille movie. These set off such an incessant buzzing among the diners that the music and lyrics of Jule Styne and Leo Robin were secondary, if not tertiary. During the three week run of this presentation the balcony seats at Meadowbrook will be at a premium. One could dwell at length on Miss

Wilson's interpretation of the role of Lorelei Lee, and her contribution to the weal of summer musicals generally . . . But of course most patrons will travel to Cedar Grove to see Miss Wilson. They had better prepare themselves to seeing very nearly all of her."

It is a shame the critic didn't decide to emphasize that there is a great deal of humor in the part of Lorelei Lee and that the star of the original production on Broadway, Carol Channing, also didn't process a first rate set of singing pipes but made the show a hit through her energy and comic ability. Marie also excelled in this role in much the same way—great energy, first rate comedy ability and she had something Miss Channing didn't—sex appeal. A year later Marie would be back with the play appearing at the Westchester (NY) Dinner Theater and the critic there compared the women who played Lorelei Lee, "In the role of Lorelei Lee, she (Marie) has two illustrious predecessors, Carol Channing who played the part on Broadway, and Marilyn Monroe, who played it in the movie. Carol Channing brought to the role an unforgettable and highly individual wackiness; Marilyn Monroe brought strictly sex. Marie Wilson brings "My Friend Irma" which should please the patrons." In fact, Marie brought both wackiness and sex to her interpretation—if not a powerful set of lungs.

When Marie wasn't playing dinner theatres or summer stock she played nightclubs around the country from New York City to Palm Springs— including an appearance at the Chi Chi Club in Palm Springs in January, 1965 with a act which included comic Peter Wood and song and dance man Dean Barlow. *Variety* reviewed her night club act, "Marie Wilson opened to a less than capacity audience, but the customers amply made up for quantity in the warmth of their applause . . . Miss Wilson weaves in and out of the other acts, displaying different costume changes. These range from an opening number in a pink, very tight, glittering gown, to a "Madame Butterfly" in a bright pink kimono and

Marie at a party in the early 1960's.
The Stumpf-Ohmart Collection.

black wig, to a ridiculous little nurse's cap and cape barely covering her shoulders. Her material is naughty, like her neckline. But her innocent style of delivery and voice takes offense out of the words. Miss Wilson's act is replete with old faves, starting with "Diamonds are a Girl's Best Friend" to ending on "Memories." There's also a memory truck from which she fishes out all sorts of mementoes, ending with a paper cigar band and a gracious tribute to Ken Murray of "Blackouts" in which she played for years."

Increasingly, Marie was content with simply enjoying her family—She, Bob and Greg enjoyed going to Big Bear and skiing. They also enjoyed taking deep-sea fishing vacations. Marie increasingly gave of herself to such charities as The Jewish Home for the Aged, The March of Dimes and the Los Angeles based City of Hope. Her generosity was legendary. In 1966, she was remembered in the will of a man who had worked as an electrician on the *Irma* radio show—why? Because Marie always gave him a ride home after work (he had no car) and because he wasn't married she always invited him to her home on holidays such as Thanksgiving and Christmas, so he wouldn't be alone. Another technician on the radio show would later recall of Marie, "She stands there in one spot for a long time, just studying the floor boards. Then she moves to some other spot and just stands there. If she was the studious type, you'd say she was going through an absent-minded professor routine . . . Then you say to yourself it's just "Irma" . . . and you forget about it . . . Two days later the sound man shows you a crib robe that Marie has given him to give his wife because they are expecting a young one in about a month. The next day the make-up man shows you a pair of hand knit slippers and a stole that Marie has given him to give to his mother who is ailing with arthritis. A week later there's a big birthday party on the set with ice cream and cake for everybody . . . Everybody is thrown for a loss. Nobody can figure out how Marie knew about the sound man's baby or the make-up man's mother or the actor's birthday . . . I guess the answer is that Marie turns statue when she's collecting news from the yakity-yak around her. Quite a girl."

Since her near death experience in 1950 her faith had become even more important to her—it gave her a sense of serenity and acceptance which she utilized when she was again fighting for her life in the late 60s and early 70s. One friend commented, "I don't think it's widely known, but Marie is deeply religious and one of the vital tenets of her faith is keeping peace. She won't argue about what she considers to be trivialities, and she won't serve as an audience to such an argument."

The offers of roles were drying up. She still would do occasional nightclub appearances and television specials (some produced by Bob), but her persona as the "dumb blonde" was becoming passé by the late 1960's Part of the reason was the woman's movement which frowned upon such stereotypes like the dumb blonde character presented—blonde and big busted equaling a tiny intellect. Yet, Marie was working and supporting her family when Gloria Steinham was still in diapers. Marie certainly didn't look upon her character as degrading to women—she

Marie, Joan Crawford and Cesar Romero at a premier, early 60's.
The Author's Collection.

looked upon them as offering a few laughs and an escape from the reality of every day life. There was also a new realism in Hollywood films and television as situation comedies moved away from the innocence and absurdity of *Irma* to the realism of ***All in the Family*** and increasingly even comedy series would tackle important social issues such as racism, religion, poverty, and drug abuse. Marie herself was aware of the changing times and didn't necessarily think it was bad, "Irma had to be a virgin for the network. I guess if I noted any changes in television today it's the fact that a girl can work as a secretary in a series and not be cast as a virgin. That's progress."

Friends were dying off too. Sid Tomack and Gloria Gordon were both gone by the mid 1960's. Cathy Lewis died of cancer in 1968. Marie herself had been diagnosed with cancer in late 1967 and she would fight the disease for the last five years of her life. The first three years she thought she had it in check as she would go into remission and then it would suddenly come back again and repeat itself. By late 1970 however, she was increasingly ill, but she didn't let on to friends and to the world when she did go out, she presented the same happy, bubbly personality and sweet spirit she always did. She also didn't totally give up on her career. In the late 1960's Bob produced television specials starring Jack Cassidy which were syndicated around the country and featured Marie as a guest star. In 1970, she leant her voice to a Hanna Barbara cartoon series about an average American family called *Where's Huddles?* In September, 1972 she made her final professional appearance in an episode of *Love American Style*—which was broadcast in November.

By the time Marie's appearance on *Love American Style* was broadcast she was fading fast. Up until mid October she had tried to keep busy around the house and go out for lunch and see friends and work on charitable projects. But now she was spending more and more time in bed. By the third week of November, 1972 she was admitted to Mount Sinai Hospital where her doctor leveled with she and Bob—she had only a matter of time left. Marie decided she didn't want to die in the hospital, but wanted to die at home. Bob would later state, "Marie fought her battle with cancer for five years—quietly and with simple dignity . . . she asked to be discharged from Mt. Sinai Hospital . . . so she could die at home."

On Thanksgiving morning, November 23, 1972 at six a.m. Marie died in Bob's arms, she was 55. Fallon had maintained a night long vigil when it became clear that Marie was slipping fast. The loss hit Bob hard. They had been married for 21 years. Years later when he was dating Debbie Reynolds and there was speculation in the press that they might marry, Bob told a reporter that "Debbie didn't have marriages as good as mine was." Though out of the limelight for several years the *Los Angeles Times* and other newspapers across the country put the news of her passing on the front page. The *New York Times* obituary on November 23rd stated, "She was the pride and joy of press agents. No stunt was too crazy, no cheesecake too 'cheesy' . . . smart, witty and kind-hearted. As a young starlet she was the sole support of her family, and in later years, she was known for her generosity to friends, strangers, and any charity that approached her."

When notified of Marie's death Ken Murray told the press that he was "devastated" and that he had just recently visited Marie at her home, "she was very ill but bright and cheerful as always, she was a wonderful girl, a warm person." Hans Conried told a reporter, "I just can't talk about it—she was so sweet and wonderful. We all loved her." Plans were made for a memorial service to be held on Sunday in the Old North Church Memorial Park in the Hollywood Hills. Among those who attended the memorial were Jack Lord, William Demarest, Cesar Romero and Ken Murray. Rabbi Edgar F. Magnin, a family friend, gave the eulogy, "People who bring laughter are bringing a kind of prayer to God. I don't know if Marie even had a religion, in the sectarian sense, but she loved God and she loved people, and I guess that's as good a religion as you can have . . . despite her popular image as 'the dumb blonde' friends knew Marie as a sweet, lovable, thoughtful girl whose concern for people transcended all races, all nations and all creeds."

Marie Wilson: 1916–1972. The Author's collection.

MY FRIEND IRMA
EPISODE SYNOPSES

Episode synopses from the KNS Radio Scripts in the Radio and Television Achieves of the Thousand Oaks (CA) Library

Note: Script titles and comments in brackets—e.g., **(IRMA MEETS JANE)**—are supplied by the Reviewers and are not material from the original scripts. Script titles, ect., without brackets surrounding them—e.g., **KROPOTIKIN GETS SICK**—are shown as stated on the original scripts. When a script is reworked and or rebroadcast, the notation "Reprise" is made. While most of the scripts for the series were available, a few couldn't be found in the collection. My Thanks to Elizabeth K. Miller and Caroline Mekhiel for all of their work in going through the radio scripts.

CAST

IRMA	MARIE WILSON (1947–1954)
JANE	CATHY LEWIS (1947–1948, 1949–1953)
JANE	JOAN BANKS (1948–1949)
AL	JOHN BROWN (1947–1952)
AL	SID TOMACK (1952–1953)
MRS. O'REILLY	GLORIA GORDON (1947–1954)
PROFESSOR KROPOTKIN	HANS CONRIED (1947–1952)
MR. CLYDE	ALAN REED (1948-1954)
WANDERKIN	KENNY DELMAR
KAY	MARY SHIPP (1953–1954)
JOE	HAL MARCH (1953–1954)

(IRMA MEETS JANE)
Broadcast: 4/11/47

Irma Peterson who is beautiful, sweet, loyal and incredibly dumb bumps into plain, loyal, hardworking and practical Jane Stacy. The two decide to share a small, run-down New York City apartment to share expenses. Irma hopes to marry her boyfriend Al, who refuses to work a regular job and is always trying to scam somebody. Jane works as a secretary for wealthy Richard Rhinelander III, who she also is secretly smitten with. Irma invites Jane's boss to dinner at the apartment. When Al drops by, Jane is embarrassed, because she wants to impress Richard. However, Richard takes a liking to Al and Irma because they're "real" people.

(AL'S PRIZEFIGHTER)
Broadcast: 4/18/47

Al has yet another idea for quick money. He is managing a prizefighter and wants to enter him into the fights that night. Problem is the always broke Al has no money so he convinces Irma to lend him the entry fee which she pays for by dipping into the rent money. When the landlady comes to the apartment to collect the rent money she gets the cash from the wallet that Richard, Jane's boyfriend had accidentally left behind. Richard comes back to the apartment to get his wallet and Irma is saved when Al shows up with the winnings from the fight. His fighter lost, but Al had bet on him not to win.

(AL MAKES RICHARD JEALOUS)
Broadcast: 4/25/47

How should Jane get Richard to make a commitment to her and ask her to marry him? Al's answer—make Richard jealous. Al gets his friend Joe to pretend to be Jane's long-time boyfriend. In the ensuing confrontation, Richard declares to everyone that he's Jane's boyfriend. Note: This episode introduces Leif Erickson taking over the role of Richard—a part he would play for most of the rest of the series run. Also introduced is Hans Conried as Irma and Jane's upstairs neighbor, music teacher Professor Kropotkin. Note that this is the third actress to play landlady Mrs. O' Reilly in as many weeks—as they continued to search for the right actress for the part.

(IT'S JANE'S BIRTHDAY, ALMOST)
Broadcast: 5/2/47

Irma's convinced it's Jane's birthday even though Jane keeps telling her it's the next day. Irma pretends to be injured to get sympathy and to get Jane, Al, and Richard to go along with her birthday plans for Jane. Everyone finally gives in to humor Irma, and as they leave to go out to dinner, Irma falls and injures herself, this time for real.

(IRMA ENTERS A CONTEST)
Broadcast: 5/9/47

Irma enters a contest to win a car. She has to write an essay titled, "How I Met My Boyfriend," in fifty words or less. Irma thinks she has won the contest, but she has not—she is a runner-up. Al, believing that Irma did win the contest tries to make a deal with a friend to trade the Grand Prize for a new apartment for the girls. When the deal fall through, Al placates Mrs. O' Reilly with the prize Irma really won—fifty pounds of soup chips. Note: Yet another actress plays Landlady O'Reilly. Jim Backus guest voices as Mr. Sanford—later went on to play Thurston Howell, III on *Gilligan's Island* and was the voice of the near-sighted Mr. Magoo.

(OUT OF WORK)
Broadcast: 5/16/47

Both girls are out of work after Jane quits her job and Irma is fired. Jane decides to start her own secretarial service from home. Unfortunately, Irma and Al have taken Jane's typewriter to a pawnshop. Irma and Al also visit Richard to plead for Jane's job back, but Jane has already spoken to Richard and arranged to return. Irma also (miraculously) regains her job. Irma also returns Jane's typewriter, but confesses that she had to sell Jane's pearls to get it back! (Jim Backus plays the part of Mr. Clyde, Irma's boss).

(IRMA'S DATE WITH SEYMOUR)
Broadcast: 5/23/47

Irma mistakenly thinks her boyfriend Al has another girlfriend named Sally Rose. So Irma decides she's through with Al and agrees to go on a date with Jane's old school friend, Seymour. Al explains to Irma that Sally Rose is a race horse.

(HOW TO SPEND A HOLIDAY WEEKEND)
Broadcast: 5/30/47

Irma and Jane discuss where they will spend the Memorial Day weekend. Jane's boyfriend Richard tries to get everyone a reservation at the upper crust Camp Nautilus, while Irma's boyfriend Al wants them to go to the NYCUA—New York Camp for Underprivileged Adults. But before they can be admitted to either place, Mrs. Vandy from the Nautilus must first interview Jane while Mrs. Klump from the NYCUA must interview Irma to determine if they fit the guest profile. Due to a mix up, Mrs. Klump interviews Jane and Mrs. Vandy interviews Irma. Mrs. Vandy thinks Irma is refreshing, and the four friends end up having a rainy weekend at Camp Nautilus.

(IRMA GOES TO NIGHT SCHOOL)
Broadcast: 6/6/47

Jane wants to go to night school, but Richard likes her the way she is and besides he will be lonely while she is gone. Irma decides to help the situation and in typical Irma fashion she takes Jane's school exam for her. Irma fails the exam, but so impresses the professors with her bizarre answers that they ask her to attend the University—as a subject for study. Note: Guest voice Alan Reed later went on to voice the character of Fred Flintstone and eventually was cast as the voice of Irma's boss, Mr. Clyde.

THE FUR COAT
Broadcast: 6/13/47

Irma gets a fur coat, and then loses it.

(IRMA'S ACCIDENT INSURANCE POLICY)
Broadcast: 6/30/47

Irma buys an accident insurance policy. Irma boyfriend Al wants her to fake an accident to collect the insurance money, but honest Irma will have no part of it. Then Irma really falls and hurts her shoulder. The Insurance representative is willing to pay the claim, but says they will sue the building's owners. Jane is afraid that the apartment manager then won't renew their lease, so Irma drops the claim. It turns out that landlady Mrs. O'Reilly would have approved suing the building owner! Note: Irene Tedrow who did guest voices in the previous two episodes gets a shot at Mrs. O'Reilly. Also, the show now was moved from Friday nights to Monday. (Bill Johnstone, who took over for Orson Welles as "The Shadow" and was a popular radio actor in his own right, plays the part of the Insurance representative).

(THE BEAUTY CONTEST)
Broadcast: 7/7/47

Irma and Al want to help Jane look more important to Richard's family. So they send in a photo of Irma in a bathing suit to a beauty contest—but put Jane's name on the photo. The contest managers like the photo, so Irma has to enter the contest, but under her own name. Irma wins the contest and a big trophy cup. She tells Jane she wants to enter another beauty contest, but this time a little one—so she can win a saucer for the cup!

(WHAT HAPPENED TO JANE'S WATCH?)
Broadcast: 7/28/47

When Richard consults Irma about getting a present for Jane, Irma tells him that Jane has been meaning to get a wristwatch converted into a lapel watch. Richard likes the idea but wants it to be a surprise, so he swears Irma to secrecy. Irma gives him Jane's watch, which he takes to his jeweler. Jane comes home just as Mrs. O'Reilly tells them that thieves have been in the apartment building. Jane discovers her watch is missing. The police take the report and end the description out over the teletype. Acting on information received, the police arrest Richard in the middle of his spech on "Good Citizenship" to the Park Avenue Civic Association.

Note: This episode introduces Gloria Gordon as landlady O'Reilly. Gordon stays for the duration—they finally have found a keeper! Gordon is the mother of veteran radio and television actor Gale Gordon who was working with Lucille Ball on *My Favorite Husband* and would later join Eve Arden on *Our Miss Brooks*.

(IRMA GETS LOST ON TRAIN)
Broadcast: 8/4/47

Irma, Jane and Al leave the city to go on vacation in the Adirondacks. As they change trains, Irma gets back on the original train to retrieve a lost item, and the train pulls out, leaving Jane and Al behind. Jane and Al try to catch up with Irma by hopping on a bus to the next train stop, but miss her when Irma finds a way back to the place where she left Jane and Al. They then go in cirlces trying to catch up with each other. Irma ends up in Canada and the Travelers' Aid flies her back to Jane and Al and they spend their vacation recuperating in the Adirondacks.

(AL'S BIRTHDAY)
Broadcast: 8/11/47

Irma plans to give Al a surprise birthday party. Meanwhile, at Jane's urging, Professor Kropotkin talks Al into ending his lengthy unemployment and look for a job. Al leaves Irma a brief note telling her where he's going, just saying he's "going to end it all." Naturally Irma jumps conclusions and thinks that Al is really going to "end it all." Note: The role of Professor Kropotkin is not credited in the script, but it's probable that it was played by Hans Conried.

(THE MONEY IN THE CABINET)
Broadcast: 8/18/47

Mrs. O'Reilly kicks out some tenants because they haven't kept up their apartment. Irma and Jane decide they'd better redecorate their apartment so they won't be the next evicted. Al finds an interior decorator, who arrives at the apartment when only Jane is there. The decorator buys all their furniture for his used furniture shop and carts it away. Irma returns and tells Jane that the rent money was in a cabinet she just sold to the decorator. They get the cabinet back from an auctioneer, but the rent money is gone. The decorator finds the money and gives it to the girls. He brings new furniture with him, which they move into the apartment. The landlady is so impressed with the new look that she raises their rent!

(IRMA FINDS A DOG)
Broadcast: 8/25/47

Irma takes a walk in the part, and a dog follows her home. Jane and Irma are not allowed to keep pets in their apartment so they enlist Al to help them get rid of the dog. Al and Irma find a lost dog notice in the newspaper and take the dog to its owner, expecting a reward, but the owner thinks they love the dog and insist that they keep it. So they place an ad to find the dog a home, but no one responds. Irma and Jane attempt to leave the dog at the pound but don't have the heart. When they take the dog back to the apartment, Mrs. O'Reilly, to their surprise is not angry. She says she'll take it to her brother in the country.

(JANE MEETS RICHARD'S MOTHER)
Broadcast: 9/1/47

Mrs. Rhinelander, just returned from Europe, calls Jane and asks if she could come over to meet her. Jane nervously agrees and persuades Irma and Al to leave the apartment for the afternoon. However, Irma and Al come back while Jane's out and take the phone message that Mrs. Rhinelander is coming an hour early. Irma forgets to tell Jane, so Jane is unprepared and flustered by Mrs. Rhinelander's early arrival. To make matters worse (from Jane's perspective) Irma, Al, and several neighbors barge into the apartment. Mrs. Rhinelander leaves soon after and Jane is miserable. Richard calls Jane and says his mother wants her to bring her friends over, and, at Al's suggestion they all end up having a great time at Coney Island.

(IRMA WINS AN ESSAY CONTEST)
Broadcast: 9/8/47

Irma enters an essay contest which offers a $1,000 first prize. The contest is sponsored by Glitter Furniture Polish and the subject is "I Like Glitter Furniture Polish Because . . . ." She ends up winning second prize but thinks she has actually won the contest. Instead of $1,000 she wins second prize, several gallons of furniture polish. Al begins selling the polish on the street corner.

(PROFESSOR KROPOTKIN'S VIOLIN)
Broadcast: 9/15/47

Professor Kropotkin quits his job playing violin in a restaurant. Jane wants him to audition for the Philhamonic, but Kropotkin says his violin is unworthy. When Jane tells Richard about it, he has his family's Stradivarius delivered to the girl's apartment, so that it can be lent to Kropotkin so he can audition for the Philharmonic's conductor who is coming by that evening to hear him play. Irma and Al return home find the rare Stradivarius and take it to the pawn shop to trade it for a cheap new violin. The audition is a disaster and Irma and Al explain what they did and Richard manages to get the Stradivarius back from the pawn shop where he auditions again for the conductor—but it is too late—a new violinist was hired, and Kropotkin goes back to the restaurant.

(Al Serves a Summons)
Broadcast: 9/22/47
Jane insists that perennially unemployed Al take a job serving summons for Irma's boss, Mr. Clyde. After a run-in with a dog while attempting to serve his first summons Al determines to quit. But he has to determine that the job is just too dangerous and hires some friends to rough him up when he delivers his next summons. However, before he can do so, Richard finds the summons, which is for a competitor of his and determines to deliver it himself, and is roughed up. Al proves his point and is allowed to quit.

(Irma Goes to Court)
Broadcast: 9/29/47
Jane is about to go on a business trip to Boston when Irma is summoned for jury duty. Jane is afraid that Irma will screw up the system, but Irma is excused. Irma accompanies Jane to the train station and witnesses a traffic accident. Irma and Jane are sent to give evidence before a judge, and Irma so muddles the courtroom that court is adjourned and the case settled without their testimony. On their way to catch Jane's train, Irma picks some flowers as a going away present for Jane and is arrested. Jane pays the fine and takes Irma on the train with her before anything else can happen!

(Al Forgets Irma's Birthday)
Broadcast: 10/6/47
It's Irma's birthday and friends and neighbors arrive to wish her a happy birthday. Al arrives but has forgotten it's her birthday. Irma is hurt and breaks up with Al. Jane advises Al to get Irma a present. Meanwhile Al's friend arranges for Katie to stop by the apartment and make Irma jealous by pretending to be Al's new girlfriend. The resulting misunderstandings are resolved.

(The New Refrigerator)
Broadcast: 10/13/47
Jane takes her half of the money that Irma and she had been saving and deposits it on a new refrigerator. She then goes to be outfitted for a fashion show. Irma returns to the apartment and discovers the money missing and then jumps the conclusions when some expensive clothing is delivered for Jane (for the fashion show). Irma decides that if Jane can use the money to buy expensive clothing then so can she and does so. Jane returns home and explains the situation to Irma and Irma attempts to return the clothes she bought, but can't get refunded until the next day. Without being able to get a refund the girls cannot pay for the refrigerator when it is arrived, but the refrigerator delivery man feels sorry for them and loans them one, which turns out to be a lemon (which Irma and Jane are unaware of). Richard's mother comes for dinner and brings ice cream for dessert, which in the meanwhile melts when put in the defective refrigerator

and spills all over of Richard's mother when she goes to serve it.

(IRMA AND THE FORTUNE TELLER)
Broadcast: 10/20/47
Professor Kropotkin doubles as Sonia the Fortune Teller at the Gypsy Tea Room, tells Irma's fortune. Kropotkin tells Irma that she will either get married in two years, two months or two days—something with a two in it. Al calls, but says he can't talk right now and that he will "ring you tomorrow." Of course, Irma jumps the conclusion thinking that Al is going to ask her to marry him and give her an engagement ring. She even goes out to find Jane a new roommate.

(RICHARD'S NEW CAR)
Broadcast: 10/27/47
Richard buys a new car, and Al wants to borrow it to help him swing one of his deals. When that doesn't work out, Al borrows the luxury car of the boss of a mechanic friend (which the boss is unaware of). When Richard sees the car he declares it's just the type of car his mother is looking for, and without Al's knowledge, Richard asks Irma if he can borrow it to show his mother, and she agrees. When the owner of the car comes to the garage to pick up his car, the mechanic, trying to cover up, says it was stolen. And, of course, Richard's mother is arrested for driving a stolen car!

(MRS. O'REILLY IS FIRED)
Broadcast: 11/3/47
It's so cold in the apartment building that the tenants want to get a new apartment manager. Before they can complain at the bank, which owns the property, Mrs. O'Reilly tells Irma and Jane that she has been fired for trying to improve conditions and that a new manager is coming. All the tenants then want to retain Mrs. O'Reilly, so Jane and her wealthy boyfriend Richard meet with the bank manager and arrange for Mrs. O'Reilly to stay on. The bank manager wants to visit the apartment building to check on the tenants. Meanwhile, Irma and Al, wanting to get rid of the new manager, have arranged for Irma's obnoxious friend Amber to immediately move into the vacant apartment above. When the bank manager arrives at Irma and Jane's apartment, he is treated to wild overhead noises. When he complains to Amber, she roughs him up. Irma and Jane explain what's happened and send Amber away. Everyone is happy that Mrs. O'Reilly's back.

(IS JANE TWO-TIMING RICHARD?)
Broadcast: 11/10/47
When Richard has a schedule conflict, he asks Jane to do him the favor of entertaining Mr. Girard, his biggest client, at the El Morocco that evening until he can arrive. Richard, though asks that she not tell Irma and Al what she is going to do, because he is afraid they might interfere. So when she goes out, Jane tells them that

she is going to a movie. Naturally Irma and Al find out that Jane is meeting a man at the El Morocco and jump to the conclusion that she is two-timing Richard.

(THE FUR NECKPIECE)
Broadcast: 11/17/47
Al lectures Jane about criticizing Irma's taste, so Jane promises she'll be more supportive of Irma's choices. Irma shows Jane a ghastly fur neckpiece she's brought from an unscrupulous vendor, and Jane remembers to say that she thinks it's "one of a kind." Irma is pleased that Jane likes it and tells Al that she intends to give the fur to Jane for Christmas.

(JANE AND RICHARD GET A LICENSE)
Broadcast: 11/24/47
Irma and Al overhear Jane and Richard making a date to meet the next day at City Hall to get a license. They, naturally, jump the conclusion and assume they are getting a marriage license. They even write up a marriage contract to protect Jane's future financial interests. It turns out that Richard is getting his mother a poodle for her birthday and they're just getting a dog license.

(THE REWARD)
Broadcast: 12/1/47
Irma finds a handbag on the street. She and Al phone the number in the purse, and the owner says she'll send her secretary to get the purse. Meanwhile, Richard has arranged with Jane for Peggy from his office to drop off $100 for him to pick up later at the apartment. Peggy arrives while Jane is out. Irma and Al think she is giving them a reward and insist that she take the purse in exchange. The bewildered Peggy accepts the purse and Irma and Al leave with the money. Of course then the real secretary comes for the purse.

(IRMA AND THE EYEGLASSES)
Broadcast: 12/8/47
Irma's having headaches, and Jane thinks she needs glasses. Jane can't get Irma to go to the eye doctor, because Irma's afraid Al won't love her anymore (or find her attractive) if she wears eyeglasses. Richard suggests that Jane go to a five and dime and get some eyeglasses for Irma to try on and when she wears them they'll tell her how great she looks in them. They finally get Irma to the eye doctor and she passes the eye exam with flying colors. Jane questions Irma further and finds out that Irma hasn't been eating lunch all week—her chronically unemployed boyfriend Al was "buying" the lunches.

(DANCING FOOLS)
Broadcast: 12/15/47
Richard wants Jane to help him entertain a big client at a nightclub to close

a deal. He asks Jane if she can recommend another couple to expand their party. Naturally she thinks of Irma and Al. Al, however, doesn't know how to rumba, so he take instructions and still can't do it correctly, so he invents his own form. They all go to the nightclub where Al dances his "unique" rumba with the client's wife—who is put through odd contortions and occasionally seems to fall to the floor. When Al and the client's wife return to the table she declares she has had a great time and her husband doubles his original order with Richard's firm. Guest voice Jerry Hausner would be recognizable from the first two seasons of *I Love Lucy* playing Ricky's manager, Jerry.

(CHRISTMAS EVE)
Broadcast: 12/22/47
Irma wants to give a Christmas Eve party, but everyone has plans. After Irma leaves the apartment feeling very sad and lonely, Jane breaks her date with Richard, and Al, Kropotkin and Mrs. O'Reilly each come by to say they've changed their plans as well, so Irma won't be alone on Christmas Eve. The gang decides to throw a surprise party for Irma. Meanwhile, Irma is so depressed that she tries to buy a train ticket back home to Minnesota, but doesn't have enough money. So she aimlessly wanders the streets. When Irma doesn't show up back at the apartment everyone goes searching for her. Al bumps into a friend, who said he panhandled money from a blonde. Al realizes this is Irma, and the gang alerts the police. Irma is brought home in a squad car and walks in to find everyone yelling, "Surprise!" Irma is overcome with emotion, and says it's the best Christmas she ever had. (this episode would be reprised several times over the next seven years).

(IRMA'S DEPRESSED)
Broadcast: 1/5/48
Irma believes that life is passing her by, and she is meant for bigger and better things than working as a stenographer.

(IRMA WANTS TO BE A BRIDE)
Broadcast: 1/12/48
Irma enters the KNX radio contest, "I Want to be a Bride, because. . ."

(IRMA IS FIRED)
Broadcast: 1/19/48
Just after Irma buys a piano, Mr. Clyde fires her when she asks for a raise.

(LONELY HEARTS CLUB)
Broadcast: 1/26/48
Irma and Al split up and both join a lonely-hearts club.

(JANE BREAKS UP WITH RICHARD)
Broadcast: 2/2/48

Richard phones Jane to tell her that he can't make their date because he is working late with the new secretary, who is very attractive. Jane interprets this as a brush off and writes a letter to Richard resigning her position as both Richard's secretary and girl friend. Irma takes the letter to the mail and in the meanwhile Richard comes to the apartment to explain that the new secretary is a relative of an important client and will soon be sent to another office. Jane is frantic to retrieve the letter and a series of misadventures ensue, but it turns out that Irma didn't mail the letter—it's still in her purse.

(BILLY BOY, THE BOXER)
Broadcast: 2/9/48

Richard loans Al $1,000 to start a business, and Al uses the money to buy the contract of a weak-kneed fighter named Billy Boy. Jane warns Richard of Al's poor business decision, and when they arrive at the fight, Richard bets on Billy Boy to lose. Meanwhile, Irma has been giving Billy Boy a pep talk, and during the fight, Irma shouts encouragement to him from ringside. Billy Boy wins the fight, and Jane is distressed that Richard lost his bet, but Richard says it's okay because he made up the money on stock exchange activity during the fight.

(PROFESSOR'S CONCERTO)
Broadcast: 2/16/48

Professor Kropotkin finishes a violin concerto which took him years to compose. He takes it to a publishing company which turns it down. Richard has a client that publishes music, and he and Jane arrange a meeting between the client and Kropotkin. The client loves the concerto and promises a $1,000 advance for it. Meanwhile, Irma and Al decide that no one will publish the composition, because it doesn't have lyrics. They boil the concerto down to song-length, write some lyrics for it, and manage to sell it for $100 to a publisher that will get it played on a radio program that night. Richard's client has the contract drawn up and brings it to Irma and Jane's apartment for Kropotkin to sign. Irma and Al confess that they sold the piece for $100 just as the client gets a phone call from a partner, telling him the concerto had been plagiarized. The client leaves and Kropotkin is crushed. Further discussion reveals that the concerto's theme is a rehashing of an old Hungarian lullaby that Kropotkin's mother sang to him.

(IT'S ALL RELATIVE)
Broadcast: 2/23/48

Irma wonders why Al never mentions his family. Al always tries to avoid the conversation. After Irma leaves the apartment he tells Jane the truth. Al, who is perpetually unemployed, doesn't want hsi mom to be ashamed of him and has been telling his mom that he's the president of General Motors *and* General Electric! Also, he sends half of his unemployment checks to his Mom. Jane is touched and tells Al to invite his mother over and she (Jane) will back up everything that Al says. Irma returns and finds a letter to Al from a strange woman, who, Al explains, is his mother. When Al's mother arrives at the apartment, Jane duly informs her that her son is a great success, to Irma's perplexity. In spite of all the misunderstandings they all end up having a nice evening.

(IRMA LOSES CLYDE'S TUX)
Broadcast: 3/1/48
Mr. Clyde asks Irma to pick up his new tuxedo. Shouldn't he know better by now?

(THE DINNER PARTY)
Broadcast: 3/8/48
Just prior to a dinner party, Irma and Jane have fights with Al and Richard. Making things worse at the dinner party, Professor Kropotkin is paired with Mrs. O'Reilly.

(BUY OR SELL)
Broadcast: 3/15/48
Irma and Jane's phone is on a party line, and they're always having trouble making or receiving calls. Irma and Al are so worried that Jane won't be able to get Richard's important long distance call that evening that they go to the phone company to demand a private line. A misunderstanding ensues, and the phone company representative disconnects the line. Irma and Al pretend to take a call from Richard and tell Jane that Richard said for her to tell an important client to sell a certain stock. Jane delivers the message to the client on his yacht. Then a telegram from Richard arrives, with instructions for the client to buy, not sell. At work the next morning Jane is clearing out her desk when the client arrives and tells Jane he wants to congratulate Richard—the client made a fortune by selling the stock.

(THE ELECTION CONNECTION)
Broadcast: 3/22/48
Richard asks Jane to help him with Colby's election to the city council. Al, who has been signed up to campaign for the rival Councilman Blake, asks Irma to help him. Blake's campaign publishes a slur against Colby, and Irma, Jane, Al, and Richard all go to a rally at Sloan's Hall for a showdown. Colby tries to speak, but can't because of the booing. Blake's speech is well received, and he calls for anyone in the audience to confirm his honest record. Irma, who has been coached to respond to this, stands up and, of course, scrambles her speech, so it makes Blake appear to be just as what he is: dishonest.

THE BIG SECRET
Broadcast: 3/29/48

Richard asks Jane to accompany him on a confidential trip to Washington, D.C. Richard wants to get a government approval to use a site as a center for underprivileged children before other business interests can get it first. Richard acquiesces when Irma begs to come along, but then Al, Professor Kropotkin, and even Mrs. O'Reilly want to come too. Later, when she is alone, a reporter calls and Irma spills the beans on the confidential trip. When they all get to Washington, the Senator won't take Richard's calls. Then they see a newspaper article about Richard coming to Washington on a confidential project and realize that Irma is the source of the story. Irma is upset and runs off, spending the day wandering around the city. She runs into the senator, and her scrambled explanation of Richard's project convinces him to call Richard. The Senator approves the project, saying no other New York child should grow up to be like Irma.

(IRMA'S INHERITANCE)
Broadcast: 4/5/48

A lawyer looking for an Irma Peterson whose uncle just died and left her a $50,000 inheritance, contacts Irma, and indications are that it is OUR Irma who is the missing heiress. Everyone is happy for Irma except Al, who feels he must now break off their relationship—the reason—he doesn't want everybody to think that he would marry Irma for her money. Everything turns out ok at the end when the lawyer informs Irma that she is not the heiress after all.

(IRMA, THE PHOTOGRAPHER)
Broadcast: 4/12/48

Wanting to be a photographer, Richard allows Irma to use his camera.

(DINNER DATE)
Broadcast: 4/19/48

Jane's discouraged because Richard has still not asked her to marry him, so she agrees to go out on a date with a new guy named Gilford. Gilford tells her he works for the government in financial distribution. When Irma's perpetually unemployed boyfriend Al finds out that Jane is going out with an important new beau, he asks if he and Irma can double date. It turns out that Al does know Gilford—he's the guy who hands out the unemployment checks.

(MANHATTAN MAGAZINE)
Broadcast: 4/26/48

Irma and Jane are out shopping on a Saturday afternoon when they become aware that they're being followed by a strange man. The man catches up to them and says he is a photographer for a major fashion magazine and would like to photograph them. The photographer says he will come by their apartment to photograph them. Jane goes to get ready, but Irma causes a fuse to blow out and the apartment is plunged into darkness. Al arrives and attempts to fix things. He fixes things alright—he disables the plumbing and disconnects the phone. Jane is panicky and is still in her robe with her hair in curlers when the photographer arrives. He says she's perfect because the magazine wants to do a story about today's young career girl as she prepares to go out on a date. Jane may even end up on the cover.

(Acute Love Sickness)
Broadcast: 5/3/48

Irma doesn't feel well, so Jane takes her to the doctor, who diagnoses love sickness. Jane determines that Al give Irma an engagement ring to make her feel better. Jane goes so far as to tell Al that she will give him her grandmother's engagement ring to give to Irma. Later, Al wants to make the mood in the apartment romantic and asks Irma to lower the lights, at the end of a flowery speech, Al can't find the ring to give to Irma. Irma is convinced there never was a ring and kicks him out. Jane returns and finds a crying Irma, and the two eventually find the ring inside of Irma's shoe. Al is forgiven and he places the ring on Irma's finger. (Veteran radio actor John McIntire plays the doctor).

Bon Voyage
Broadcast: 5/10/48

Richard asks Jane, Irma, Al, Kropotkin and Mrs. O'Reilly to come to the Queen Mary to see him off before he sails to England. Al decides that he should go to London because in the London fogs he's more likely to be successful promoting his crazy schemes. However, he can't afford the price of a ticket, so he decides to stowaway in one of the lifeboats. He's discovered in the lifeboat just as Irma tries to deliver a suitcase of sandwiches to him. Al and the rest of the gang are ordered off the ship, but Irma disappears. While they are searching for her, the ship sets sail. They see Irma waving to them from the shore, and they all have to be returned by the pilot boat. (The captain is played by the famous silent screen star Francis X. Bushman, who starred in several classics including the original *Ben Hur*).

New York Professional Women's Club
Broadcast: 5/17/48

Jane has been accepted into an organization of professional women, and Irma, feeling left out wants to join too. Naturally, the professional women are less than thrilled with Irma, and Jane, as usual sticks up for her friend.

(Aunt Harriet)
Broadcast: 5/24/48

Jane's Aunt Harriet is coming for a visit, and Jane wants everything to go well, and with Irma around that is difficult to achieve.

(THE COUNTRY CLUB CAPER)
Broadcast: 5/31/48
Irma is jealous when Richard invites Jane to play golf with him at the country club. Al, suggests that they go and surprise Jane and Richard at the club. Richard and Jane are playing with Mr. Bailey and Kay Collins, and Mr. Bailey takes Richard aside and convinces him to invest $1,000 in one of his projects. Irma and Al show up, and while Irma is talking to Jane, Al runs ito Mr. Bailey, who has just cashed Richard's check. Al convinces Bailey to invest $1,000 in one of his deals. Meanwhile, the club manager informs Richard that Bailey is a crook and has been asked to resign from the club. Richard is relating the sad facets to Jane and Irma about his recent investment when Al joins them. Al responds by putting the $1,000 that he got from Bailey into Richard's hand. Al even refuses an award!

(HEAT WAVE)
Broadcast: 6/7/48
The gang visits Coney Island to get relief during a heat wave.

(IS IRMA GETTING MARRIED?)
Broadcast: 6/14/48
Jane jumps the conclusion when Al and Irma come home with a wedding ring—but it turns out that they bought it for Amber.

(RESORT VACATION)
Broadcast: 6/28/48
The gang wants to go to the Moose Head Lodge for their vacation. Jane plans to impress the fancy resort by writing them a cultured letter requesting reservations. Al thinks he can write an even better letter. When Jane finds out that Al also wrote a letter she believes that the resort will not admit them. Jane receives a reply denying her request for accommodations. Then a letter comes to Al and Irma. The resort administrators found Irma and Al's letter to be so amusing and original that they are delighted to welcome them to the hotel.

END OF SEASON, SHOW GOES ON A TWO MONTH SUMMER HIATUS.

(JANE'S NEW JOB)
Broadcast: 8/30/48
Jane breaks up with her boyfriend and boss Richard and quits her job. Irma, Al, Kropotkin and Mrs. O'Reilly all pitch in to help her find a new job. Jane signs up with an employment agency and accepts a job with the Fidelity Bond Investment Company. She writes a note about the job and abbreviates the firm's

name as "FBI" and leaves the apartment. Irma and Al find the note and are convinced that she is going to work for J. Edgar Hoover's FBI.

(JANE'S NEW BOYFRIEND)
Broadcast: 9/6/48

Jane who has broken up with Richard has met an interesting new guy named Mike. Jane's afraid Mike will be turned off by Irma and Al, so Jane doesn't tell them about Mike. While waiting for Mike to call her, Jane tries to get Irma and Al out of the apartment. Mike calls and Jane asks him to come over. While Jane's out, Irma and Al return. When Mike knocks at the door, Irma tells him what Jane said about men, when she was mad at Richard and to go away. When Jane returns, she learns what has happened, and tells Irma that Mike is her new boyfriend. Luckily, Mike found Irma so unbelievable that he returns and the foursome spend the evening getting to know one another. *(Joan Banks replaces Cathy Lewis as Jane for the remainder of the season. Cathy Lewis, one of the busiest radio actresses of her day, had a breakdown and took the season off to recuperate).*

(SAVINGS ACCOUNT)
Broadcast: 9/13/48

Jane spends $200 in the girl's joint savings account to pay off a loan on the piano, but then Irma takes the same $200 out of the bank and buys a half pound diamond.

(UNEMPLOYED KROPOTKIN)
Broadcast: 9/27/48

When Professor Kropotkin loses his job at the Gypsy Tea Room, Irma gets the idea of opening a new restaurant—The Café Kropotkin. Part one of two.

(CAFÉ KROPOTKIN)
Broadcast: 10/4/48

The professor has his new restaurant, but finds he's losing money—could it be because Irma is his bookkeeper? Needless the say, Krop's restaurant goes under, but he gets his job back at the Tea Room. Part two of two.

(MASQUERADE BALL)
Broadcast: 10/11/48

Irma and the rest of the gang attend a charity Masquerade Ball.

(MISSING GLASSES)
Broadcast: 10/18/48

Irma's in jeopardy of losing her job (yet again) if she can't find Mr. Clyde's eye glasses—which she misplaced.

(A Fortune in Bonds)
Broadcast: 11/1/48

Jane's boss asks her to take $50,000 worth of bonds home overnight (!) so she will be able to deliver them to a client the first thing the next morning. Having the bonds in the apartment terrifies Irma, who is afraid that they will be robbed. Along with Al they rig an elaborate array of booby traps in the apartment just incase a thief comes calling. In a typical Irma move she even cuts the cord to the telephone so that she will be able to throw it at the would-be thief. In the middle of the night, Irma and Jane hear a scuffle outside the apartment and when they open up the door they discover Al (who was posting guard) who tells them that he just beat up a stranger who was trying to break into the apartment. Al describes the stranger and he fits the description of Jane's new boss, who came over to the apartment because he had given Jane the wrong bonds and couldn't reach her by telephone.

(Irma Joins a Club)
Broadcast: 11/8/48

Irma is excited that she's been proposed for membership in her friend Amber Lippscott's (Bea Benaderet) club, Social Ladies of the Bronx Society, or S.L.O.B.S. Irma got glowing references from Professor Kropotkin and Mrs. O'Reilly, so it stuns Irma when Amber tells her that the other club members blackballed her—because she is dating Al, who used to be another members boyfriend. Eventually Irma is approved for membership after being told that other members are dating each other's boyfriends and they have declared it Open Season!

(Thanksgiving Dinner)
Broadcast: 11/15/48

With Thanksgiving approaching, Jane plans a nice Thanksgiving dinner for four, and to help out Irma buys a live turkey named George, and of course, the girls grow attached to George and can't sacrifice him for their dinner.

(The Contest)
Broadcast: 11/22/48

Irma enters a contest sponsored by *Wall Street Magazine* where she has to describe a secretary's most interesting experience. The prize is $150.

(Irma's Birthday)
Broadcast: 11/29/48

Jane throws a costume party in honor of Irma's birthday, and Al causes her ire to rise when he invites one of his crooked friends, Joe.

(THE PIANO)
Broadcast: 12/6/48
Irma decides to take piano lessons, but Jane, without Irma's knowledge, has returned the piano.

(JANE QUITS)
Broadcast: 12/13/48
Jane quits her job just before Christmas. Al and Irma decide to help, and just make things worse.

(THE CHRISTMAS EVE SURPRISE PARTY)
Broadcast: 12/20/48
A reprise of the December 22, 1947 episode.

(IRMA'S NEW BOYFRIEND)
Broadcast: 12/27/48
Irma is fed up with perennially unemployed boyfriend Al and makes a dinner date with a new fellow. The new boyfriend arrives for a dinner date at the apartment at the stated time and then turns around and returns to work because he is in the middle of running a test project at work. In the meanwhile Al sends Irma a telegram stating he's going to jump off a bridge in an hour. When Irma doesn't show up to "save him," Al phones and asks what's taking her so long? She hangs up on him. The new boyfriend returns in time to take Irma out to the movies, but again cuts it short because he remembers he forgot to turn off some equipment at work. Poor Irma is perplexed—first she has one boyfriend who never works, and now she has one who doesn't stop working. She decides to put an ad in the Lonely Hearts column of the newspaper advertising for a boyfriend who is employed part time. Sandra (Sandy) Gould, of *Duffy's Tavern* and later the second Gladys Kravitz on *Bewitched* is a guest voice.

(DOUBLE DATE)
Broadcast: 1/3/49
Irma and Al are still on the outs, so Irma and Jane decide to go on a double date. When Al finds out about it, he makes plans to sabotage it.

(DONE WITH MEN)
Broadcast: 1/10/49
Both Irma and Jane decide to give up men—or they think they are, until temptation comes their way.

(AL WINS BACK IRMA'S HEART)
Broadcast: 1/17/49
Irma's old boyfriend Al wants to get back together with her, but Irma says no. Yet

Irma can't stop thinking about Al and is driving everyone around her crazy be being forgetful and upset. Al pretends to be sick to get Irma's sympathy. Jane and Richard realize what he's up to and, knowing that Irma was much happier when she was with Al, they confirm to Irma that Al is sick and needs her care. Irma brings Al some homemade soup, and they make up. Then Al drinks the soup and really does become ill—distracted Irma accidentally put shoe polish in it.

(THE POOR RHINELANDERS)
Broadcast: 1/24/49

When Richard's mother, Mrs. Rhinelander turns up depressed, Irma jumps conclusions and thinks that the Rhinelander's have lost their fortune and is now broke.

(OLD MEN'S HOME)
Broadcast: 1/31/49

The gang needs to help Professor Kropotkin raise money or else he is going to be put in an "old men's home."

(LAKE PLACID OR BUST)
Broadcast: 2/7/49

Richard phones Jane from Lake Placid and asks her to bring some securities from the office for a client meeting he's having. Irma and Al ask if they can go with Jane. Jane buys some pricey winer sports gear for the trip. Jane, Irma and Al hurry to Grand Central Station and run to catch the train. After the train is underway they discover they are on the wrong train and are heading for Miami. Al meets a bathing suit salesman and swaps all their winter gear for his suitcases full of bathing suits. Jane makes arrangments with the conductor to switch trains at Philadelphia. Once they're on their way to Lake Placid, Irma and Al try to keep Jane from opening up the suitcases, but she discovers what Al has done—and even forgives him.

(THE VALENTINE'S DAY CANDY MIX-UP)
Broadcast: 2/14/49

While Irma's out her boyfriend Al stops by the apartment and leaves a box of candy for her. He tells Jane he's in a hurry to deliver a second box to his mother. When Irma gets home, she is upset when she reads the card on the candy box and thinks Al doesn't love her anymore. She decides to leave New York and move back to Minnesota. Meanwhile, Al hands the second box to his mother and she questions her son as to why he would tell her she has a great pair of legs! Al realizes that he switched boxes.

(A NEW CAR?)
Broadcast: 2/21/49

After Jane complains about being trampled on the subway, Richard suggests she buy a used car, but Jane says that she can't afford one. Irma is enthusiastic about the idea and suggests that they combine their small savings to buy one. Naturally without Jane being along, Irma purchases a broken-down vehicle from a shady used car salesman.

(INCOME TAX SHOW)
Broadcast: 2/28/49

Jane fills out income tax forms for herself and Irma. She tells Irma that she owes the government $20. Irma and Al decide that the government doesn't need Irma's $20, so Al sends her to one of his shady friends. The friend creates deductions so Irma doesn't owe a cent, and then charges Irma $35!

(IRMA'S TRIAL SEPARATION)
Broadcast: 3/7/49

Al wins $500 from a horse race bet and declares he now has enough money to marry Irma. Irma's friend Amber, who's bitter against men, suggests that Irma have a trial separation from Al to test the bond of their love. Irma goes and stays at Amber's apartment, where Al will not be given admittance. Al sends candy via his friend Mushy and asks Irma to give a final answer. Irma calls Al to say "Yes," but Al tells her they can't get married—he tried to double his winnings by betting the $500 on another horse and lost everything. Bea Benaderet guest voices as Amber.

(THE PRIZE-WINNING ORCHID)
Broadcast: 3/14/49

Al is discouraged and tells Irma he is leaving New York City and going west to his aunt's ranch. Irma tries to dissuade him, and all of their friends look for possible jobs for Al. Meanwhile Richard's horticultural efforts have resulted in a new pale green orchid, which Richard plans to enter in the horticultural society's contest that night. Richard brings the orchid to the girl's apartment and Jane puts it in the refrigerator. Irma and Al return to the empty apartment after a morning of job hunting for Al. Irma makes a sandwich for Al and discovers the orchid and thinks it's a new type of lettuce and uses it on the sandwich. Jane comes home and learns what happens and when Richard arrives she tells him the bad news. Instead of being mad—he laughs about Al eating the orchid.

(IRMA IS FIRED)
Broadcast: 3/21/49

Irma's boss Mr. Clyde runs out of patience with Irma's scatterbrained way of doing her job and fires her. Irma's friend Amber says she's used a good employment agency that assigns numbers instead of names to applicants and prospective employers to protect privacy and prevent prejudice. Irma signs up with the agency and they soon match her with a prospective employer—who turns out to be none other than Mr. Clyde. Mr. Clyde's wife Phoebe urges him to rehire Irma and to give her a raise to boost! Bea Benaderet is Amber and Alan Reed is Mr. Clyde. (Note in some episodes, Mrs. Clyde's first name is Phoebe, in others it's Martha).

(JANE'S APRIL FOOL'S PARTY)
Broadcast: 3/28/49

Jane plans an April Fool's party and invites Irma, Al, Professor Kropotkin, Mrs. O'Reilly, the Martin's and Richard. Richard says he won't be able to attend if he can't find a nurse to stay with his mother. Jane replies that she knows someone and will get the name and information to Richard. Irma wants Jane to invite her friend Amber, but Jane finds Amber brash and obnoxious and refuses to do so. Irma is commiserating with Amber when Jane phones Irma with the name of the nurse. Amber has some nursing experience and so Irma decides to give her name and number to Richard's mother. Jane is horrified when she learns this and begins apologizing to Richard, who says his mother is highly amused by the outrageous Amber and is feeling so much better that she will even come to the party—with Amber!

(MEATLOAF AND A RING)
Broadcast: 4/4/49

Irma enrolls in a cooking class at night school so she will be able to make a home-cooked meal for Al. The teacher is so confounded by Irma's bizarre mental processes that she dismisses Irma from the class. Meanwhile Al wants to give Irma an engagement ring but doesn't have any money. Professor Kropotkin says he'll take Al to a jeweler friend and vouch for him. Irma, in the meanwhile, cooks up a homemade meatloaf dinner for Al who says it's delicious until he chokes on a bite. Irma hadn't understood that she should shell and beat the egg before adding it to the meatloaf. Al presents the engagement ring to Irma. Jane asks why the center diamond is missing. Irma replies that Al said marriage is a 50-50 proposition, and it's up to her to supply the stone.

(A SPECIAL EASTER DRESS)
Broadcast: 4/11/49

Amber tells Irma she doesn't know what to wear to the Easter Parade. They call Jane at her office, and she agrees to help. Jane is surprised to see her boss' mother Mrs. Rhinelander, arrive at the office. She shows Jane six sketches of original designs and asks Jane which one she likes best. The one Jane selects is also Mrs. Rhinelander's favorite. They leave the sketch on Jane's desk for Richard to see, and go to have a cocktail. Irma and Amber stop by the office and find the sketch, which they think Jane left for them. Amber takes it and begins to make a copy of the dress.

(IRMA HELPS HER BROTHER)
Broadcast: 4/18/49
Irma gets a letter from her little brother Eddie, who asks if he can come and stay for a short visit when school's out. Irma and Jane decide he could sleep on the sofa, and Jane sends him a wire saying it's okay to come. Al (naturally) has a cash flow problem and can't pay his rent. He asks Irma if he could sleep on her sofa for a while. When Irma says her brother will be using the sofa, Al says she must choose between him and her brother. Eddie sends another letter asking Irma to help him with a class paper on wild animals. Irma goes to the zoo to research the subject and writes the composition for Eddie. Eddie later sends a telegram saying he can't come as he failed the class, because of Irma's bizarre composition. Al gets the sofa.

(PLANNING A VACATION)
Broadcast: 4/25/49
While investigating where Jane and she cold go on their summer vacation, Irma discovers that Crandall's Department Store has a vacation village resort for their employees. Irma tells Mr. Clyde that she quits and applies for a position at Crandall's. She learns that not only will her salary for her new job be only half of what she was earning working for Mr. Clyde, but that she has to be an employee for a year to qualify for the vacation resort. Jane counsels her to ask Mr. Clyde for her job back. Irma calls Jane and says Mr. Clyde has rehired her, but as a new employee, she won't get a vacation for a year. Jane privately thinks that Mr. Clyde will send Irma on a vacation in August to save his sanity. Alan Reed is the voice of Mr. Clyde.

(SPEECH SWITCHAROO)
Broadcast: 5/2/49
Mrs. Rhinelander is asked to make a fundraising appeal to a ladies' club for a children's charity foundation. When the meeting is unexpectedly moved up to this evening, Mrs. Rhinelander is unprepared and asks Jane to write the speech for her. Jane is working on the speech at the apartment when Irma's girlfriend Amber stops by and asks Jane to write an acceptance speech for her to give that evening. Since Jane can't do it, Irma writes it—and you guessed it—Irma accidentally gives Jane's speech to Amber and Jane gives Mrs. Rhinelander the speech that Irma composed.

(JANE'S 24TH BIRTHDAY PARTY)
Broadcast: 5/9/49
Irma wants to give Jane a birthday party, but the apartment is being painted, so she must look for another venue. Richard wants Jane to celebrate her birthday at his estate on Long Island and also help him entertain a client. After much discussion, Jane decides that she must be with Irma and her dearest friends.

Al's friend Mushy has a new job as a chauffeur for a man who has a mansion on Long Island. The man is currently away, so Mushy offers the mansion as the site for Jane's birthday party. Richard's mother notices lights on at the neighboring estate and calls the police. Richard and his mother go to the neighbors' house arriving just before the police—and everyone is arrested, but eventually let off with a warning.

(IRMA STUDIES YOGA)
Broadcast: 5/16/49

When everyone tells Irma she's a scatterbrained, Irma decides to take Jane's advice and take a course in concentration. Richard calls Jane and tells her that the auditors want to review the company's books the next day, and asks her if she could finish her work on the ledger tonight. She agrees and brings the ledger home with her. Irma starts doing her homework, sitting in the middle of the room and concentrating. Richard calls and says he's sending a messenger over to pick up the ledger. Jane searches all over for it but cannot find it. Irma finally breaks her concentration, and when she gets up, Jane sees that Irma has been sitting on the ledger. Irma is convinced that her course in Yoga is responsible for the ledger being found.

(AL GETS A BUSINESS MANAGER)
Broadcast: 5/23/49

Al's friend Mushy falls in love with Irma's friend Amber, but Amber won't consider marrying Mushy until he gets a job. Al has several "business deals" pending and decides he needs a business manager, so he hires Mushy. Irma wants to marry Al in a double wedding, so she asks her boss Mr. Clyde for a raise, and he refuses to give it. Al fires Mushy after Mushy tells the unemployment office that Al was in such a bad way that he died. So the double wedding is off, and Irma and Al go to the movies instead.

(MRS. RHINELANDER'S BIRTHDAY SURPRISE)
Broadcast: 5/30/49

Richard invites Jane to a surprise birthday party for his mother at the yatch club. Richard tells Jane to keep it a secret that his father's gift is a new cabin cruiser, called Helen II. Jane tells Irma that she'd going out for the evening with Richard but doesn't mention the party or the present, because she's sure Irma nor Al could keep a secret. After Jane leaves, Irma finds the invitation and Jane's notes about the party. Irma and Al are sure that Richard's father is seeing another woman—Helen II. They decide to tell Mrs. Rhineleander about it, and upsets her so much she doesn't show up at the yatch club. Jane and Richard discover what Irma and Al have done, and Richard explains it all to his parents—who have a good laugh!

(Stunning Stanley the Wrestler)
Broadcast: 6/6/49

Al finds another moth-eaten wrestler to promote and cajoles Irma, Jane, Kropotkin, Mrs. O'Reilly and Amber into investing in the project. Amber thinks that the wrestler, named Stunning Stanley, is cute and goes on a pre-fight date with him. Right before the fight, Stunning Stanley shows up with his arm in a sling, Amber says he got fresh with her, and she had to break his arm.

(Parlay Voo Frenchy)
Broadcast: 6/13/49

Mr. Clyde fires Irma (again). Irma has an interview with a woman who wants a traveling companion on her trip to Europe. The traveling companion must be able to speak French, so Al finds a Frenchman to teach Irma to speak French in one day. After Irma leaves for the interview, Professor Kropotkin stops by the apartment, recognizes the tutor, and reveals to Al the man is a phony who used to work at the café with him. The only French the tutor knows consists of insults. But amazingly Irma is hired. It turns out that the woman who interviewed Irma introduced her to her husband and asked Irma what she thought of her husband—Irma used the descriptive terms she learned from the tutor—and the woman said Irma is the only one who saw through her husband immediately. Jane is not worried that Irma will actually go to Europe. She is sure Irma will not be able to be parted from Al. Part one of two.

(The European Trip Caper)
Broadcast: 6/20/49

After Mr. Clyde fired her, Irma answered the ad to be a paid companion to a woman traveling in Europe. Mr. Clyde comes to the apartment to beg Irma to come back to work as his secretary, as he can't find anything due to the screwy filing system. Irma declines and leaves to get her vaccinations, while Jane runs an errand for Irma, picking up a package from Irma's new employer. Back at the apartment, Jane tells Irma that she doesn't have the package, as the police were there before she and arrested her new employer, a notorious smuggler. Irma tells Mr. Clyde that she will resume her position as his secretary. Part two of two.

(Irma and the Gang Go on Vacation)
Broadcast: 6/27/49

Irma and Jane have only $100 to spend on a joint vacation and are trying to decide where to go. Richard arranges for them to stay at an exclusive inn owned by a friend. Jane asks Irma and Al to take the money and book the reservation. Al's miffed he's not invited and convinces Irma to give the money to a politician, who can get all three of them a special deal at a camp. Back at the apartment, Al learns the politician was no re-elected and that they gave him the money for nothing. Jane cries when they tell her what happened, but good-old Richard arrives and invites everyone to go on a river cruise on his family's boat instead.

END OF SEASON
CATHY LEWIS WILL RETURN THE NEXT SEASON AS JANE.

(IRMA LOSES HER JOB)
Broadcast: 8/29/49

Irma and Jane return from vacation. Al tells them that he has gotten a job with an employment agency. Irma is delighted and starts planning to get married. She decides to ask her boss Mr. Clyde for a raise, but when she arrives at the office, he tells her she's fired. Al is unable to find another job for Irma but does arrange for her to collect unemployment.

(IRMA TAKES CHARGE)
Broadcast: 9/5/49

Irma feels everyone lacks confidence in her abilities so she asks Jane, Professor Kropotkin, and Mrs. O'Reilly to give her some tasks to prove that she's responsible. She goes to the bank for Jane, but can't remember whether she's to transfer money from savings to checking or the reverse, so she does neither. She takes the professor's trousers to the tailor's, but can't recall how much he wanted them shortened, so she picks a number. She takes Mrs. O'Reilly's dress to the dry cleaners, but doesn't get there in time for the same-day service, so she takes the dress to a Laundromat and washes it. When she gets home after her errands, she discovers that Jane's check has bounced, the hems of the professor's trousers are above his knees, and Mrs. O'Reilly's dress has shrunk. Jane sends Irma to her room.

(IRMA DOES THE LAUNDRY)
Broadcast: 9/12/49

Irma's still looking for a new job when Amber says she can work at the Laundromat for the afternoon and earn enough money to buy Jane a birthday present. Naturally Irma makes a shambles of it.

(THE ESTATE JOB)
Broadcast: 9/19/49

Now Professor Kropotkin loses his job. Irma's getting ready to go back to work for Mr. Clyde, when Al says he's arranged for them to work as caretakers on an estate. When Irma says no, Al says their romance is over and he'll find someone else to work with him. Irma is distracted at work all morning when Amber stops by and urges her to get Al back. Irma calls the estate office and tells them "Mrs. Al" is Typhoon Mary, the carrier of a plague. After work, Al shows up at Irma and Jane's apartment. He's not mad at Irma, because he didn't take the job. Instead he sent another couple Professor Kropotkin and Mrs.

O'Reilly to take the job. The professor arrives and says the police arrested Mrs. O'Reilly at the estate, thinking she broke in. Jane and Irma get Mrs. O'Reilly released.

(IRMA AND JANE GIVE A BIRTHDAY PARTY)
Broadcast: 9/26/49

It's Jane's birthday and Irma is giving her a birthday party. She has also bought a watch as a present. The problem is that the watch is not paid off, there is a final payment to be made, but Irma spent all the money on party arrangements, so now the finance company is sending somebody over to repossess the watch. Meanwhile, Jane finds out that her father is flying in for the party. While Jane's out her father arrives at the apartment and Irma and Al think that he's the repo man—and send him packing. Then just as the party is to begin the real repo man arrives demanding $5.00—which Richard pays. Jane's father comes back and they all have a big laugh over what happened.

(RICHARD'S NEW OFFICE)
Broadcast: 10/3/49

Richard (also Jane's boss) asks Jane to help him find new office space. While Jane's out of the apartment, Irma takes a call from Richard, who tells her to tell Jane not to bother to look, he's found a place with five rooms and a view, and they can move in it in two weeks. Naturally, Irma thinks that Richard is talking about an apartment for Richard and Jane, and assumes that they are getting married.

(IRMA AND *LOOK* MAGAZINE)
Broadcast: 10/10/49

A photographer from *Look* magazine sees Irma on the street and comes to the girls' apartment to photograph her for a story. Al is sure that Irma will be a great success and will become a star on stage and screen. Irma daydreams at work and makes many mistakes, and Mr. Clyde fires her (yet again). It's up to Jane to return the situation to normal.

(IRMA BUYS A TELEVISION SET)
Broadcast: 10/17/49

Irma and Jane decide to buy a television set because they believe that in the long run they will save money by cutting down on their entertainment budget. Jane notices a good bargain on a set at Macy's, but Al naturally knows somebody who can sell Irma a set wholesale and sends Irma to him— where she discovers that he is out of business. Irma meets a "passerby" who after learning that Irma is looking for a new set—sells her his own broken set. Jane manages to get the money back, but they decide not to buy a television set.

(Irma's Second Job)
Broadcast: 10/24/49

Jane rents a Scarlett O'Hara costume for a Halloween party. Without Jane's knowledge Irma takes a second job as a seamstress. Jane takes her costume to be altered—and guess who alters it? (Note: Mary Shipp, who in 1953 would take over the role of Jane on both the television and radio programs has a role in this episode).

(Al and the Other Woman)
Broadcast: 10/31/49

Al's friend Sandra tells Al that she's engaged to his friend Mushy, but since Mushy is shy, she asks if Al would handle getting the engagement ring. Al agrees and tells Sandra she can reach him at Irma's phone number. Irma answers the phone when Sandra calls and takes a message for Al about the engagement ring. Irma thinks that Al is two-timing her and tells him to get lost. Later, Irma talks to Sandra and learns the truth. Sandra Gould, a veteran radio actress and the second Gladys Kravitz on *Bewitched*, plays "Sandra."

(Irma Manages the Apartment House)
Broadcast: 11/7/49

While Mrs. O'Reilly is in the hospital recovering from a broken leg, Irma volunteers to take over her apartment management duties. The owner of the building tells Irma to get the tenants of 4A to pay their back rent or else evict them. Irma misunderstands and ends up redecorating their apartment. The tenants in 4A turn out to be delighted by the new look of the apartment that they not only pay their back rent, but also pay a year's rent in advance!

(Jane Goes Out with Another Man)
Broadcast: 11/14/49

Once again Jane is discouraged that her relationship with Richard is not progressing along faster so when another attractive man, Michael, asks Jane out she accepts. Irma, Al and the gang want to help the new relationship along. Professor Kropotkin stations himself out on the fire escape to play romantic music on his violin. Irma and Al get some atar of roses incense to burn in the living room. When Michael arrives and the incense is lit, Michael begins sneezing—he's allergic to roses and quickly leaves. Shortly after Michael leaves—Richard arrives with a surprise for Jane—he's giving her a raise. Hal March provides the voice of Michael.

(Irma Provides the Evidence)
Broadcast: 11/21/49

Irma decides she wants to be a writer, and enrolls in a correspondence course. Al encourages her and tells her about some of the great romances from history and mythology. While at the law office, Irma works on a story combining plot elements from the lives of Helen of Troy, Cleopatra, and Camille when her boss calls from the courthouse and asks her to bring some evidence papers vital to the success of the case, an annulment. Irma hurries to the courthouse, and the envelope with the evidence is in actuality, the story which Irma had been working on.

(AL IS ARRESTED)
Broadcast: 11/28/49

Irma is worried because Al has disappeared. Mushy tells her that Al's in jail—he had been set up as a lookout for a floating crap game. Irma and Jane try to raise funds to bail Al out, but no one has enough money, except Richard, who declines to help. Jane's mad and quits her job. Irma goes to her boss, Mr. Clyde, an attorney, and finally persuades him to represent Al. Part one of two.

(AL'S TRIAL)
Broadcast: 12/5/49

While Al is in jail awaiting trial, his attorney, Mr. Clyde, prepares Al's friends to give testimony on Al's behalf. Even though Jane wants Al's freedom, she says that Al must promise to get a job after the trial, or she won't participate—and the rest of the gang agrees with Jane's terms. At the trial, Irma is very moving when she takes the stand and the Judge lets Al go free. Part two of two.

(THE SLEEPWALKER)
Broadcast: 12/12/49

Jane gets a new job at the phone company. Meanwhile Al is supposed to be looking for a job, but he disappears. Irma's friend Amber tells her there's a rumor that Al was seen getting on a train going out west, and Irma is very perturbed. When Jane wakes up in the middle of the night and discovers Irma is missing, she suspects Irma may be sleepwalking. Jane calls the police, and they find Irma and take her home. Bea Benaderet is the voice of Amber.

(THE THEATRICAL AGENT)
Broadcast: 12/19/49

Irma is upset because Al left town without saying goodbye. She is relieved to get a letter from Al, telling her that he's looking for work in Texas. Jane informs Irma that she has a new boyfriend, Ned—a theatrical agent. Irma's boss arranges a date with his visiting nephew Robert and Irma. Ned is putting on a Broadway show and wants the gang to judge the talent. Everything is going well until Ned reveals that his backer is a Texas millionaire named Al, who'll soon be back in town. Hal March plays Ned.

(THE CHRISTMAS EVE SURPRISE PARTY)
Broadcast: 12/26/49

Yet another variation of the December 22, 1947 Christmas show.

(AL GOES ON A JOB INTERVIEW)
Broadcast: 1/2/50

Al has promised he'll go out and get a job. Irma is fretting because they can't get married until Al has a steady job. Amber stops by the apartment with a lead that the candy company where she works is looking for a salesman. Everyone pitches in to prepare Al for the big interview. Jane coaches him in speaking proper English—and the others pitch in a silk shirt or a nice suit, etc. to improve Al's appearance. Everyone anxiously awaits the results of the job interview. Al returns and says he was offered the job, but a fella who dresses as well as he does couldn't afford to work at the low wages that the company proposed—so he declined!

(PROFESSOR KROPOTKIN PROPOSES)
Broadcast: 1/9/50

Irma and Jane's lease has expired, and the girls wonder if Mrs. O'Reilly will raise the rent. Mrs. O'Reilly in turn has more bad news for the girls—he brother from Ireland is coming and since there is no lease on their apartment she is renting it to her brother—the girls will have to move. Professor Kropotkin decides to help the girls save their home and proposes marriage to Mrs. O'Reilly—who accepts. Now Mrs. O'Reilly's brother can take over Kropotkin's apartment since he will be moving in with Mrs. O'Reilly after the wedding. However, Mrs. O'Reilly receives a telegram from her brother—he's unable to come afterall. The Professor promptly cancels the marriage plans.

(IRMA ELOPES)
Broadcast: 1/16/50

Irma scans the help wanted ads to find a job requiring a married couple, because Al once said he would marry her if they could work together. When Al hears about Irma's idea he is at first upset, but then he is persuaded by Irma. Irma tells Al she wants to elope, just like in the movies—which naturally includes climbing down a ladder from her window. Al says he can get a ladder from his shady friend Joe. The morning of the elopement, however, Al fails to show up. Then Irma gets a call from Al—he's in jail. He put the ladder up under the wrong window! Needless to say Al and Irma remain unhitched.

(AUNT JENNIFER VISITS)
Broadcast: 1/23/50

Jane's prim, proper and wealthy Aunt Jennifer will be visiting. Jane is sure that Aunt Jennifer won't approve of Irma and Al, so she doesn't tell them about her aunt. Jane suggests that Irma and Al go to a movie that evening, so the girl's apartment will be empty for Aunt Jennifer's arrival. Al's shady friend Joe wants to put on a charity show for the widows and orphans of some con men and asks Al to organize it. Irma thinks Jane will be out for the evening and tells Al that the charity show performers can rehearse at her apartment. Irma and Al are waiting for the performers to arrive when Jane returns from the train station with Aunt Jennifer. Jane and the Aunt are surprised as the brash and uncultured amateur performers enter. Amber begins to sing a version of a vulgar song, and Aunt Jennifer stops her and demonstrates the singing of the correct lyrics! The rehearsal is a success, and Aunt Jennifer gives Al a $100 for the charity.

(IRMA TAKES UP ASTROLOGY)
Broadcast: 1/30/50
Irma buys an astrology book which tells her she needs to take on more responsibility. When Mr. Clyde becomes ill, he tells Irma that she will have to fly to Washington, D.C., in his place to deliver some legal papers to the Pentagon. Irma packs and promises to get souvenirs for her friends, and leaves by herself. Two days pass and no one has heard from Irma. Mr. Clyde is frantic because he is getting calls from Washington asking where the legal papers are! Irma phones Jane and says she can't find the Pentagon, but she knows she's three blocks from the Pacific Ocean—she went to Washington State. Irma flies home and her boss goes to D.C.

(MONKEY BUSINESS)
Broadcast: 2/6/50
Irma's friend Amber stops by with a monkey which belongs to her boyfriend, Sam. It seems that Sam is away and put Amber in charge of looking after the monkey, but Amber explains to Irma, her apartment doesn't allow pets—Will Irma look after the monkey for a few hours? Irma agrees. Jane returns home and reminds Irma that their apartment lease doesn't allow pets either, so they go to great lengths to hide the fact that they have a monkey in the premises. They dress the monkey as a baby and are trying to keep Mrs. O'Reilly at bay when Amber arrives to get the monkey. Professor Kropotkin smoothes things over with the irate Mrs. O'Reilly by taking her to dinner and a show.

(MR. CLYDE'S BIRTHDAY PRESENT)
Broadcast: 2/13/50
Irma bakes a birthday cake for her boss, Mr. Clyde, but he ends up sitting on it. Mrs. Clyde phones and asks Irma to help her by picking up the rare piece of Dresden China that an antique shop is holding for her to give her husband. Irma takes Al with her, and when Al sees all the cracks in the piece, he says Mrs. Clyde could do better. Al gets Irma to buy a piece of "16th Century plastic" instead. Jane is furious and tries to explain things to Mrs. Clyde. Mrs. Clyde has her maid send over another piece of Dresden for Irma to take to Mr. Clyde, but this piece has no cracks, so Al decides to give it a few, to make it more valuable. Fortunately, the maid sent the wrong piece of china, so Mr. Clyde's birthday is saved. Mary Shipp plays Mrs. Clyde.

(RUDOLPH'S RACING TIP)
Broadcast: 2/20/50

Professor Kropotkin's cousin Rudolph is coming on a short visit from Europe. The professor tells Irma, Jane and Al that his cousin is practically a millionaire and that it has something to do with horses. Al figures that Rudolph could give him a sure tip on the horse races and borrows a hundred dollars from his friend Joe to wine and dine Rudolph. Rudolph speaks almost no English, but Al tries to pump him for racing tips, without much success. When Joe calls Al to find out what he has learned from Rudolph, Al tells him that Rudolph will only say, "Comme ce, comme ca." It turns out that Rudolph's involved with carousel horses—not race horses, but it ends up that a horse named Comme Ce Comme Ca wins the last race—so Al is off the hook to his friend Joe. Jay Novello plays Cousin Rudolph.

(HEM LENGTHS)
Broadcast: 2/27/50

Irma and Jane plan to go to the Spring Fashion Show and Dance. Their evening gowns are at the tailor's to have the hems shortened to the new length. The trouble is, various sources such as *Vogue Magazine* cannot agree what the correct new length is. After Jane has phoned the tailor a few times to request a different hem length, Al gets the bright idea for an invention and goes to see the tailor. Al brings the girls' evening gowns back with him, with his new invention installed. Like the cord on Venetian blinds, Al's invention allows the wearer to alter the length of the corded hem from low to high, although, unfortunately, the cord ends trail behind the wearer. Irma and Jane decide to stay home and not go to the dance.

(THE MONEY IN THE CABINET)
Broadcast: 3/6/50

Reprise of the August 18, 1947 episode.

(IRMA'S ACCIDENT INSURANCE POLICY)
Broadcast: 3/13/50

This is a reprise of the June 30, 1947 episode.

(THE VACUUM CLEANER SALESMAN)
Broadcast: 3/20/50

Irma thinks that Al won't marry her because she isn't smart enough, so she decides to improve her mind. Jane and Professor Kropotkin try to persuade her that it isn't necessary. Irma's friend Amber comes by the apartment to announce that she is engaged to be married, and that motivates Irma to propose to Al. Al explains that she can't marry until one of his big deals goes through. A handsome man shows up at the apartment asking for Irma, whom he had met at her job. Al leaves in a huff. The man says he's not there to ask for a date, as he's married, but to try and sell Irma a vacuum cleaner. The mix up is explained to Al, and all returns to normal.

KROPOTKIN GETS SICK
Broadcast: 3/27/50

Professor Kropotkin comes to Irma and Jane's apartment to get the shirt with the torn chest pocket that Irma was mending for him. He tells the girls he's about to go out on a date and tries on the shirt while he's in their apartment. The girls hear him moaning in pain in the other room, and after checking on him, Jane calls the doctor. It turns out that Irma left a sewing needle stuck in the shirt, causing Kropotkin's pain and discomfort.

GETTING JANE BACK WITH RICHARD
Broadcast: 4/3/50

Jane is fed up with her job, her lack of love life, and New York, and tells Irma she's moving back home to Connecticut. Irma, Al, Professor Kropotkin and Mrs. O'Reilly try to dissuade her. Irma is sure that Jane is still in love with Richard, and that's why she is dissatisfied. Irma finds a newspaper that Jane was reading; with a society feature commenting that Richard is going to marry a certain girl. Irma and Al determine to bust up the engagement and start planting rumors via phone calls. Meanwhile, the professor meets Richard and talks with him. The professor tells Jane that Richard is not engaged and he still loves her. Richard calls and offers Jane her gold job back. Jane manages to untangle Irma and Al's rumor mill with smiles all around.

(AL GETS AMNESIA)
Broadcast: 4/10/50

It's Jane's first day back at work with her old boss and boyfriend Richard, and Jane has also gotten a job at the office for Irma's perpetually unemployed (and happily so) boyfriend Al. Al is desperate to find a reason not to take the job and pretends he has amnesia.

KROPOTKIN INHERITS AN OIL WELL
Broadcast: 4/17/50

Professor Kropotkin tells Irma and Jane that he's just learned he's inherited an oil well, and everyone is thrilled that he will be wealthy. While everyone except Irma and Al are away from the apartment, a messenger delivers a telegram from the drilling company saying they have found water. Al is sure this means the well is a dud, and he and Irma go off to try to sell the deed on the professor's behalf. Meanwhile, the professor finds the telegram and tells Jane that this is good news. Irma returns and tells them what Al is trying to do, to their consternation. Then another telegram arrives from the drilling company saying the well has no oil. Al arrives triumphantly at the apartment and says he sold the deed for $50 to his shady friend Joe. So all's well—and Kropotkin makes a little money afterall.

JEALOUS OF JIM
Broadcast: 4/24/50

Richard invites Jane, Irma and Al to dinner to celebrate Jane's birthday. Irma buys a new dress, but it's tight on her, so Amber invites Irma to go to her gym for a workout and sauna to take off a few pounds. Irma, who's a poor speller, leaves a note for Al, saying she'll be back later when she's through with Jim. Al finds the note, thinks Irma's going out with another guy, and storms off. Well Irma meant gym, not Jim.

(JANE TRIES TO MOVE OUT)
Broadcast: 5/1/50

Jane decides she can no longer be Irma's roommate, because living with Irma is like living with a small child, not an adult. Irma is upset and gets Professor Kropotkin and Mrs. O'Reilly to plead with Jane not to move, but their arguments are ineffective. While Jane goes to check out some possible apartments, Irma walks about the city and comes upon a soapbox in the park. She creates a disturbance just as Jane is passing by on her way to see an apartment. As a policeman is about to arrest Irma, Jane comes over and convinces him not to by saying she'll take care of Irma and take her home. Everything is back to normal. (Hans Conried plays two roles in this broadcast—Kropotkin and an orator Irma meets in the park).

(IRMA ENTERS ANOTHER CONTEST)
Broadcast: 5/8/50

Although Irma has promised Jane not to enter any more contests, she can't resist one that promises a free wedding and honeymoon in Las Vegas She writes an essay on why "My Boyfriend Would Make the Best Husband Because . . . ," but her friend Amber says it's too prosaic and she should make Al look like a hero, such as Robin Hood. So Irma says Al robs banks to give money to the poor. When Al hears about the contest, he says he's not ready to be married, so Irma and Al decide to enter the contest on behalf of Jane and Richard. A week later, Jane discovers what Irma has done and shows a copy of the essay to Richard, who thinks it's funny. The police knock on the door and arrest Richard and Jane. After a lot of explaining they are released. Veteran radio and television actor Parley Baer (Chester on the radio version of *Gunsmoke*) plays a police officer.

THEY TAKE UP OIL PAINTING
Broadcast: 5/15/50

Irma learns that a representative of the Paris Art Commission is coming to New York on a talent search and will award scholarships to selected students to study art in Paris. Irma urges Jane to enter one of her paintings and says she'll do a painting too. Jane is skeptical, but Professor Kropotkin urges the girls to give it a try. Everyone loves Jane's still life of flowers, but Irma's landscape showing the nearby brewery has everyone puzzled. Well, it turns out that when the commission representative finds Jane's painting is pedestrian but that Irma's painting was brilliant and wold have won first prize.

PICNIC WITH MUSHROOMS
Broadcast: 5/22/50

Mrs. O'Reilly is trying to raise money to pay for a neighborhood boy to have an operation. Everyone thinks it's a great idea, and forming a committee, they decide to hold a picnic at a park and sell tickets to the public. The day of the picnic begins well, with steaks grilling on the barbeque, etc. Mrs. O'Reilly misplaces the mushrooms, but Irma finds them for her. The picnic is a success, and everyone enjoys the feast. When Mrs. O'Reilly thanks Irma for getting the mushrooms, Irma discloses she got them from the base of a tree. Everyone panics and goes to the hospital to get their stomachs pumped. Later, Irma explains that she didn't pick the mushrooms, she found the bag of mushrooms at the base of the tree.

IRMA WRECKS A BORROWED CAR
Broadcast: 5/29/50

Irma borrows a car to get into a drive-in movie, but she doesn't know how to drive and damages the car. Irma is unsuccessful when she tries to borrow money from each of her friends and her boss to pay the damages, so she turns to a loan shark. Everyone is angry with her when they hear what she's done, including Al, who calls his shady friend Joe for help. Al learns that Joe's mother is the loan shark and gets Irma released from the contract. Jane pays for the damages, and Irma takes driving lessons, until she wrecks the teacher's car.

AL'S BIRTHDAY
Broadcast: 6/5/50

This is a reprise of the August 11, 1947 program.

BALL GAME
Broadcast: 6/12/50

Richard has a box for the baseball season and invites Jane, Irma, and Al to see the Giants play the Dodgers. Irma's friend Amber and Al's friend Mushy are interested in each other, but they have not been seeing each other after an argument. Irma and Al decide they can smooth things over if they can get the couple together, so they invite Amber and Mushy to the ball game. Things start off well until it's revealed that Amber roots for the Giants and Mushy for the Dodgers. A new argument culminates with Amber hitting Mushy on the head with Al's coke bottle. Mushy is all right, but Al moans that he's out of the two-cent deposit on the bottle.

KROP WRITES A CONCERTO
Broadcast: 6/19/50

This episode is a reprise.

THE GIRLS LEAVE FOR HOLLYWOOD VACATION
Broadcast: 6/26/50

Irma and Jane decide to go to Hollywood for a vacation. They bid the gang a tearful farewell and board the bus west. When they reach Las Vegas, the bus breaks down, and they have to wait for the next bus. Jane can't find her purse, which has all their travel funds in it, and discovers that Irma got mixed up and threw it away. Jane reminds Irma about the time and number of the next bus before she goes to phone Richard to wire some money to them. Having no paper, Irma decides to use a big table with numbers on it to remember about the bus and places quarters on the various relevant numbers. Jane is unable to reach any of the gang in New York and returns to Irma, who has inadvertently made a small fortune at the roulette table! The girls look forward to finishing their trip and seeing the new movie, *My Friend Irma Goes West.*

END OF SEASON

JANE RENTS AN OFFICE
Broadcast: 8/27/50

Jane decides to leave her job and start her own secretarial agency. She finds a perfect office, but the rent is $75/mo. and Jane is afraid she won't be able to afford it. Al and Irma attempt to help, but as usual make a shambles of everything.

MUSHY GETS DRAFTED
Broadcast: 9/4/50

While Al is visiting Irma he gets a call from his landlady telling him he has a notice to report to the Draft Board. Al leaves, and Irma decides to join the WACS, so she can be near him. Al returns to report that the draft notice is really for his roommate, Mushy. It ends up that the WACS won't accept Irma. All's well in the end.

(JANE'S NEW DATE)
Broadcast: 9/11/50

Jane and her client Steve Baxter are interested in each other, and Steve tells his father about her. However, when Mr. Baxter, Steve's father, decides unexpectedly to drop by the apartment to check Jane out, Irma and Al are there instead. Trouble arises when Irma and Al mistake Steve's dad for Steve and the father thinks Irma is Jane. Joseph Kearns the voice of the "Man in Black" on *Suspense* and the original Mr. Wilson on *Dennis the Menace* plays Steve's dad.

KROP HOCKS HIS VIOLIN
Broadcast: 9/18/50

Mrs. O'Reilly needs $100 more to pay the lease on the apartment building and asks all the tenants in turn for a loan. No one has an extra $100 to loan her, and the building owner won't give her an extension on the payment. If she can't pay the $100 by the next morning, there'll be a new landlady. Kropotkin, who constantly bickers with the landlady, quietly goes and pawns his violin and slips an envelope containing $100 under Mrs. O'Reilly's door.

(THE SONG CONTEST)
Broadcast: 9/25/50

Irma and Al enter a song contest, which requires them to compose a patriotic song. Then Irma is fired (again) because she is so preoccupied with the contest. When Irma and Al submit their song, the judges are displeased with it as a patriotic song, but love it as a comedy routine.

AL BUYS A SECOND-HAND SUIT
Broadcast: 10/2/50

Jane lands a great contract for her secretarial service and gets a large advance payment. She tells the gang that she's taking them all out to the Copa that night to celebrate, but she'll only take Al on the condition that he replaces his disreputable suit with a new one. Al arrives at the apartment with a new suit, but then finds someone else's wallet in the pocket. The suit is "hot" and Irma tells Al she won't go anywhere with Al until he returns the wallet to its owner.

(IRMA JOINS THE WACS)
Broadcast: 10/9/50

Irma is upset with Jane and decides to try and join the WACS again. The gang decides to throw her a big farewell party. However, Irma tells them she will be leaving in three months, so there is plenty of time for farewells.

(COLONEL IRMA)
Broadcast: 10/16/50

The gang goes to Camp Lee, Virginia, to see Irma graduate from the WACS, but they arrive too late. Irma wrote the wrong time on the invitations to prove she could keep a military secret. Private Irma Petersen is transferred to New York, and as part of the Quarter Master Corps, she's instructed to purchase two eagles for her shoulder insignia at the PX. Irma sees some pretty silver ones and has the salesperson pin them on her. Irma is amazed when everyone starts saluting her and calling her colonel!

ATOMIC ATOMIZERS
Broadcast: 10/23/50
Irma does secretarial work for the General as part of her WACS duty Irma is suspicious of a package with the words "atomic bombs" written on it. Prepared to defend her country, Irma decides to spy on the man she suspects is responsible for the package. Naturally it's a big misunderstanding.

HALLOWEEN SHOW
Broadcast: 10/30/50
Jane's boyfriend Steve is throwing a Halloween bash and everyone is invited. When Jane tells Irma that she will be the thirteenth person at the party, Irma refuses to go because she of her superstition. Jane goes through a frenzy trying to find a fourteenth person.

IRMA AND THE WAR HERO
Broadcast: 11/6/50
Irma's a civilian again and back working for Mr. Clyde in the law office. He gives her his brother-in-law's dog Mike to care for over the weekend. The dog was part of the Canine Corps and is a war hero. Jane gets upset when Irma tells her she's got a war hero staying for the weekend and he'll sleep under her bed. Then when Irma tells Al that Mike, the War Hero, has been kissing her all day, Al jumps the conclusions and tells Irma that they are through.

KROP AND O'REILLY GET HANDCUFFED
Broadcast: 11/13/50
Irma and Jane decide to throw a charity benefit show to raise money for starving children. Everyone must contribute to the show by performing in it. Irma will perform a magic act and while performing her routine she accidentally handcuffs Mrs. O'Reilly and Professor Kropotkin together, and is unable to free them.

IRMA LOSES THE LETTER
Broadcast: 11/20/50
Irma is assigned to deliver a very important letter to her boss, Mr Clyde in Boston. Irma is eager to see Boston for the first time, but she keeps losing the letter. Fortunately she is able to find it, and Jane drops Irma off at the airport. Irma is unwilling to go and is anxious to tell Jane the reason, but Jane ignores her and sends her through the gate. Irma decides to give the security guard a note to give to Jane. In the note, Irma explains that she has already mailed the important letter to Mr. Clyde and there is no need for her to travel.

AMBER SUES VIOLET
Broadcast: 11/27/50
Al tells Irma that they can plan on being able to get married pretty soon, thanks

to a hot new business deal with his friend Mushy. But then Amber shows up at the law office where Irma works because she is suing Mushy for breach of promise, because although he promised to marry her, Mushy is now dating Violet. Bea Benaderet voices Amber and Sandra Gould voices Violet.

IRMA GETS A PART TIME JOB
Broadcast: 12/4/50

Irma needs some money to buy Christmas presents, so she gets a part time job demonstrating cosmetics at a local department store. To get time off of her regular job, she tells Mr. Clyde that she needs to be with her sick grandmother. Naturally Mr. Clyde comes to the department store while Irma is demonstrating a face cream. Fortunately for Irma, Jane talks Mr. Clyde into giving Irma her job back, for the umpteenth time.

(FIGHTING A DUEL OVER MRS. O'REILLY)
Broadcast: 12/11/50

Mrs. O'Reilly tells Irma, Jane and Professor Kropotkin that a new tenant will be renting the empty apartment in the building and she leaves the key with Irma and Jane while she's out. When Henri, the new tenant, appears and Jane gives him the key, he mistakenly assumes Jane is Mrs. O'Reilly. Henri gets into an argument with the Professor when Kropotkin offends Henri by disparaging Mrs. O'Reilly's looks, and Henri challenges him to a duel. Veteran radio, film and television character actor Fritz Feld voices Henri.

IRMA TAKES A COURSE IN TELEVISION
Broadcast: 12/18/50

Mr. Clyde fires Irma for the fiftieth or so time (a slight exaggeration). Irma takes her severance pay and enrolls in a course that a shady character says will prepare her for a career in television. At the conclusion of her course, Irma goes to the television studio and is accepted as a contestant on a quiz show, and through no fault of her own ends up winning the jackpot of $300.

(THE CHRISTMAS EVE SURPRISE PARTY)
Broadcast: 12/25/50

Yet another reworking of the 12/20/47 show.

CLYDE THREATENED
Broadcast: 1/1/51

Mr. Clyde lets Irma know that he is hiring a bodyguard because a man he sent to prison and had pledged to get him when he is released has been released. He describes both the prisoner and the bodyguard to Irma, so she will know who is who. Irma tells Al and Mushy about the threat and describes both the guard and prisoner to them—but gets their descriptions mixed up and when Al and Mushy go to Clyde's office and see the bodyguard they assume it's the ex-prisoner and attack him—they wind up in the hospital.

IRMA THINKS JANE'S TAKING GAS
Broadcast: 1/8/51

Irma and Jane are despondent over their love lives, so when Irma overhears Jane speaking with a warehouseman on the phone ordering a stove and says she wants a gas stove—Irma, naturally, thinks that Jane is planning to kill herself.

(IRMA MEETS HER CONSCIENCE)
Broadcast: 1/15/51

Irma has told Al she won't see him until he gets a job. She enjoys going out with Steve's friend Jim, but she still loves Al. Al and Jim both send packages to Irma. Jim's contains a jewelry box with a silver anklet; Al's contains his dirty laundry. Al phones Irma and tells her he has gotten a job and asks her to go out that night, but Irma has already made plans with Jim. Jane and the rest of the gang tell Irma she should consult her conscience about breaking her date with Jim. Irma does break the date, and then Al confesses that he really doesn't have a job—and Irma sends him away. Irma tells Jane that she's going to the doctor, because her conscience is even dumber than she is.

IRMA AND HER PHOTOGRAPHY HOBBY
Broadcast: 1/22/51

Irma takes up photography as a hobby. Mr. Clyde is handling a lawsuit and asks her to send a photographer to take pictorial evidence of damage done to a house next door to a Judge's house. The photographer is away, so Al urges Irma to take the photographs herself. Furthermore, at the scene, Al doesn't think the house looks bad enough, so he pulls up a fence and throws mud and rocks at the house. As it turns out Irma got the addresses mixed up and Al vandalized the judge's house next door. Irma is fired again!

KROP'S ROYAL BLOOD
Broadcast: 1/29/51

Professor Kropotkin is informed that he has inherited the title of Baron and an estate in Europe; everybody is excited for him until they find out that to claim his inheritance he will have to live in Europe. They have a bon voyage party on the Queen Mary for him, and after the boat sails the gang assembles back at Irma and Jane's apartment—when in walks the professor who tells tehm his true fortune is here in America with his friends.

INCOME TAX
Broadcast: 2/5/51

This is a reworking of the 2/28/49 episode.

LINCOLN'S BIRTHDAY
Broadcast: 2/12/51

Irma's irritated that she has to work on a holiday. Mr. Clyde tells her she has to deliver some securities to Mr. Green's business by three O' Clock. After lunch, Jane and Irma discuss Lincoln's life, and Jane tells Irma that he was famous for being called "Honest Abe." Irma wants her boyfriend to be famous, too, so she hatches a scheme to have Al rescue the securities as she's making her delivery. Naturally confusion ensues and Irma winds up in jail.

LOVE BIRDS
Broadcast: 2/19/51

Irma finds a half-frozen sparrow outside her apartment window and brings it inside to keep warm. Jane says it's an English sparrow, so Irma names it Cecil. When Mushy stops by to give Irma Al's invitation to go to a dance contest that night, Irma tells him she can't go as Cecil is staying with her and she's keeping him warm. When Mushy delivers this message to Al—he assumes that Irma is talking about another man.

IRMA RUNS A TELEPHONE SERVICE
Broadcast: 2/26/51

Irma breaks the mirror in the furnished apartment she shares with Jane. Since Irma's already broken the TV, Jane tells her she's on her own as far as replacing the mirror. Irma doesn't have any money to pay for a new mirror and is unable to borrow any, so she starts a 24-hour answering service. Business is brisk, and Jane asks Irma when the customers will begin to make payments, and Irma tells her that she told everyone that the first month was free. Jane ends up paying for the mirror and the phone bill.

MR. O'REILLY SHOWS UP
Brodcast: 3/5/51

Professor Kropotkin tells Irma and Jane that he's going to propose to Mrs. O'Reilly, and Jane says she'll throw an engagement party for them that night. After Irma leaves, Mrs. O'Reilly stops by the apartment and shows Jane a letter from her brother Patrick O'Reilly, who has been missing since WWI. He writes in his letter that he has had amnesia and is looking forward to being reunited with her. Later Al and Irma come to the apartment and find the letter and assume that Patrick O'Reilly is Mrs. O'Reilly's long lost husband. Needless to say the Professor and the Irish landlady do not marry.

SAVING A TREE
Broadcast: 3/12/51

Mrs. O'Reilly tells Irma and Jane that a neighbor has complained about the tree in the apartment house's backyard, and she has received a notice from the city that they will be coming out to cut it down. This upsets Irma and she vows to fight for the tree's life.

AL AND IRMA SEE A MOVIE
Broadcast: 3/19/51

Irma and Al go to a romantic movie but get into an argument, and Irma breaks up with Al—again. Al is down in the dumps when his mother visits. She tells him that if he marries a sensible, down-to-earth girl to steady him, she is prepared to give them a nice apartment and $1,000 if they marry. Al and his mother go and see Irma, who puts on a disdainful, high society manner which totally turns Al's mother off and she rescinds her offer. Irma says she is through with culture.

(DOES IRMA NEED A NEW BOYFRIEND?)
Broadcast: 3/26/51

Irma is depressed because she has broken up with Al and has no boyfriend. She reads that the key to romantic success is to learn to speak a romantic language. She goes to a language school to investigate and perhaps meet someone new, but the instructors are too old for her. Mrs. O'Reilly tells Jane that he well educated brother Patrick doesn't have a girlfriend. The two arrange for Irma and Patrick to go out together, with Jane hoping that Patrick will improve Irma's mind. Well, the opposite happens and after a time with Irma, Patrick's intelligence begins to falter!

JANE'S BOOKSTORE
Broadcast: 4/9/51

Irma is in the hospital recovering from an accident; Jane inherits $10,000 and decides to open a bookstore. (Marie Wilson doesn't appear in this episode).

SPRING CLEANING
Broadcast: 4/16/51

Jane thinks the furniture looks dirty and decides to have it cleaned, and she's inviting her boyfriend Steve to dinner the next day. Irma looks up phone numbers for furniture cleaners, while Jane goes to see Mrs O'Reilly. The landlady tells Jane that a big furniture sale is going on, and the two ladies go shopping. Jane finds a new living room set, and the next day, the new furniture is delivered and the old is carted off. Meanwhile, Irma still thinks the furniture needs cleaning and ships it all away to be cleaned. Later, Steve and Jane enter the apartment and find no furniture.

CLYDE SENDS IRMA FOR MINK
Broadcast: 4/23/51

Irma is depressed because she doesn't feel like a success and she asks Mr. Clyde for a raise. Mr. Clyde is concerned that everything costs more and decides to cut back on expenses. He tells Mrs. Clyde to stop shopping at expensive stores. A business partner tells Clyde that a big deal will probably come through if they can give one of the female clients a sweetener. The partner suggests a mink coat. Clyde sends Irma to shop for a mink coat, but she can't decide which one to get and ends up calling Mr. Clyde's house where she speaks with Mrs. Clyde. Mrs. Clyde misunderstands and ends up hitting her husband over the head with a rolling pin.

IRMA GETS LOST ON A TRAIN
Broadcast: 4/30/51
This is a reworking of the 8/4/47 program.

IRMA AND THE S.P.C.S.
Broadcast: 5/7/51
Irma and Jane are concerned that their neighbor is mistreating their dog, and Irma decides to write a complaint to the S.P.C.A. At the office, Mr. Clyde informs Irma that he may be appointed to the Racing Commission and sternly orders her to get all her work done while he's at the state capital. Irma gets her girlfriends together to form the S.P.C.S. (The Society for Prevention of Cruelty to Secretaries). Naturally, somehow Mr. Clyde is accused of cruelty to animals and is not appointed to the commission.

IRMA IN THE HOSPITAL
Broadcast: 5/21/51
Irma's in the hospital and to cheer her up, the gang pool their money to get her unemployed boyfriend Al a hospital room next to hers. (Marie Wilson doesn't appear in this episode which was broadcast during Marie's health scare, see Chapter Six).

(THE S.P.C.S. MEMBERS BOYFRIENDS GO ON STRIKE)
Broadcast: 5/28/51
Irma and her secretary friends hold a meeting of the S.P.C.S. and vote to go on strike against their bosses. Jane thinks they'll all lose their jobs and Al, is alarmed at the prospect. he calls a meeting of all the boyfriends of the S.P.C.S. members, and they vote to have nothing to do with their girlfriends until they all come to their senses. (This episode was originally written to be broadcast May 14, 1951, but was delayed due to Marie Wilson's illness).

DEEP SEA FISHING
Broadcast: 6/4/51
Mrs. O'Reilly's brother Patrick has bought a boat and invites the gang to go deep-sea fishing. Everyone accepts, happily, except Irma, who is convinced she'll be seasick. Well, everybody ends up seasick—except Irma, who ends up steering

the boat back to shore, with one hand on the wheel and the other holding a hotdog with mustard and marshmallow sauce.

MURDER
Broadcast: 6/11/51

Irma's been reading a murder mystery where a body was stuffed in a truck. She's concerned that Professor Kropotkin will become violent when he gets angry with Mrs. O'Reilly for renting the vacant apartment in the building to a new tenant and says he'll have his revenge. The girls can't find Mrs. O'Reilly, and when the Professor borrows a butcher knife from them, Irma fears the worst—especially when the Professor ask Al and Mushy to help carry down a heavy trunk.

MUSHY, THE PRIZE FIGHTER
Broadcast: 6/18/51

Mrs. O'Reilly is organizing the entertainment for the fireman's widows and orphans. She tells Irma and Jane that she's looking for major attractions. Irma informs her that Al has been training Mushy to be a prizefighter, and Mrs. O'Reilly says she'd like to arrange a match between the inexperienced Mushy and the Fire Department's champion.

(IRMA WANTS A MINNESOTA VACATION)
Broadcast: 6/25/51

Irma and Jane discuss where to go on vacation. Irma wants to go back to her parents' farm in Minnesota and invites the gang to come too. Jane is worried that several people suddenly descending on Irma's parents will be an imposition and says she'll only go if her parents agree in advance. Irma sends a telegram. When there's still no response after a few days, Al reads what Irma wrote. He discovers that Irma has screwed up again, and the telegram invites her whole family to vacation in New York with the gang.

END OF SEASON

KISS AND TELL
Broadcast: 9/16/51

Irma and Jane return from vacation eager to see their boyfriends, Al and Richard (Leif Erickson returns as Richard). Jane warns Irma not to say anything to the boys about their harmless vacation romances at the lake. Naturally, Irma discloses that she and Jane went out on some dates with Barney and Harry while on vacation.

(MUSHY AND VIOLET TRY TO GET MARRIED)
Broadcast: 9/23/51

Violet calls Irma and asks her to be a bridesmaid at her wedding to Mushy.

Al will act as best man. Irma's never been a bridesmaid and is afraid she'll mess it up. Violet tells Irma they can't afford a honeymoon. Al's shady friend Joe says they can use his gang's hideout on the lake. Al and Irma plan to surprise the bridal couple by "kidnapping" them right after the ceremony and driving them in the back of a truck to the honeymoon cabin. Unfortunately the Judge performing the ceremony is late, so when Al and Irma drive up and "kidnap" Violet and Mushy, they haven't been married yet. A forest ranger arrives at the cabin in the nick of time and rescues the blushing couple.

Six Convicts
Broadcast: 9/30/51

Jane tells Irma that her father wants to expand his business, and Jane is upset that she's unable to loan him any money. Jane phones a friend and arranges for the friend to return Jane's book, My Six Convicts, that day in front of the bank where the friend works. Irma overhears the last part of Jane's phone conversation and is sure that Jane is going to hold up the bank with six convicts. To save Jane from a life of crime, Irma reports her to the welfare office.

Horseback Riding
Broadcast: 10/7/51

Irma and Al discover that Jane has entered herself in a horseback riding meet. First prize is $1000. If Jane wins, Al and Irma would like her to donate $150 towards their marriage plans. After going to the stables to take a look at Jane's horse, Al sends Mushy to get energy pills for the horse. Mushy brings sleeping pills instead.

Clyde Runs for the State Senate
Broadcast: 10/14/51

Mr. Clyde decides to run for the State Senate. Clyde promises to take Irma with him if he wins. Clyde gives Irma her first campaign task. Irma must give Clyde's campaign slogan to the newspaper. Clyde receives the paper only to find that Irma has made damaging mistakes to the slogan. Clyde fires Irma. Irma finds another job with Clyde's opponent and she makes the same error. This pleases Mr. Clyde and he rehires Irma.

(Jane Goes on a Diet)
Broadcast: 10/21/51

Richard asks Jane out on a date, but Jane is unable to fit into her black velvet dress. Mr. Stern, the tailor, would make a new dress for $100. Instead, Jane decides to go on a diet, and Irma joins in. They must eat wheat germ and yogurt. However, Jane finds herself gaining weight on the diet. Irma tells Jane that Al didn't like the yogurt, so he added sweet cream to it.

(IRMA AND THE EYEGLASSES)
Broadcast: 10/28/51
This is a reworking of the 12/8/47 script.

(IRMA'S UNCLE WILL)
Broadcast: 11/4/51
Mr. Reed, an attorney looking for an Irma Peterson of Minnesota, arrives at the apartment while Irma is away. Mr. Reed explains to Jane that Irma's uncle has died, leaving half of his estate to his widow and half to his niece. However, Mr. Reed must verify that he has located the correct Irma Peterson. Mr. Reed then finds Irma and asks her age. Irma takes Jane's previous advice and lies about her age. Mr. Reed is convinced this is not the Irma he wants and leaves.

(JANE CATCHES A COLD)
Broadcast: 11/11/51
Jane has a stubborn cold and is waiting for a call from her doctor for some test results. Jane considers going on a cruise to Havana to recuperate. Mrs. O'Reilly wants to make a meat broth for Jane and has the butcher call Jane for her choice of meat. While Jane is out, Irma takes the phone call and she thinks she is talking with Jane's doctor who tells her that the liver and heart are no good. Naturally Irma assumes that Jane is dying.

(IRMA GETS MORE RESPONSIBILITY)
Broadcast: 11/18/51
Irma demands that Jane give her more responsibility in running their apartment. Jane agrees to give Irma a trial period and hands her the cash to pay all the utilities plus the week's groceries. On her way to the grocery store, Irma is waylaid by a couple of shady vendors. After buying their wares, Irma has only a few dollars left for groceries. As she enters the store, someone pops out and declares Irma the 100,000[th] customer, and she wins $100 worth of groceries. Well everyone is pretty amazed, until they arrive home to find no lights or phone working; Irma forgot to pay the utility bill.

(SWIMMING LESSONS)
Broadcast: 11/25/51
Jane receives tickets for a free Florida vacation and offers to take Irma along, but only if Irma learns to swim first. Irma refuses, because she is afraid of water. Al convinces Irma to take swimming lessons. Irma wears earplugs for her lesson, but forgets to take them out when she comes to work, and Mr. Clyde asks her to take shorthand notes for an important criminal case. She takes it down wrong and Clyde (once again) fires her.

(IRMA'S NURSING CLASS)
Broadcast: 12/2/51

Irma wants to be a nurse and, despite Jane's advice, signs up for a nursing class. While Jane is busy after work helping Richard's mother to organize her charity event, Irma attends night class. The school wants Irma to drop out, but Irma persists. Before leaving the apartment to go to class one evening, Irma makes Jane a sandwich. Jane phones Irma to ask the contents of the sandwich. Irma says she put garlic in it. As Jane will be operating the charity event's kissing booth, Jane asks Irma to bring home some chlorophyll to freshen her breath. Instead, Irma brings home chloroform, and puts Jane to sleep.

(THE HISTORY PAPER)
Broadcast: 12/9/51

Irma meets a boy crying on the stairs in her apartment building. He tells Irma that he's visiting his grandmother for a while. He's crying because his grandmother is working and there's no one to talk to his teacher at his schools Open House. Irma decides to be a mother to him, and visits his school. Later, Irma gets a note from the boy's teacher saying the boy is bright but that he needs help in history to get perfect grades. When the boy comes down with measles, Irma and Al write his history paper for him, and Irma takes it to school to present it to the class. The paper is badly inaccurate, and upon discussing it with the teacher, Irma confesses that she wrote it. When the teacher says she'll try to get Irma a seat in the first grade, Irma cries.

(THE CLYDE'S DIVORCE)
Broadcast: 12/16/51

Mr. Clyde tells Irma his wife is divorcing him. Irma decides to visit Mrs. Clyde, hoping to convince her to stay with Mr. Clyde, but the visit turns sour. Mrs. Clyde sends her attorney to her husband's office to collect evidence that Mr. Clyde is a "spendthrift," her grounds for divorcing him. Meanwhile, a man from the Internal Revenue arrives at the Clyde's office to discuss his business expenditures. At this moment, Mrs. Clyde calls to say the divorce is over. Clyde is happy and leaves the man with Irma. Irma thinks the man is Mrs. Clyde's attorney and tells him that Mr. Clyde is "cheap" and not a spendthrift. The man from the IRS decides to audit Mr. Clyde.

(THE CHRISTMAS SURPRISE PARTY)
Broadcast: December 23, 1951

Another reprise of the 1947 episode.

(CUB SCOUTS SAVE THE DAY)
Broadcast: 12/30/51

Young Irving is upset because he must get rid of his only friend, a rabbit. Irma sympathizes with the boy's loneliness. Irma signs Irving up with the Cub Scouts and becomes Den Mother. When the apartment tenants are threatened with a rent increase, Jane decides to show the apartment isn't worth an increase by making it messy. Irma and the scouts unknowingly tidy the mess, but then a bunch of boys let their wild animals run loose. The superintendent thinks the apartment is a wreck and does not increase the rent.

(MEMOIRS)
Broadcast: 1/6/52
Irma writes her memoirs and has trouble finding a publisher.

(KROP NEEDS A BRIDE)
Broadcast: 1/13/52
Professor Kropotkin wants to adopt a boy from Europe, but to be able to do so he needs to be married—something he told immigration he is, so the gang tries to help him come up with a bride. Of course, Mrs. O'Reilly is more than willing.

(THE GIRLS ARE ROBBED)
Broadcast: 1/20/52
A burglar breaks into the girl's apartment and makes off with Jane's new brooch.

(LONELY HEARTS CLUB)
Broadcast: 1/27/52
This is a reprise of the 1/26/48 show.

(IRMA WRITES A COLUMN)
Broadcast: 2/3/52
Irma gets the opportunity to write a newspaper column.

(MAGICIAN'S ASSISTANT)
Broadcast: 2/10/52
Irma quits her job working for Mr. Clyde for a job in show business—getting sawed in half by a magician.

(JANE BREAKS UP WITH RICHARD)
Broadcast: 2/17/52
This is a reprise of the 2/2/48 episode.

(THE FRIENDSHIP RING)
Broadcast: 2/24/52
Irma thinks that Al bought her an engagement ring, but he says it's a friendship ring. She accidentally drops it down the drain and then has to study plumbing

(because she can't afford a plumber) to retrieve it.

(THE LOST BABY SHOES)
Broadcast: 3/2/52
Jane promises Richard that she will get his niece's baby shoes cast in bronze. When Mrs. O'Reilly and Kropotkin get into a fight, the baby shoes are accidentally thrown out the window. O'Reilly and Krop are upset with each other, and each decides to move out. Fortunately, Mushy has just gotten a job with the sanitation department, and he found the baby shoes.

(THE COMPOSER)
Broadcast: 3/9/52
Mrs. Rhinelander fails to invite Jane to an opera party. Jane feels she is not cultured enough, but things perk up when a composer by the name of Tschaikowsky moves into the building. The gang quickly sets up their own opera party and invite Mrs. Rhinelander. The guest of honor is the composer. When Mrs. Rhinelander arrives, the man admits he is neither a composer nor is his name Tschaikowsky.

(THE CIGAR)
Broadcast: 3/16/52
Al and Mushy invent an exploding cigar for April Fool's Day. Irma unintentionally gives the gag cigar to Mr. Clyde, who then gives it to Richard. Richard then bumps into Mr. Flugel, the man who will soon by the "Gypsy Tea Room," where Kropotkin works. Richard gives the cigar to Mr. Flugel and recommends Krop as a reliable worker. Mr. Flugel is pleased with Krop and gives him the cigar and promotes him to headwaiter. Krop takes the cigar home and it explodes.

(MOOSE HEAD JANE)
Broadcast: 3/23/52
Irma receives a moose head as a gift from her parents. Jane is not fond of the gift. When Jaen hears that Mrs. Rhinelander is holding a charity auction, she persuades Irma to donate her moose head. Irma feels charitable and buys the remaining tickets. When the moose head is auctioned off, Jane is holding the winning ticket. Jane goes home with the moose head.

(MRS. O'REILLY'S FACELIFT)
Broadcast: 3/30/52
Mrs. O'Reilly has an unknown pen pal. Before meeting him, she wants to have a face-lift. Irma and Kropotkin try and stop her. The gang decides to tell Mrs. O'Reilly a sad story of someone in need, hoping she would cancel the operation and instead give the money to charity. After hearing the sad story, Mrs. O'Reilly readily donates the money. When someone expresses surprise at her quick

response, Mrs. O'Reilly confesses that her pen pal decided to call off the rendezvous once he found out her real age.

IRMA, CAREER WOMAN
Broadcast: 4/6/52
Mr. Clyde goes on a trip and leaves the office in Irma's care. After Irma reads an article about a successful and mannish businesswoman, she is determined to emulate her and become efficient. She believes she can do anything a man can, just like the woman in the article. Al wants to change her attitude. With Mushy's help, Al decides to dress like a woman, hoping to put Irma back in her place. Irma gets the point and gives up the act.

(THE EASTER EGG HUNT)
Broadcast: 4/13/52
The gang gets ready for the Easter holidays. Irma decides to organize an Easter Egg hunt for the neighborhood children. Things go wrong when Mrs. O'Reilly's brother, an archaeologist, wins an award for discovering a rare "Floona" bird egg. When the egg is missing, they suspect Irma has taken it for the hunt.

(MISERY SONG)
Broadcast: 4/20/52
Al decides he's a failure and that he must leave Irma to marry a woman with money. He wants to escape to California, with a wealthy woman by the name of Libby Klinebocker. Libby was formerly the fiancée of Al's best friend, Mushy. In hopes of winning their loves back, Irma and Mushy attempt to become rich by entering themselves in a "misery" song-writing contest. Because the lyrics are so miserable, Irma does not win. However, she plans to enter a few more in the future and begins working on a new song, entitled, "You Dropped Me in a Concrete Mixer, and I've Just Gone to Pieces Over You."

(VOTE FOR IRMA!)
Broadcast: 4/27/52
Irma wants to run for President of the United States, as she thinks that way she could win back Al. Mushy gets involved with Irma's plan too. Irma spends $250 on pencils with her campaign slogan on and asks Mushy to distribute them to voters. When she is surprised to find only two people voted for her, Mushy explains that he handed out all the pencils to his friends, who could not write.

(THE LOST BIRTH CERTIFICATE)
Broadcast: 5/4/52
Al has left Irma for a wealthy woman, so Irma tries to find a new job which pays more, so she can get Al back. She finds a potential job, which requires her to present her birth certificate. Irma sends a letter to the state records office, requesting

a copy of her birth certificate, and is very upset when they state they cannot locate it. Irma decides this means she doesn't exist and runs away. Al shows up at the apartment and tells Jane he wants Irma back. Al and Jane find Irma in the Internal Revenue Office. Because they have no proof of her age, Irma claimed to be 65 so she could begin receiving social security!

(MOTHER'S DAY)
Broadcast: 5/11/52

It's Mother's Day, and Irma is homesick for her mother. Richard, Jane's wealthy boyfriend, decides to surprise Irma by flying her mother in from Minnesota. Richard tells his friend Higgins in Minneapolis to phone Irma and get her to describe her mother. Meanwhile, Al warns her not to give the right information to anyone about anything, because he is being investigated. When Higgins calls Irma, she purposely gives him the wrong information. Higgins accompanies a bewildered old woman from Minnesota to New York. Irma declares that this not her mother and she had lied to him about her appearance. When the old woman tells them her only child died in the war, Jane says today they'll all treat her as if she's their mother.

(LOST AND FOUND)
Broadcast: 5/18/52

Irma buys a book on navigation and suggests that the gang go on a picnic. At the picnic, Irma and Mrs. O'Reilly decide to go bird watching. The situation turns grim when Mrs. O'Reilly relies on Irma's navigational skills, which lead them far out in the woods. Finally, Mrs. O'Reilly finds her way back to the picnic grounds. However, when she realizes that Irma didn't follow her, the gang breaks into teams and goes with rangers to locate her. Everyone is terrified until they find Irma asleep back at the picnic grounds. Irma insists her superior navigational skills allow her to lose her way.

(THE MARTIN'S FIGHT)
Broadcast: 5/25/52

Irma and Jane invite their neighbor, Mrs. Martin, into their apartment after she has been beaten up by her husband. Irma and Jane want to help the Martin's reconcile. After reading a book about the role environment plays in changing behavior, Irma decides to show Mr. Martin how two people in a loving environment behave. Irma and Al demonstrate their love for each other, using cutsy endearments. The plan fails when both couples end up getting in a fight with each other.

(ROMANTIC AL)
Broadcast: 6/1/52

Irma desperately wants Al to propose. Mrs. O'Reilly suggests that Irma make him jealous by pretending to see other men. Irma asks Violet to phone her and pretend to be a man. When Al overhears the conversation he runs off. Saddened, Irma decides a trip to Europe will make her feel better. When Al finds out that Irma is going to Europe, he gets worried that she'll marry a European prince. Al's friend Mushy advises him that the only way to win Irma back is to recite love poems, which Mushy will whisper to him line by line, while standing outside her window. The plan works until Violet switches papers on Mushy. Al ends up reciting an essay written about a cocker spaniel.

(GOD BLESS AMERICA)
Broadcast: 6/8/52
Stella Jabolowski, a refugee from Europe, moves into the apartment building. Mrs. O'Reilly tells Jane and Irma that Stella must familiarize herself with America to get a job with the refugee service. Stella loses her opportunity to work with the refugee service after Irma explains her wacky version of American history. Stella then decides to move out of the building.

(RESORT VACATION)
Broadcast: 6/15/52
This is a reprise of the 6/28/48 episode.

END OF SEASON

AL SUBLETS GIRL'S APARTMENT
Broadcast: 10/7/1952
While Irma and Jane were vacationing in Europe, Al sublet their apartment, without their knowledge. Irma and Jane return to find the apartment lock changed, and the tenant won't answer their knocking on the door. The tenant loves music and wears earphones, blocking out other sounds. Al tries to get the man to move out, but he's a tough guy and refuses to budge. After various ideas are proposed, the gang makes a tape of Mrs. O'Reilly singing, which Kropotkin calls "America's answer to the Spanish Inquisition." When the tenant takes off his ear phones, the gang plays the recording at full volume outside the door, but the plan backfires. The tenant thinks he was hearing an air raid siren and locks himself in the closet! Irma and Jane find a room at the YMCA. (Note: Sid Tomack replaces John Brown as Al).

IRMA TRACKS A KILLER
Broadcast: 10/14/52
Irma's father is stuck in St. Paul and needs money to go home. Irma doesn't have any money, but she learns that a reward of $1,000 is being offered for finding "Willie the Whistler," a suspected murderer. So naturally, Irma tracks him down—and gets so far as to being trapped with Willie in a back room. Willie

finds it torture to be locked up with airhead Irma.

GENEALOGY SHOW
Broadcast: 10/21/52

Irma gets fired and then finds a want ad in the paper, seeking a person of "distinguished ancestry" to be the companion of a wealthy widow. Meanwhile, Richard asks Jane if she would be his lonely Aunt Agatha's companion, and Jane agrees. Irma wants to work for the widow in the ad, but she lacks a dynamic family tree. However, Al knows a man who forges impressive genealogy charts. Irma goes to the address listed in the ad and enters Aunt Agatha's home. Aunt Agatha throws Irma out, because she is unimpressed with Irma's fake family tree. Jane once again arranges for Irma to get her job back with Mr. Clyde.

HALLOWEEN SHOW
Broadcast: 10/28/52

Richard is throwing a Halloween party and the gang is invited. Jane looks at the newspapers for the inspiration for her costume, and Irma does the same for Al's costume. The headlines warn of an infamous burglar called the "Masked Robin Hood." The gang goes to the party, while Irma waits for Al. Al is on his way to Irma's apartment, dressed like Robin Hood, when he is mistaken for the burglar and arrested. Coincidentally, the real burglar has found himself in Irma's apartment, and she takes him to the party thinking he is Al.

The 11/4/52 show is pre-empted due to the 1952 Presidential election returns.

JOINT CHECKING ACCOUNT
Broadcast: 11/11/52

Irma has convinced Jane to sign up for a joint checking account. When the girls bump into Mrs. Rhinelander at the bank, she tells Jane that she can be the official treasurer of their charity drive. Jane is pleased and uses he new financial confidence to pay off all of her bills in advance. However, Irma uses the money from the joint account to surprise Jane with a new television set. When Mrs. Rhinelander unexpectedly shows up at the apartment, asking for a credit reference, Jane is thoroughly embarrassed to find some bill collectors at the door. Then the TV set is delivered, and Jane realizes all the money in the account has been spent. Mrs. Rhinelander decides that Jane is not suitable for the position. The finances are eventually resolved, and Irma learns how to deal with her new joint account more responsibly.

MRS. O'REILLY GETS ARRESTED
Broadcast: 11/18/52

The long-time quarrel between the two landladies, Mrs. Hogan and Mrs. O'Reilly, has resulted in Mrs. O'Reilly being arrested for allegedly "disturbing the peace" with her singing. After bailing her out, the gang decides to defend Mrs. O'Reilly at her trial. During the trial, Mrs. O'Reilly pleads "not guilty" to all charges. Mrs. O'Reilly sings for the court, and the judge is appalled by her voice and is about to pass judgment, when Professor Kropotkin suggests that she only be allowed in her apartment after it has been sound proofed. The judge agrees, and the case is dismissed.

THANKSGIVING SHOW
Broadcast: 11/25/52

Irma wants to host Thanksgiving dinner, but everyone she has invited cancels. Feeling depressed and alone, Irma goes to the home of her boss, Mr. Clyde. She begins to feel accepted until she burns the turkey and the Clyde's are left with no dinner. Convinced she is unworthy of anyone's friendship; Irma runs away and spends Thanksgiving dinner at a homeless mission. Eventually, the gang arrives at the mission and brings her home.

THE REFUND SHOW
Broadcast: 12/2/52

Irma wants to buy Al a Christmas gift, but has no money. When Violet tells her that her CPA got her a $50 rent refund because her landlord overcharged her, Irma is persuaded to seek a refund. Jane warns Irma that asking for a refund from the city will get Mrs. O'Reilly in trouble. Making matters worse, Violet files a $68 claim on Irma's behalf. When Irma tries to stop the claim, she ends up in the marriage license department. However, Jane finds the right department and stops the claim. (Brooks West assumes the role of Richard).

BOTH GIRLS QUIT JOBS
Broadcast: 12/9/52

After Irma is fired, and Jane quits, both girls are jobless and reluctant to tell each other the truth. When Jane catches Irma at home, they are forced to confess their secret. However, they must hide their status from Mrs. O'Reilly, or risk being evicted. When Jane and Irma are certain that Mrs. O'Reilly will be traveling on Saturday, they think it would be safe to lie to her about throwing a lavish party, hoping this will convince her that they are still making money. But then the girls find themselves in a predicament when Irma persuades Mrs. O'Reilly to stay. Luckily, both girls get their jobs back.

(DEPARTMENT STORE SANTA)
Broadcast: 12/16/52

Irma wants to earn extra money for the Christmas holidays. Mr. Clyde reluctantly gives her the opportunity by serving a summons on the notoriously untraceable Mr. Murdock, who works part-time in Lacy's Department Store. Al tries to help Irma deliver the summons while Irma works another job in the store, but he gives up. Irma feels that a visit to the department store Santa will lift her spirits. The Santa is actually Murdock. When Irma reaches into her bag, she accidentally gives him the summons.

CHRISTMAS SHOW
Broadcast: 12/23/52

Irma is sad when Al tells her he cannot afford a Christmas gift. Jane persuades Al to find a job to pay for the gift. Al is working as a street Santa Claus, raising money for charity, which means working during Christmas Eve. After searching through the entire Santa's in the city, Irma finds Al and decides to take his place. Irma's "ho, ho, ho-ing" is disturbed when a bunch of robbers try to take her money. Fortunately, the Christmas spirit subdues the robbers, and they drop all the money they've stolen in Irma's charity pot. Irma takes the robbers home, singing Christmas carols.

IRMA OPENS A BANK VAULT
Broadcast: 12/30/52

Irma's New Year's resolution for 1953 is that she will be a doer. When the adding machine and the typewriter break down at work, Irma fixes them. However, some of the pieces from the typewriter end up in the adding machine, and vice versa, so 310 divided by 16 equals "Dear Sir." Irma minds a locksmith's shop while the locksmith is testifying for Mr. Clyde in court, when an emergency call comes in from a bank. A vice president is locked in the vault. Al goes with her and using nitroglycerin they do open the vault but also cause a big hole in the bank building. Later, Jane locks Irma in the bathroom until Irma promises not to be a doer for 1953.

IRMA THE ARCHITECT
Broadcast: 1/6/53

Dissatisfied with her current job, Irma applies to be an architect's secretary and gets the job. Irma immediately starts making design suggestions of a bizarre nature to the clients. While her boss is away on a trip, Irma is supposed to mail the plans for an apartment building in Cleveland to the construction boss, but she loses the plans. In desperation, Irma tries to redraw the plans, making some alterations of her own. The architect is furious, but soon cools off when he wins an award from *Architectural Digest* magazine for winning the "Outstanding Achievement of the Month" award because of the innovative design of the apartment building. But, Irma decides she would be better off working for Mr. Clyde, and gets her job back.

MRS. O'REILLY IS ROBBED
Broadcast: 1/13/53

Jane's father is coming to visit her, but Jane will be unable to pick him up at the train station. Jane asks Irma to meet him and gives her a piece of paper with his complete physical description. That night, Mrs. O'Reilly tells them she was robbed. Mrs. O'Reilly is unwilling to involve the police, but Irma reports the robbery and gives the police a written description of the robber. However, the paper Irma gives the police is the one with the description of Jane's father. Jane's father is arrested at the station, and Jane spends the visit with her dad in his jail cell.

AL IMPRESSES MINNESOTA
Broadcast: 1/20/53

Irma's family in Minnesota writes to her, saying they're sending their neighbor, Walter Schenson, to meet Al. Irma is worried because she has lied to her family about Al's job. Fortunately, Richard agrees to let Al use his office for a short time, so he may impress Schenson. After a wonderful evening, Al takes Schenson to the train station. All goes well until Al makes a call and gets arrested for slipping slugs into a telephone box.

IRMA GETS A RAISE
Broadcast: 1/27/53

Irma is stuck going out on a date with her boss's nephew Hector. Worried about Al, Irma pleads with her friend Eloise to go out with Hector instead, and Eloise is willing to pretend to be Irma for the evening. After confusing Hector with a series of identify shifts, Eloise abandons the plan when her boyfriend shows up, and the real Irma is left to go out with Hector. Meanwhile, Al's friend checks up on Irma, making sure she is not cheating on Al. Jane decides to help by telling him that she is Irma, and they go out. Mrs. O'Reilly is the only gal left in the apartment when a friend of Jane's boyfriend Richard shows up to take Jane out on Richard's behalf. Mrs. O'Reilly feels she has no choice but to tell him she is Jane, and they go out!

(IRMA THE REDHEAD)
Broadcast: 2/3/53

Irma has not heard from Al in a week, and Eloise tells Irma she has seen a vivacious redhead knocking at Al's door. Irma decides to dye her hair and change her manner. Irma gets fired after her new look causes her boss to lose a conservative client. When Al sees Irma with red hair, he leaves. Irma is bewildered, until Professor Kropotkin explains that the woman knocking on Al's door was from the finance company, threatening to take away his bed.

IRMA GOES TO CONFER WITH EISENHOWER
Broadcast: 2/10/53

Irma goes to Washington D.C. to deliver a document for her boss, and she is determined to speak with President Eisenhower while she's there. Jane also goes to D.C. to pick up a package for Richard. The package contains the prototype of a valuable and sensitive timing device. Irma takes a tour of the post office, where she is told that ticking packages are dangerous and should be put in water. While Jane is out, Irma arrives back at the hotel just in time to receive the package for Richard. She hears ticking coming from inside of it, and throws it in water. Jane comes back to find that Irma has damaged the device, and she faints from the shock.

VALENTINES DAY SHOW
Broadcast: 2/17/53

Jane is certain Irma will not receive a Valentine from her perpetually unemployed Al. Irma and her friend Hazel decide to prove Jane wrong by sending a Valentine signed with Al's name to Irma. So, Hazel goes out to get the card, but she chooses a card for a dog and signs it "Lover boy." Al surprises Irma with a half-full box of chocolates and sees the Valentine sent by Hazel. Irma attempts to convince him that she sent it to herself. However, when Al reads the message signed by "Lover Boy," he becomes upset. Irma says she's through with men.

AL'S YOUTH RESTORER
Broadcast: 2/24/53

Al invents a drink that he says will restore one's youth. Mrs. O'Reilly buys it, but it worsens her appearance. After she complains to the Better Business Bureau, Al is arrested. When Irma tells her that it's Al's product, Mrs. O'Reilly decides she must help Al. Mrs. O'Reilly dresses and acts childishly, to demonstrate that Al's youth formula does work. When the man from the bureau finally shows up, Kropotkin tells Jane to pretend to be Mrs. O'Reilly. The man looks at the younger Jane and is convinced the formula works. He is about to exonerate Al, until he sees the real Mrs. O'Reilly and is shocked by her true appearance. Al doesn't go to jail, but his formula is taken off the market.

BICYCLE SHOW
Broadcast: 3/3/53

When Jane goes bike riding in the park, she accidentally collides with a woman who threatens to sue Jane for every penny she's got. Jane must convince the woman's lawyer that she's broke. Jane alerts the gang that when the lawyer comes to the apartment, they must act as if she's quite poor. When a man arrives, Irma doesn't know he is the lawyer, but instead believes he's a potential boyfriend. Irma gets her Al, Eloise and Barney to pretend that they are Jane's servants. The lawyer, convinced that Jane is wealthy, threatens to sue for even more money. When Jane explains Irma's ploy, he drops the case. (Note: This is Hans Conried's last appearance as Professor Kropotkin).

INCOME TAX SHOW
Broadcast: 3/10/53

This is a reprise of the 2/28/49 show. This episode introduces a new character, Wanderkin, who in effect takes over for Hans Conried's Professor Kropotkin, as the girl's upstairs neighbor. Wanderkin is played by Kenny Delmar.

St. Patrick's Day Show
Broadcast: 3/17/53
Mrs. O'Reilly and Mrs. Hogan are vying in an election to be the St. Patrick's Day parade leader. Al tells Mrs. O'Reilly that he will bring her a green cloth for good luck. The election results in a tie vote. Mr. Kelly, the deciding vote, votes for Mrs. Hogan, because some fool on Mrs. O'Reilly's team ripped the green cloth off the billiards table. The gang is pleased when Mrs. Hogan and Mrs. O'Reilly both end up leading the parade.

School Teacher Show
Broadcast: 3/24/53
Irma's old teacher, Miss McClusky, is visiting from Minnesota, and Irma must prove to her that she is the successful, cultured woman her parents rave about. Then, at work, a sophisticated woman client shows up. Responding to Irma's enthusiasm and honesty, the woman gives her a crash course on culture. Meanwhile, a secret document, which Jane worked on for her boss, has apparently been stolen. An FBI agent tells Jane he must investigate Irma, but Jane insists that her roommate is neither intelligent nor malicious enough to steal the document. When Jane and the agent find Irma having an intelligent conversation with Miss McClusky, she becomes suspect. After looking around the apartment, Jane finds that Irma has used the document for a bookmark. The document is safely returned, and Irma's teacher is impressed with her accomplishments.

Al's Rich Uncle
Broadcast: 3/31/53
Al's wealthy Uncle Ethelbert is coming to New York from Australia, and he expects to bequeath money to his nephew, if he is a married man, so Irma and Al get a marriage license. Uncle Ethelbert arrives and begins to talk about his millions, but every time Ethelbert tells them about how he made money, he mentions how he subsequently lost it. Ethelbert's financial rollercoaster stories make it increasingly difficult for Irma and Al to decide to get married. However, after hearing the story in which his uncle mistook glass for diamonds, the gangs realize he is an eccentric and not a millionaire. Irma and Al don't get married.

Irma Is Fired
Broadcast: 4/7/53
This is a reprise of the 3/21/49 episode.

AL GETS A JOB
Broadcast: 4/14/53

Jane and Irma are going to a dance, and Jane, who dislikes Al, fixes her up with Paul. Irma reluctantly agrees. When Al tells Irma he is working the night shift at the Blue Star Garage, Jane and Irma have a new respect for him. After the dance, Paul's car breaks down and he takes it to the nearest mechanic, which is the Blue Star Garage. Irma tells Paul that she loves the mechanic at the garage. Paul sympathizes and brings the mechanic over to her. Irma takes one look at the aged mechanic and tells Paul that this is not Al. The old man informs her that Al quit. Al is once more unemployed.

WAY TO A MAN'S HEART
Broadcast: 4/21/53

Irma decides to take cooking lessons after her tomato surprise is a disaster. Then Irma is fired, and Richard allows her to take Jane's place as secretary for a day. The Westbrook Caterers call Richard's office and tell Irma that they need a cook for a special luncheon being held for Richard's mother, and Irma agrees to go work for them. Jane is worried that Irma's creations will poison the crowd. Richard and Jane scramble to relocate the people to a new restaurant before it's too late. When Jane gets back from the party, she is furious with Irma, until Irma tells Jane that she was only hired as a dishwasher.

IRMA TAKES UP YOGI
Broadcast: 4/28/53

Irma finds a letter to Mr. Clyde about being chosen to serve on the Draft Board, and she misinterprets it, thinking her boss is being drafted into the army. When Mr. Clyde's doctor shows up to administer an examination by the Board, Irma convinces the doctor that Mr. Clyde is very sick. He believes her and cancels Mr. Clyde's nomination. Mr. Clyde is angry, but forgives Irma. Irma decides to study yoga. Jane tries to hide Irma's yoga practices from Mrs. Rhinelander when she visits the apartment. But when Mrs. Rhinelander sees Irma, she admits that she also practices Yoga, to Jane's relief.

IRMA WANTS OLDER MEN
Broadcast: 5/5/53

When Al cancels Irma's birthday lunch and gets into a cab with another girl, Irma suspects he's dating her. Frustrated with younger men, Irma calls up Mr. Clover, an "old" love, who's 62 years old. While Irma and Mr. Clover are at the museum, Jane receives a telegram that Irma's father is coming to New York that night. Jane leaves a note for Irma, but Irma never receives it. When Al catches Mr. Clover and Irma saying goodbye to each other, Irma tells Al that was her father. Irma's real father arrives, and Al finds him and Mr. Clover standing together. Angered and bewildered Al socks both Mr. Clover and Irma's father in the face. The misunderstanding is resolved, and Irma and Al are still in love.

THE PICNIC
Broadcast: 5/12/53

When the gang decides to go on a picnic, Irma is reluctant to go because she fears she will not have time to finish her night school homework, which involves listing important sites in New York. Al borrows a car for the day of the picnic, and Irma drives it. Irma and the gang arrive at a secret military base that they think is a public park. The army fires on them, and they try to escape. They are caught and taken in for questioning. When the Lieutenant reads Irma's school assignment, he suspects that Irma is a spy preparing an attack on the places listed on the paper. Jane and Irma try to explain that the paper is a harmless homework assignment. Irma is released, and the gang enjoys their picnic in the safety of Irma and Jane's apartment.

IRMA'S BROTHER LECTURES
Broadcast: 5/19/53

Irma's intelligent brother, Gerald, is wrapping up his nation-wide lecture tour in New York. Jane takes this opportunity to invite Irma and her brother to her philosophical society meeting. However, when Gerald arrives, his much-anticipated lecture turns out to be a marketing scheme to sell a snake oil potion. The society's members disapprove, and Jane resigns her membership.

CORONATION SHOW
Broadcast: 5/26/53

Irma wins an all-expense paid trip to see the Coronation in England, from the Secretarial Club raffle. Jane decides to help Irma make her arrangements for the trip, but Irma insists on doing it all herself. When Jane gets a phone call from Irma, she thinks Irma's calling from overseas. Hoever, Irma tells her that when she bought her ticket, the man at the counter asked if she was going to "merry old England," Irma replied that she did not like anything old. Irma informs Jane that she is in New England.

LAUGHING BOY
Broadcast: 6/2/53

Mr. Clyde has just purchased a racehorse named Laughing Boy. Irma becomes upset when she finds out that Laughing Boy will be replaced in a race by a younger horse named Dancing Girl. When Mr. Clyde orders Irma to go to the stables and tell them to enter Dancing Girl into the race, she tells them to enter Laughing Boy instead. When the gang places their bets, they are horrified to see that the older horse has replaced Dancing Girl. Everyone is upset with Irma, until Laughing Boy miraculously wins the race. Irma explains that she had married off the two horses, and Laughing Boy was anxious to get back to his honeymoon.

THE MARTIN'S FIGHT
Broadcast: 6/9/53
This is a reprise of the 5/25/52 show.

GHOST SHOW
Broadcast: 6/16/53
Irma, Jane and Wanderkin are spooked after seeing a ghost in a ling sheet pacing through the hallway of their apartment building. As a result, Irma is fired for sleeping on the job, since she can't sleep at night. Jane quits her job out of frustration. When the gang approaches Mrs. O'Reilly, she suspects the ghost is her late husband Clancy. After they hold a séance, Jane realizes that the ghost is really Mr. Martin wrapped up in a white sheet. Jane explains that Mrs. Martin hides his clothes to deter him from going to his weekly poker game, thus all he can find to wear is a white sheet.

IRMA WRITES A COLUMN
Broadcast: 6/23/53
This is a reprise of the 2/3/52 episode.

IRMA BUYS AN AIR CONDITIONER
Broadcast: 6/30/53
Jane discovers that Irma has spent all their vacation money on an unreliable air conditioner. When the gang sees Jane and Irma in distress, they decide to raise some money, but tell the girls the block party is a fundraiser for two little orphans. Jane and Irma get the two winning raffle tickets to an all-expense-paid vacation, and they both begin to suspect the truth. The gang confesses that the event and the raffle were both rigged. Jane and Irma go on their vacation and are thankful for having such wonderful friends. (This is Cathy Lewis' final episode as Jane Stacy, her character will be written out next season—having moved to Panama. This is also Sid Tomack's last episode as Al. The show will have an unusually long hiatus—until December—the "My Friend Irma" television show will introduce the new characters that Fall, so the radio show will not have to explain the changes).

IRMA GETS A RAISE
Broadcast: 12/1/53
This episode introduces Mary Shipp playing Irma's new roommate, Kay Foster. Kay had already been introduced in the fall on the television series, so no elaborate explanation is given as to why there is no Jane. Also, Hal March is cast as Irma's new boyfriend, Joe Vance—who was also introduced on the television show. The character of Professor Kropotkin is back, but not played by Hans Conried, instead, radio veteran Benny Rubin takes on the part. Interestingly, the Kropotkin character is not part of the television show that season. Also most of the remaining episodes

are reprises of earlier scripts, with few original episodes written for this, the final season of the radio show. This episode is a reprise of the 1/27/53 show.

IRMA TRACKS A KILLER
Broadcast: 12/15/53

This is a reprise of the 10/14/52 show.

CHRISTMAS SHOW
Broadcast: 12/22/53

This is yet another reworking of the 12/22/47 Christmas episode.

(IRMA AND KAY FIND A HOBBY)
Broadcast: 12/29/53

This is a reprise of the 1/10/49 show.

(IRMA AND THE S.P.C.S.)
Broadcast: 1/5/54

This is a reprise of the 5/7/51 show.

(RUDOLPH'S RACING TIP)
Broadcast: 1/12/54

This is a reprise of the 2/20/50 show.

(BOTH GIRLS QUIT THEIR JOBS)
Broadcast: 1/19/54

This is a reprise of the 12/9/52 show.

(GOD BLESS AMERICA)
Broadcast: 1/26/54

This is a reprise of the 6/8/52 show.

(JOINT ACCOUNT)
Broadcast: 2/2/54

This is a reprise of the 11/11/52 show.

(IRMA SINGS)
Broadcast: 2/9/54

This is a reprise of the 12/6/48 show.

(IRMA AND THE EYEGLASSES)
Broadcast: 2/16/54

This is a reprise of the 12/8/47 show. (Richard Deacon, Mel Cooley from "The Dick Van Dyke Show" is a guest voice).

(Income Tax)
Broadcast: 2/23/54

This is a reprise of the 2/5/51 show.

(Irma's Memoirs)
Broadcast: 3/2/54

Irma decides to publish her memoirs. However, all of her attempts to get a publisher are rejected. The future brightens for Irma when a publisher, Professor Nichols, tells her that he has published her work for $100 in the newspaper. Irma and Kay are ecstatic until they learn that Nichols used a sample of Irma's writing in order to advertise his grammar school.

The Girls are Robbed
Broadcast: 3/9/54

A robber breaks into Irma and Kay's apartment in the middle of the night. While Irma is covering the robber with a lighter shaped like a pistol, Kay runs to get the police. The robber outsmarts Irma and runs away, taking Kay's expensive watch, which was a gift from her boyfriend. Kay feels threatened and decides to move out of the apartment. Irma tries to pawn her things to be able to buy a new watch for Kay. Coincidentally, Joe and Irma see the robber trying to pawn Kay's watch, and Joe catches him. Meanwhile, Kay decides to stay in the apartment and buys a pistol. When Mr. Clyde, asks Irma to light his cigarette, Irma takes the pistol, thinking it's the lighter. Luckily, Irma is a poor shot.

Irma Is Fired
Broadcast: 3/16/54

This is a reprise of the 3/21/49 show.

(Irma's Fling with Astrology)
Broadcast: 3/23/54

This is a reprise of the 1/30/50 show.

(Spring Cleaning)
Broadcast: 3/30/54

This is a reprise of the 4/16/51 show.

(Mrs. O'Reilly's Face-lift)
Broadcast: 4/6/54

This is a reprise of the 3/30/52 show.

(The Vacuum Cleaner Salesman)
Broadcast: 4/13/54

This is a reprise of the 3/20/50 show.

(IRMA, CAREER WOMAN)
Broadcast: 4/20/54

This is a reprise of the 4/6/52 show.

(MR. AND MRS. CLYDE'S DIVORCE)
Broadcast: 4/27/54

This is a reprise of the 12/16/51 show.

(IRMA MANAGES THE APARTMENT HOUSE)
Broadcast: 5/4/54

This is a reprise of the 11/7/49 show.

(THE LOST BIRTH CERTIFICATE)
Broadcast: 5/11/54

This is a reprise of the 5/4/52 show.

(KAY CATCHES A COLD)
Broadcast: 5/18/54

This is a reprise of the 11/11/51 show.

(LOST AND FOUND)
Broadcast: 5/25/54

This is a reprise of the 5/18/52 show.

(CUB SCOUTS SAVE THE DAY)
Broadcast: 6/1/54

This is a reprise of the 12/30/51 show.

(SCHOOL TEACHER SHOW)
Broadcast: 6/8/54

This is a reprise of the 3/24/53 show.

(JOE'S RICH UNCLE)
Broadcast: 6/14/54

This is a reprise of the 3/31/53 show.

(A MOVING EXPERIENCE)
Broadcast: 6/21/54

This is a reprise of the 1/9/50 show.

(IRMA WANTS AN OLDER MAN)
Broadcast: 6/28/54

This is a reprise of the 5/5/53 show.

(JOE'S BIRTHDAY)
Broadcast: 7/5/54
This is a reprise of the 9/11/47 show.

(IRMA'S BROTHER LECTURES)
Broadcast: 7/12/54
This is a reprise of the 5/19/53 show.

(KROPOTKIN'S ROOM)
Broadcast: 7/19/54
This is a reprise of the 1/31/49 show.

JEALOUS OF JIM
Broadcast: 7/26/54
This is a reprise of the 4/24/50 show.

JOE'S SHRINK
Broadcast: 8/2/54
This is a reprise of the 4/2/51 show.

(KISS AND TELL)
Broadcast: 8/9/54
This is a reprise of the 9/16/51 show.

(LAUGHING BOY)
Broadcast: 8/16/54
This is a reprise of the 6/2/53 show.

(JOE'S YOUTH RESTORER)
Broadcast: 8/23/54
This is a reprise of the 2/24/53 show. This is also the last episode of the "My Friend Irma" series.

Marie on Television

THE ED WYNN SHOW (April 22, 1950, CBS)
Marie makes her television debut on Wynn's variety show.

MY FRIEND IRMA (January 8, 1952 – June 25, 1954, CBS)
Seasons one and two center on the misadventures of Irma Petersen and her roommate Jane Stacy and the characters established in the long running radio series. However, during the start of the third and final season (53-54) major changes occurred. Jane Stacy is gone, having moved to Panama and Irma gets a new roommate, Kay Foster (played by Mary Shipp) and Irma's seven year old nephew, Bobby (Richard Eyer). Irma also dumps long time boyfriend Al, for the more handsome and somewhat more reliable Joe Vance (Hal March). Professor Kropotkin is played on television by Sig Arno also is gone in the final season and replaced by an unsuccessful Shakespearian actor, Mr. Corday (played by John Carradine). The television series never attained the popularity of the radio show—and was never a top 25 program, but did well enough to produce approximately 70 episodes.

THE ED SULLIVAN SHOW (March 3, 1957, CBS)

THE TENNESSEE ERNIE FORD SHOW (October 16, 1957, NBC)

THE LUX SHOW Starring Rosemary Clooney (December 5, 1957, NBC)

THE ED SULLIVAN SHOW (February 28, 1960, CBS)

THIS IS YOUR LIFE (May 18, 1960, NBC)
Marie was part of the surprise for honoree Ken Murray.

THE ED SULLIVAN SHOW (August 7, 1960, CBS)
Marie appeared with Ken Murray.

THE COMEDY SPOT (July 3, 1962, CBS)
A summer replacement series for *Red Skelton* which showed previously unaired pilots. CBS aired the 1959 pilot for *Ernestine*.

THE ED SULLIVAN SHOW (August 12, 1962, CBS)

EMPIRE (March 26, 1963, ABC)
Marie appeared in an episode titled, "Hidden Assets" in this western series which starred Richard Egan.

BURKE'S LAW (February 28, 1964, ABC)
Episode Title: "Who's Killing Marty Kelso?"
Marie plays Chuchi Smith in an episode about a Hollywood agent who is murdered shortly after attending a dinner party attended by three of his ex-wives. Gene Barry stars.

BURKE'S LAW (February 3, 1965, ABC)
Episode Title: "Who Killed Wimbeldon Hastings?"
Marie plays Ramona Specks in an episode about a tennis pro who is killed when one of his tennis balls explodes.

WHERE'S HUDDLES? (July-September, 1970, CBS)
This animated series was the summer replacement for *The Glen Campbell Goodtime Hour* and told the story of Ed Huddles, quarterback fro a pro football team. His next door neighbor is Bubba McCoy, the team's center. The couples are married and socialize together. Another neighbor was Claude Pertwee, who was not a member of the team. Marie voiced blonde and ditzy (what else?) Penny McCoy. Other voices included Cliff Norton (Ed), Mel Blanc (Bubba, among others), Jean Vander Pyl (Marge Huddles), and Paul Lynde as Claude. About nine episodes were produced by Hanna-Barbara.

LOVE, AMERICAN STYLE (October 6, 1972, ABC)
Episode Title: "Love and the Girlish Groom."
A man dressed is dressed in drag when he meets his fiancés parents (played by Vincent Gardenia and Marie, in her final performance).

ADDITIONAL APPEARANCES
No specific dates.

CELEBRITY TIME (1951, CBS)
A prime-time quiz program.

THE FRANK SINATRA SHOW (1951, CBS)

THE KEN MURRAY SHOW (1953, CBS)

THE JOHNNY CARSON SHOW (1955, CBS)

THE RED SKELTON SHOW (1957, CBS)

THE EDDIE FISHER SHOW (1957, NBC)

THE GARRY MOORE SHOW (1959, CBS)

ARTHUR MURRAY PARTY (1960, NBC)

HERE'S HOLLYWOOD (1961, NBC)

ART LINKLETTER'S HOUSE PARTY (1967, CBS)

THE MERV GRIFFIN SHOW (1967, Syndicated)

BUDDY GRECO SPECIAL (1969, Syndicated)

JACK CASSIDY'S ST. PATRICK'S DAY SPECIAL (Feb, 1969, Syndicated)

THE FILMS OF MARIE WILSON

BABES IN TOYLAND
Released: November 30, 1934 (MGM)

CAST

STANNIE DUM	Stan Laurel
OLLIE DEE	Oliver Hardy
MOTHER GOOSE	Virginia Karns
BO-PEEP	Charlotte Henry
TOM-TOM PIPER	Felix Knight
SILAS BARNABY	Henry Kleinbach
SANTA CLAUS	Ferdinand Munier
TOYMAKER	William Burress
LITTLE BOY BLUE	Johnny Downs
MARY QUITE CONTRARY	Marie Wilson

Musical-Comedy based on the operetta (music by Victor Herbert) starred Laurel and Hardy and was set in the village of Toyland where evil Silas Barnaby attempts to evict the widow Peep from the shoe she and her family live in unless her daughter Bo-Peep marries him. Enlisted to aide the widow is her boarders Stannie Dum and Ollie Dee. The film also known as March of the Wooden Soldiers has since become a Christmas time viewing perennial. The film was produced by Hal Roach but distributed through MGM and Directed by Gus Meins and Charles Rodgers. The film was written by Frank Butler, Nick Grinde and (uncredited as usual) Stan Laurel. Without a doubt, Marie was cast in her small role as Mary, Quite Contrary, through her association with Grinde. Film historian Leonard Maltin gives this film ***1/2 stars and writes, "L&H version . . . looks better all the time, compared to lumbering "family musicals" of recent years." Also watch for the Attack of the Bogeyman!

STARS OVER BROADWAY
Released: November 23, 1935 (Warner Brothers)

CAST

AL MCGILLEVRAY	Pat O'Brien
JOAN GARRETT	Jane Froman
JAN KING	James Melton
NORA WYMAN	Jean Muir
OFFKEY CRAMER	Frank McHugh
FREDDY	Eddie Conrad
MINOTTI	William Ricciardi
MOLLY	Marie Wilson
ANNOUNCER	Frank Fay
ROMEO	Phil Regan
LUIGI	Paul Porcasi

This was a top studio release with one of Warner's top directors (William Keighley) and a screenplay by Jerry Wald and Julius J. Epstein. The musical numbers were staged and directed by Busby Berkeley and gowns were by Orry-Kelly. Al McGillevray is a failed theatrical manager about to commit suicide when he hears hotel porter Jan King singing and so taken with his beautiful voice offers to make him a star. When Al is told that it will take five years of extensive study before Jan can become an accomplished opera singer, he decides to take Jan on a round of radio stations intending to make him a crooner (ala Bing Crosby) rather than an opera singer. The original title of this film was *Radio Jamboree*.

BROADWAY HOSTESS
Released: December 7, 1935 (Warner Brothers)

CAST

WINNIE WHARTON	Winifred Shaw
IRIS MARVIN	Genevieve Tobin
LUCKY LORIMER	Lyle Talbot
FISHCAKE CARTER	Allen Jenkin
TOMMY BLAKE	Phil Regan
DOROTHY DUBOIS	Marie Wilson
MRS. DUNCAN-GRISWOLD-WEMBLY-SMYTHE	Spring Byington
BIG JOE	Joseph King
RONNIE MARVIN	Donald Ross

The Broadway Hostess is Winnie Wharton who becomes a successful nightclub singer with the help of Lucky Lorimer. Lucky becomes her manager and is instrumental in getting hard boiled night club owner Big Joe to pay her a huge salary. Winnie loves Lucky, but Lucky loves a socialie Iris Marvin while poor but proud piano player Tommy Blake loves Winnie. The film takes a melodramatic, yet typical Warners turn. Marie is cast as not too bright fellow night club singer Dorothy Dubois.

MISS PACIFIC FLEET
Released: December 14, 1935 (Warner Brothers)

CAST

GLORIA FAY	Joan Blondell
MAE O BRIEN	Glenda Farrell
MR. FREYTAG	Hugh Herbert
KEWPIE WIGGINS	Allen Jenkins
SGT. FOSTER	Warren Hull
DUTCH	Eddie Acuff
VIRGIE MATTHEWS	Marie Wilson
SADIE FREYTAG	Minna Gombel
NICK	Guinn Williams

Blondell and Farrell play two former showgirls working a booth on at a seaside amusement park. Kewpie Wiggins, a sailor, decides to show off and with his skill at throwing rings he wins all of the girls prizes—and they lose everything. Kewpie has fallen in love with Gloria and tries to help them by suggesting that Gloria enter the "Miss Pacific Fleet" contest. Marie plays fellow "Miss Pacific Fleet" contestant, Virgie Matthews—giving her plenty of opportunity to show off her voluptuous body.

COLLEEN
Released: March 21, 1936 (Warner Brothers)

CAST

DONALD AMES, 3RD	Dick Powell
COLLEEN REILLY	Ruby Keeler
JOE CORK	Jack Oakie
MINNIE HAWKINS	Joan Blondell
CEDRIC AMES	Hugh Herbert
ALICIA AMES	Louise Fazenda
PAUL DRAPER	Paul Gordon
MABEL	Marie Wilson

Businessman Cedric Ames buys a dress shop for Minnie Hawkins, a gold digger. His nephew, Donald Ames, III, wants to close the shop down and enlists the support of the book keeper, Colleen, who is initially opposed to his taking such action. Colleen even attempts to help Minnie by staging a fashion show to help attract business. In the meanwhile Donald and Colleen fall in love. In true Powell-Keeler fashion the rest of the plot is typical "boy meets girl, boy loses girl and boy gets girl back." Leonard Maltin gives this film *** and calls it a "neglected Warner Bros musical."

THE BIG NOISE
Released: June 22, 1936 (Warner Brothers)

CAST

JULIUS TRENT	Guy Kibbee
KEN MITCHELL	Warren Hull
BETTY TRENT	Alma Lloyd
DON ANDREWS	Dick Foran
DAISY	Marie Wilson
CHARLIE CALDWELL	Henry O'Neill
HARRISON	Olin Howland
MRS. TRENT	Virginia Brissac

Julius Trent, the president of Trent Mills objects to plans of his manager Walford Andrews, to manufacture a synthetic wool called Woolex. The stockholders believing that Julius is behind the times vote Andrews in as the new president. Julius and his family retire to California on doctors orders. On the advice of his gardener, Julius buys a small business to run as an amusement and to keep him active and vital. His "small business" goes so well that he eventually gets his job back at Trent Mills.

SATAN MET A LADY
Released: August 8, 1936 (Warner Brothers)

CAST

VALERIE PURVIS	Bette Davis
TED SHANE	Warren William
MADAME BARABBAS	Alison Skipworth
ANTHONY TRAVERS	Arthur Treacher
MISS MURGATROYD	Marie Wilson
ASTRID AMES	Winifred Shaw
AMES	Porter Hall
DUNHILL	Olin Howland
POLLOCK	Charles Wilson
BABE	Barbara Bane

This film was loosely based on Dashiell Hammett's classic novel ***The Maltese***

Falcon. Private detective Ted Shane returns to his old partner Ames, but it is not a happy homecoming since Shane and Ames' wife had a previous fling. But Ames allows him in since Shane brings in business. One client is Valerie Purvis, who asks help in finding a man who jilted her. Ames follows her to a meeting and winds up dead and Shane becomes the primary suspect. Along the way Shane meets up with Anthony Travers, an Englishman who is on the hunt for a rams horn rumored to be filled with jewels. Shane suspects that Valerie is also searching for the elusive horn. Marie has a fine comic turn as Miss Murgatroyd, Shane's dim but beautiful secretary. This film was directed by William Dieterle. Leonard Maltin gives this film ** and pronounces it "far below the 1941 remake" which starred Humphrey Bogart (and was much more faithful to the original novel).

CHINA CLIPPER
Released: August 22, 1936 (Warner Brothers)

CAST

DAVE LOGAN	Pat O'Brien
JEAN LOGAN	Beverly Roberts
TOM COLLINS	Ross Alexander
HAP STUART	Humphrey Bogart
SUNNY AVERY	Marie Wilson
JIM HORN	Jospeh Crehan
MR. PIERSON	Joseph King
B.C. HILL	Addison Richards
MOTHER BRUNN	Ruth Robinson
SECRETARY	Anne Nagel
PILOT	William Wright
NAVIGATOR	Wayne Morris
RADIO OPERATOR	Milburn Stone

A cast full of familiar faces are half the fun of this Warner's B. Importer Dave Logan (O'Brien) arrives in Shanghai late and ruins a business deal. He realizes that there can be a gold mine in commercial air service. This plan fails, but the ever optimistic Dave decries to start a second airline based in Key West, Florida to deliver mail in the Caribbean. He is aided by his buddy Hap Stuart (Bogart). Milburn Stone who plays one of the radio operators went on to play "Doc" in the television version of "Gunsmoke" for twenty years.

KING OF HOCKEY
Released: December 19, 1936 (Warner Brothers)

CAST

GABBY DUGAN	Dick Purcell

KATHLEEN O'ROURKE	Anne Nagel
ELSIE	Marie Wilson
JUMBO MULLINS	Wayne Morris
NICK TORGA	George E. Stone
MIKE TROTTER	Joseph Crehan
PEGGY O'ROURKE	AnnGillis
DR. NOBLE	Gordon Hart
MRS. O'ROURKE	Dora Clemant
MR. O'ROURKE	Guy Usher
TOM MCKENNA	Harry Davenport

Hockey player Gabby Dugan takes his team to first place. A gangster offers him a payoff to throw a game. Gabby turns the ganster down, but is seen talking to him by his teammate, Jumbo. Jumbo doesn't hear Gabby's refusal and when Gabby deliberately fouls so he can spend time talking to the beautiful Kathleen O' Rourke—it is assumed he did it to try and throw the game. Star Dick Purcell was a former hockey player for Fordham University.

MELODY FOR TWO
Released: May 1, 1937

CAST

TOD WEAVER	James Melton
GALE STARR	Patricia Ellis
CAMILLE CASEY	Marie Wilson
REMORSE RUMSON	Fred Keating
MEL LYNCH	Dick Purcell
LORNA WRAY	Winifred Shaw
SCOOP TROTTER	Charles Foy
EXODUS JOHNSON	Eddie Anderson
OPERATOR	Marjorie Weaver

Bandleader Tod Weaver fires his arranger Mel Lynch when Lynch demands a new contract with a bonus. Tod believes Mel drinks too much and further alienating him is the fact that Mel also dated Gale Starr, Tod's current girlfriend. Tod's impulsive act leaves him without an arranger so Gale contacts Mel and asks him to use an anonymous name on his arrangements so that Tod will use them. But Tod finds out and refuses to use the arrangements. Eventually he loses all, but puts his life and career back together when he is persuaded to organize an all-girl's (composed of all blondes) band including Camille Casey (Marie Wilson), a bass player. Eddie Anderson is best known as Jack Benny's valet "Rochester." Also appearing are the O' Connor Brothers—including a young Donald O' Connor.

PUBLIC WEDDING
Released: July 10, 1937 (Warner Brothers)

CAST

FLIP LANE	Jane Wyman
TONY BURKE	William Hopper
JOE TYLOR	Dick Purcell
TESSIE	Marie Wilson
POP LANE	Berton Churchill
NICK	James Robbins
THE DEACON	Ramond Hatton
REPORTER	Horace MacMahon

Pop Lane and his daughter Flip run a concession stand at an amusement park. To attract attention and customers they decide to hold a public wedding in the mouth of a whale skeleton which they display. Flip will be a phony bride and a phony groom is one of her group. However, the phony groom takes the money from the concession and goes on the run and Flip is groom less. The crowd has gathered for the phony wedding and if it doesn't take place they will want their money back—money they don't have. Pop finds artist Tony Burke who agrees to the charade—but it turns out that the judge who performs the ceremony is a real judge and Flip and Tony are really married! Marie Wilson plays Tessie, a stripper, who avoids arrest during a police raid by donning a wedding dress.

William Hopper is the son of famed Hollywood gossip columnist Hedda and later went on to play Paul Drake on the long-running TV series, *Perry Mason*.

THE GREAT GARRICK
Released: October 30, 1937 (Warner Brothers)

CAST

DAVID GARRICK	Brian Aherne
GERMAINE DUPONT	Olivia de Havilland
TUBBY	Edward Everett Horton
M. PICARD	Melville Cooper
BEAUMARCHAIS	Lionel Atwill
BASSET	Luis Alberni
AUBER	Lana Turner
NICOLLE	Marie Wilson
INNKEEPER (TURK HEAD)	Harry Davenport

A major "A" picture directed by James (*Frankenstein*) Whales. Aherne plays the famous eighteenth century English actor whose reputation precedes him. A group of French actors he will be working with take over a roadside inn determined to teach him a lesson in the art of "realistic acting." Garrick almost immediately recognizes that he is being put-on and decides to play along. Aherne later became de Havilland's brother in law when he married her sister, Joan Fontaine.

THE INVISIBLE MENACE
Released: January 22, 1938 (Warner Brothers)

CAST

JEVRIES	Boris Karloff
SALLY PRATT	Marie Wilson
EDDIE PRATT	Eddie Craven
LIEUTENANT MATTHEWS	Regis Toomey
COLONEL HACKETT	Henry Kolker
COLONEL BOB ROGERS	Cy Kendall
DR. BROOKS	Charles Trowbridge

"B" mystery about soldier Eddie Pratt smuggling his new wife Sally on an army base so that they can have their honeymoon. While looking for a quiet place where they can be alone they discover a dead body. Who done it?

FOOLS FOR SCANDAL
Released: April 16, 1938 (Warner Brothers)

CAST

KAY WINTERS	Carole Lombard
RENE	Fernand Gravet
PHILLIP CHESTER	Ralph Bellamy
DEWEY GELSON	Allen Jenkins
LADY PAULA MALVERTON	Isabel Jeans
MYRTLE	Marie Wilson
JILL	Marcia Ralston
AGNES	Tola Nesmith
LADY POTTER-PORTER	Heather Thatcher

Movie star Kay Winters is in Paris, incognito, and meets Rene who offers to show her "the real Paris." They fall in love. Into the mix , and in his usual sap role, is Ralph Bellamy as Phillip Chester, an insurance salesman who is also in love with Kay. Marie plays Lombard's maid, Myrtle, who is in charge of serving an engagement dinner for Kay and Phillip which Rene does his best to ruin. This "A" feature was directed by veteran Warner's director Mervyn LeRoy, just before he left and joined MGM. Leonard Maltin gives this film a **1/2 rating and calls it "generally a misfire."

BOY MEETS GIRL
Released: August 27, 1938 (Warner Brothers)

CAST

ROBERT LAW	James Cagney
J.C. BENSON	Pat O'Brien
SUSIE	Marie Wilson
C. ELLIOTT FRIDAY	Ralph Bellamy
ROSSETTI	Frank McHugh
LARRY TOMS	Dick Foran
RODNEY BEVIN	Bruce Lester
ANNOUNCER	Ronald Reagan
PEGGY	Penny Singleton

This film was widely considered to be Marie Wilson's big break. A comedy about two screen writers, Robert Law and J.C. Benson, assigned to write a story for a cowboy star, Larry Toms. However, nothing they write satisfies the films producer, C. Elliott Friday. They are inspired when a pregnant, divorced waitress, Susie (Wilson) arrives to deliver lunch. She inspires Law and Benson to come up with the idea of writing a western where Larry finds a lone baby. The baby is born and is signed to a studio contract in the movie that the screenwriters wrote and the baby becomes a big star. Susie and Larry are encouraged to marry by the studio even though they don't love each other—Susie is more taken with an English actor—Rodney Bevin. The film is based on a highly successful Broadway play which was produced by George Abbott. Marion Davies was considered for the leading lady role of Susie, but her lover, William Randolph Hearst believed the part was too racy for her image. Penny Singleton went on to play *Blondie* for several years in films and radio. Leonard Maltin gives this film **1/2 and writes that this "Screwball spoof of Hollywood sometimes pushes too hard, but has enough sharp dialogue, good satire."

BROADWAY MUSKETEERS
Released: October 8, 1938 (Warner Brothers)

CAST

ISABEL DOWLING	Margaret Lindsay
FAY REYNOLDS	Ann Sheridan
CONNIE TODD	Marie Wilson
STANLEY DOWLING	John Litel
JUDY DOWLING	Janet Chapman
VINCENT MORRELL	Dick Purcell
PHILLIP PAYTON	Richard Bond
GURK	Horace MacMahon

Isabel Dowling and Connie Todd grew up together in an orphanage; they are reunited when they arrive at the city jail to bail out another orphan, Fay Reynolds, who was arrested for doing a strip tease. Isabel is married to a wealthy man and has a daughter. Connie is a secretary who is in love with her boss. They all have birthdays in June and when Fay gets a job singing in a club, Connie and Isabel celebrate by coming to see her act. At the club, Isabel catches the eye of a gambler which leads to her leaving her husband—who, in turn, eventually falls in love with Fay. This film is a remake of another Warner's film *Three on a Match* which had starred Bette Davis (in the role which Marie plays) and Joan Blondell.

SWEEPSTAKES WINNER
Released: May 20, 1939 (Warner Brothers)

CAST

JENNIE JONES	Marie Wilson
MARK DOWNEY	Johnnie Davis
"TIP" BAILEY	Allen Jenkins
"JINX"	Charley Foy
NICK	Jerry Colonna
CHALKY WILLIAMS	Frankie Burkel
MRS. MCCARTHY	Vera Lewis

When her grandfather dies a waitress from Athens, Nebraska, Jennie Jones, inherits $1,000 and a old nag named "Firefly" which she travels to California with to race. However, before she can race the horse two conmen fleece her of her inheritance. Jennie thinks that she has lost everything and takes a job in a restaurant waiting tables. She soon finds out she has won $15,000 and can qualify for a jackpot of $150,000 if her horse wins the sweepstakes race. This leads to unscrupulous types trying to get their hands on her sweepstakes ticket.

WATERFRONT
Released: July 15, 1939 (Warner Brothers)

CAST

ANN STACEY	Gloria Dickson
JIM DOLEN	Dennis Morgan
RUBY WATERS	Marie Wilson
MARIE CORDELL	Sheila Bromley
FRANKIE DONAHUE	Larry Williams
FATHER DUNN	Aldrich Bowker
SKIDS RILEY	Frank Faylen
MART HENDLER	Ward Bond

When Longshoremen Jim Dolen and Mart Hendler, opponents for president of association of dockworkers get into a fight when Hendler refuses an order. Jim's friend Frankie Donahue tries to stop the fight, Jim slugs him and Frankie's head hits an anchor as he falls and Jim is jailed for assault. Father Dunn goes to the jail and speaks with Jim and the effect helps turns him around and he decides to marry his girlfriend Ann Stacey and settle down at a ranch. Jim even goes as far as to endorse Hendler for the presidency—but a drunken Hendler insults Jim in his acceptance speech which leads to the death of Jim's brother. Jim seeks vengeance on Hendler.

THE COWBOY QUARTERBACK
Released: July 29, 1939 (Warner Brothers)

CAST

HARRY LYNN	Bert Wheeler
MAIZIE WILLIAMS	Marie Wilson
EVELYN COREY	Gloria Dickson
RUSTY WALKER	William Demarest
STEVE ADAMS	Eddie Foy, Jr.
HANDSOME SAM	De Wolf Hopper
COL. MOFFETT	William Gould

Rusty Walker, a scout for the Chicago Packers football teams, hears about the football prowess of Harry Lynn who lives in Montana. Walker treks to Montana to sign Lynn as quarterback but runs into difficulty when Harry won't leave unless his sweetheart, Maizie Williams goes with him—he is afraid that Maizie will marry another local boy, Handsome Sam, if he leaves. Bert Wheeler is best known as one part of the comedy team Wheeler and Woolsey. Woolsey had died a few months before and this was Wheeler's first solo film.

SHOULD HUSBANDS WORK?
Released: July 26, 1939 (Republic)

CAST

Joe Higgins	James Gleason
Lil Giggins	Lucile Gleason
Sidney Higgins	Russell Gleason
Grandpa	Harry Davenport
Myrtle	Marie Wilson
Jean Higgins	Mary Hart
Tommy Giggins	Tommy Ryan
J.B. Barnes	Berton Churchill

Joe Higgins fears that he will lose his job with a cosmetics company when J.B. Barnes takes over the company. But Barnes soon offers Joe a job as general manager in Chicago. Joe's son Sidney is also elated since the company stock has increased enough so he can afford to marry his girl friends, Myrtle. But soon the good news turns bad and Joe loses his job and Sidney can no longer afford to marry Myrtle. When it turns out that too many men are competing for the same jobs, the women decide to seek work—thus the title, "Should husbands work?" being the 1930's the men eventually become the breadwinners again. Marie was borrowed by Republic from Warners, her home studio, to appear in this film.

VIRGINIA
Released: February 21, 1941 (Paramount)

CAST

CHARLOTTE DUNTERRY	Madeleine Carroll
STONEWALL JACKSON ELLIOTT	Fred MacMurray
NORMAN WILLIAMS	Sterling Hayden
THEO CLAIRMONT	Helen Broderick
PRETTY ELLIOTT	Carolyn Lee
CONNIE POTTER	Marie Wilson
JOSEPH	Darby Jones
THOMAS	Paul Hurst
CARTER FRANCIS	Tom Rutherford
EZECHIAL	Leigh Whipper
LOAFER	William D. Russell

Marie Wilson's first film after being released from her Warner Brothers contract. This is the story of Charlotte Dunterry who returns to her family home in Fairville, Virginia after living among "Yankees" in New York City for many years. She is now considered a city sophisticate who has forgotten her southern ways and plans to see her family home (which has become rundown). She meets up with an old friend Stonewall Jackson Elliott, whose wife lives abroad and he lives with his daughter, Pretty, in a nearby cottage. Through Stonewall and a former black servant, Joseph, who has returned to die at the Dunterry homestead he worked at for so long, Charlotte comes to appreciate the southern way of life and history. Marie Wilson is once again comedy relief, while Sterling Hayden (who later married Carroll) plays MacMurray's main competition. Leonard Maltin gives this film ** and writes that it is "well mounted but tedious."

ROOKIES ON PARADE
Released: April 17, 1941 (Republic)

CAST

DUKE WILSON	Bob Crosby
LOIS ROGERS	Ruth Terry
MARILYN FENTON	Gertrude Niesen
CLIFF DUGAN	Eddie Foy, Jr.
KITTY MULLOY	Marie Wilson
JOE MARTIN	Cliff Nazarro
MIKE BRADY	William Demarest
AUGUSTUS MOODY	Sidney Blackmer
TIGER BRANNIGAN	Horace MacMahon
BOB MADISON	William Wright

Pretty decent Republic musical about a song writing team (Crosby and Foy) who lose all their earnings by gambling. Duke's fiancée, chorus girl Lois Rogers calls off their engagement. Soon afterward the duo audition for Augustus Moody who hires them to write songs for a new play. Duke also gets a job as a singer for Lois, and they patch things up. Things take a turn when the song writing duo are drafted—and coincidentally their new sergeant is the husband of their former landlady (played by Demarest). Meanwhile, Lois and her friend Kitty Mulloy (Wilson) end up at the same camp entertaining the recruits.

FLYING BLIND
Released: August 29, 1941 (Paramount)

CAST

JIM CLARK	Richard Arlen
SHIRLEY BROOKS	Jean Parker
ERIC KAROLEK	Nils Asther
VERONICA GIMBLE	Marie Wilson
MISS DANILA	Kay Sutton
CHESTER GIMBLE	Grady Sutton
ROCKY DRAKE	Roger Pryor
RILEY	Eddie Quillan
BOB FULLER	Dick Purcell
MISS DANILA	Kay Suton

Aviator drama about Jim Clark who is fired from his job after he takes the blame for mistakes made by his co-pilot, Rocky Drake. Jim and a stewardess (Parker) form their own airline called Honeymoon Air Service, which makes round-trips flights from Los Angeles to Las Vegas for couples to marry and honeymoon.

Shirley loves Jim, and he loves her, but his work precludes romance and Shirley accepts a marriage proposal from Bob Fuller. Jealous and wanting to stop an immediate marriage Jim sends Bob away to Hackensack, NJ for a publicity job at a friends firm. Among the people making a honeymoon run to Las Vegas are Eric and Danila, who are actually foreign spies trying to steal a prototype transformer. Also on the run, are honeymooners Veronica and Chester Gimble (Wilson and Sutton).

HARVARD, HERE I COME
Released: December 18, 1941 (Columbia)

CAST

"SLAPSIE" MAXIE	··············	Maxie Rosenbloom
FRANCIE CALLAHAN	··············	Arline Judge
HARRISON CAREY	··············	Stanley Brown
HYPO MCGONIGLE	··············	Don Beddoe
ZELLA PHIPPS	··············	Marie Wilson
MISS FRISBIE	··············	Virginia Sale
EDDIE SPELLMAN	··············	Larry Parks
LARRY	··············	Lloyd Bridges
BATHING GIRL	··············	Yvonne DeCarlo

The Harvard Lampoon bestows a "special award" on nightclub owner "Slapsie" Maxie. Maxie is delighted but his friends believe he is being made a butt of an ivy-league joke. Their fears are realized when the award given to Maxie is for "Supreme Pediculousness"—or being infested with lice—which Slapsie happily accepts thinking since it is a big word it must be some prestigious honor. The next day the newspapers report on Maxie's humiliation, but rather than becoming angry, Maxie decides to enroll at Harvard and become educated. Marie plays undergrad, Zella Phipps, who falls for Slapsie.

BROADWAY
Released: May 8, 1942 (Universal)

CAST

GEORGE RAFT	··············	George Raft
DAN MCCORN	··············	Pat O'Brien
BILLIE MOORE	··············	Janet Blair
STEVE CRANDALL	··············	Broderick Crawford
LIL	··············	Marjorie Rambeau
PEARL	··············	Anne Gwynne
NICK	··············	S.Z. Sakall
GRACE	··············	Marie Wilson

DOLPH	Ralf Harolde
PETE DAILEY	Arthur Shields
ANN	Dorothy Moore
MACK (KILLER)	Mack Gray

George Raft plays himself, a Hollywood actor, who flies from Hollywood to New York with his friend and aide, Mack Gray (who plays himself). One day while walking the streets of Broadway, Raft discovers that "The Paradise" a night club he used to work at, is about to be converted into a Bowling alley. He then reminisces with the night watchman about the days when he worked there, the days of prohibition and gangsters. Crawford plays a ruthless gang lord. Leonard Maltin gave this film *** and writes that it is "full of colorful characters and incidents but not made with an eye towards believability."

SHE'S IN THE ARMY
Released: May 15, 1942 (Monogram)

CAST

SGT. HANNAH WINTERS	Lucille Gleason
SUSAN SLATTERY	Marie Wilson
DIANE JORDAN	Veda Ann Borg
LT. JIM RUSSELL	Robert Lowery
CAPT. STEVE RUSSELL	Lyle Talbot
BUCK SHANE	Warren Hymer
SAILOR	Eddie Acuff
HELEN BURKE	Charlotte Henry
WALLY LUNDIGAN	John Holland

To generate publicity for her nightclub act, debutante Diane Jordan enlists in an Army volunteer group, hoping to work for a week or two and then have the Flamingo nightclub request her return to sing for morale boosting purposes. Gossip columnist gets wind of the stunt and bets Diane $5,000 she can't last six weeks in the corps—a bet that Diane can't help but take. Diane enlists with the scatter-brained hat check girl Susan Slattery (played by Marie Wilson).

YOU CAN'T RATION LOVE
Released: 1944 (Paramount)

CAST

BETTY HAMMOND	Betty Rhodes
JOHN "TWO POINT" SIMPSON	Johnnie Johnston
MARIAN DOUGLAS	Marjorie Weaver
KEWPIE	Johnnie Scat Davis

BUBBLES KEENAN	Marie Wilson
PETE ALLEN	Bill Edwards
PICKLES	Roland Dupree
CHRISTINE	Christine Forsyth
MISS HAWKS	Sarah Edwards

SHINE ON HARVEST MOON
Released: April 8, 1944 (Warner Brothers)

CAST

NORA BAYES	Ann Sheridan
JACK NORWORTH	Dennis Morgan
THE GREAT GEORGETTI	Jack Carson
BLANCHE MALLORY	Irene Manning
POPPA KARL	S.Z. Sakall
MARGIE	Marie Wilson
DAN COSTELLO	Robert Shayne
DESK SARGEANT	Bob Murphy

Period musical, set in 1905 about a songwriter/performer Jack Worworth who is taken by a magician friend, The Great Georgetti, to see a singer named Nora Bayes, who performs at a local honey-tonk. Jack is impressed by Nora and offers her help breaking into vaudeville. This doesn't go over very well with the owner of the honky-tonk, Dan Costello. Eventually Nora and Jack marry and travel around the country performing to great success. But then Costello convinces club owners to blacklist the couple, and Jack and Nora hit hard times. Marie plays Margie, and assistant to the Great Georgetti.

MUSIC FOR MILLIONS
Released: December 21, 1944 (MGM)

CAST

MIKE	Margaret O'Brien
"BABS" AINSWORTH	June Allyson
ANDY	Jimmy Durante
ROSALIND	Marsha Hunt
UNCLE FERDINAND	Hugh Herbert
DOCTOR	Harry Davenport
MARIE	Marie Wilson
LARRY	Larry Adler
ELSA	Katharine Balfour
HELEN	Helen Gilbert
CONDUCTOR	Jose Iturbi

Seven-year old "Mike" travels to New York from her home in Connecticut to see her sister "Babs" who is a bassist in a Symphony orchestra. When "Mike" arrives at the symphony hall with a concert under way, she can't resist interrupting the concert to let her sister know she is there. This outrages conductor, Jose Iturbi—who's prepared to fire Babs. The quick witted stage manager, Andy, prevails on Iturbi to keep Babs, reminding him that many of the male members of the orchestra are fighting in the war, so they can't afford to lose Babs. Babs and her fellow female orchestra roommates sneak little Mike into their "no children" boarding house. Eventually, Babs finds out she is pregnant (her husband is off fighting the war too). Babs is in fragile condition and Mike and all of her roommates attempt to keep bad news from her, especially when a telegram comes regarding bad news about her husband. Eventually all turns out well, but the movie takes a sentimental turn with a scene which includes little Mike urging a tearful Babs to pray to God for the safe return of her husband. Marie plays a clarinet player, who also worries about "Babs" and instructs her alcoholic, petty crook Uncle Ferdinand to compose a letter supposedly from Bab's husband. This film was produced by Joe Pasternak and directed by Henry Koster, who would later direct Marie in her final feature film, *Mr. Hobbs Takes a Vacation*.

Young Widow
Released: March 1, 1946 (United Artists)

CAST

JOAN KENWOOD	Jane Russell
JIM CAMERON	Louis Hayward
GERRY TAYLOR	Jim Cameron
PETER WARING	Kent Taylor
MAC	Marie Wilson
AUNT CISSIE	Connie Gilchrist
AUNT EMELINE	Cora Witherspoon
SAMMY	Norman Lloyd
PEG MARTIN	Penny Singleton

Joan Kenwood's husband was killed during the war. She returns home to New York from England and is met at the dock by her old friend, Peter Waring, a managing editor of the newspaper that both she and her husband had formerly worked for. Peter offers Joan her old job, but she turns him down, deciding to stay instead with her two old aunts on their Virginia farm—as she is still haunted by her husband's death. Her stay in Virginia is short and she shortly thereafter returns to New York by train where a young Lieutenant (Jim Cameron) makes a pass at her which she rebuffs. While in New York Joan stays with a friend Peg, whose husband is on a submarine in the South Pacific and her roommate Mac (Marie) a man-crazy show girl. The infatuated Jim, finds out where Joan is staying and comes to see her where he insensitively suggests that she get on with her life. When Joan tells him that the man who he wants her to get over was her husband who died during the war, Jim leaves in shame. The next day Jim comes by to tell her he is leaving and apologizes and Joan accepts the apology and follows him to the train station, where he saves the life of a woman who falls on the tracks. Joan's old reporter instincts kick in and she writes up the story and gives it to Peter and accepts his invitation to return to the paper. The production of this film was quite interesting with filming beginning with Ida Lupino in the title role and taken off the picture. Producer Hunt Stromberg attempted to then talk Joan Fontaine into taking on the role, but she declined it, and finally Jane Russell was borrowed from Howard Hughes.

NO LEAVE, NO LOVE
Released: October 1, 1946 (MGM)

CAST
SGT. MICHAEL HANLON	Van Johnson
SLINKY	Keenan Wynn
SUSAN	Pat Kirkwood
ROSALIND	Marie Wilson
COL. ELLIOTT	Leon Ames
COUNTESS STROGOFF	Marina Koshetz
SELENA ROYLE	Mrs. Hanlon
MR. CRAWLEY	Wilson Wood
HOBARD CANFORD STILES	Edward Arnold/Guy Lombardo

Michael Hanlon is a World War II veteran living in New York, who rushes to the hospital when he learns that his wife, Susan, is delivering a baby. While he awaits the birth he tells another expectant father the story of how he met Susan during the war. Marie plays Rosalind the girl friend of "Slinky."

THE PRIVATE AFFAIRS OF BEL AMI
Released: March 7, 1947 (United Artists)

CAST
GEORGES DUROY	George Sanders
CLOTILDE	Angela Lansbury
MADELEINE FORESTIER	Ann Dvorack
CHARLES FORESTIER	John Carradine
SUZANNE	Susan Douglas
MONSIEUR WALTER	Hugo Haas
LAROCHE-MATHIER	Warren William
MARIE DE VARENNE	Frances Dee

RACHEL	Marie Wilson
MADAME WALTER	Katherine Emery
PHILIPPE DE CANTEL	Richard Fras

This film is an adaptation of the Guy de Maupassant novel about a man who uses sex to gain power. The setting is 1880's Paris. Ex-soldier Georges Duroy (Sanders) meets and old army comrade, Charles Forestier, who helps him get a job at a newspaper owned by Monsieur Walter. Soon Duroy is introduced into Paris society by Charles' young and beautiful wife Madeleine. One of the women who Duroy is introduced to is a young widow and mother named Clotilde de Marelle (Lansbury), who is the best friend of Madeleine. Through the help of Madeleine, Duroy, starts a gossip column called "Echoes" and he will use this position and the dirt he discovers on prominent citizens to gain favor and power. Duroy and Clotilde eventually fall in love and plan to marry, but then Clotilde discovers that at the Folies Bergere that Georges has been involved with a young dancer (Wilson)—and realizes that Duroy will never be faithful to her—she breaks it off with him. When Charles Forestier dies, Duroy takes advantage of the situation marries Madeleine—but tells Clotilde that it is "a marriage of convenience" and that his love for her has not dimmed. From there he seduces several prominent women to gain power and wealth—until it finally catches up with him and Duroy is challenged to a duel by the husband of one of his conquests—and is mortally wounded—as he is dying he murmurs that he could have been happy with Clotilde.

Leonard Maltin gives this film ***1/2 and calls it a "Delicious, literate adaptation" of the novel, with a "fine gallery of performances."

THE FABULOUS JOE
Released: August 29, 1947 (Hal Roach Studios)

CAST
MILO TERKEL	Walter Abel
EMILY TERKEL	Margot Grahame
GORGEOUS GILMORE	Marie Wilson
HENRY CADWALLADER	Donald Meek
LOUIE	Sheldon Leonard
GEORGE BAXTER	Howard Petrie
MRS. BELMONT	Nana Bryant

After twenty-years of marriage, Milo and Emily Terkel are in the middle of a divorce proceedings and Milo is explaining to the court how their marriage fell apart. Through flashbacks he tells the story of the previous July on his anniversary, Milo returned home from his bank job carrying an expensive necklace for his wife. His wife is not at home, and Milo is forced to have dinner at his club, and with him is his dog, full name being Joseph McMasters, "The Fabulous Joe" of the title. while at the club he defends the honor of a young woman named Gorgeous Gilmore—after his dog Joe "tells" him to be a brute "like Humphrey Bogart." This leads to his wife telling him that the family will not tolerate his "brutal and abusive behavior" any longer. One thing leads to another with Gorgeous' boyfriend convinced that Milo has been corrupting his girlfriend and Milo taking advice from his dog "The Fabulous Joe."

LINDA, BE GOOD
Released: November 8, 1947 (Cameo Productions)

CAST

LINDA PRENTISS	Elyse Knox
ROGER PRENTISS	John Hubbard
MARGIE LaVITTE	Marie Wilson
SAM THOMPSON	Gordon Richards
JIM BENSON	Jack Norton
NUNNALLY LaVITTE	Ralph Sanford
MRS. LA VITTE	Joyce Compton
OFFICER JONES	Alan Nixon

Authoress Linda Prentiss returns home to New York City after conducting research for her latest book on the psychology of Eskimos in Alaska. Her husband, Roger urges her to give up her writing career to concentrate on being a wife, so they can start a family. When attending a book signing, Linda meets a burlesque dancer Margie La Vitte (Wilson), who saves the life of the bookshop owner from a holdup by a gangster whom she knows. Margie suggests that Linda join her dancing troupe in order to gain "life experiences" for her writing. This leads to one adventure after another, and leads to Linda writing a best seller titled, "I Was a Burlesque Queen." (the working title of this film). Wilson met her future husband Alan Nixon, who has a small part as a police officer, on this film.

MY FRIEND IRMA
Released: October 14, 1949 (Paramount)

CAST

IRMA PETERSON	Marie Wilson
AL	John Lund
JANE STACEY	Diana Lynn
RICHARD RHINELANDER	Don Defore
STEVE	Dean Martin
SEYMOUR	Jerry Lewis

PROFESSOR KROPOTKIN	Hans Conried
MRS. RHINELANDER	Kathryn Givney
MRS. O'REILLY	Gloria Gordon

This film should have been Marie Wilson's second big break in motion pictures (after *Boy Meets Girl*). After all it was based on her very popular radio series and she was the lead—except that two brash young nightclub performers making their film debuts stole the film from under her and went on to highly successful careers. The plot is the same as the radio series; Jane Stacey's perky, sweet, but dimwitted friend Irma (Wilson) constantly creates problems due to her stupidity. She has a fiancé, Al, who has been unemployed for four years. One day Irma is taken by the singing voice of Steve Laird (Martin) who runs an orange juice stand with his loony partner Seymour (Lewis). Al appoints himself Steve and Seymour's partner and moves the boys into Jane and Irma's apartment. Jane, unaware of what happened is furious to have two men rooming with them. Jane is in love with her employer, wealthy investment broker Richard Rhinelander III (Defore), whom she hopes to marry. But Steve complicates matters by falling in love with Jane—but she resists his advances and is true to Richard. Jane uses her connections to Richard to advance Steve's career by introducing him to a Broadway producer. Seymour meanwhile is unhappy because he isn't included in all of this—after all he is Steve's partner. But Steve rejects this because he loves Jane and doesn't want to take charity from Richard. He and Seymour return to their orange juice stand. Irma misunderstands what is going on and comes to consider her friend Jane a gold digger—only interested in Richard's money and this leads to more problems. This film includes many actors from the radio show (Wilson, Conried and Gordon) but playing Jane is not Cathy Lewis, but Paramount contractee, Diana Lynn, who was deemed more "attractive for the screen" than her radio counterpart. Nevertheless, the film is completely stolen by newcomers Martin and Lewis with the *New York Times* signaling out Lewis in particular, "a new comedian, Jerry Lewis . . . is the funniest thing in this film." (One big change from the radio show is that Jane ends up with Steve rather than her radio love interest Richard Rhinelander III).

MY FRIEND IRMA GOES WEST
Released: July 4, 1950 (Paramount)

CAST
IRMA PETERSON	Marie Wilson
AL	John Lund
STEVE LAIRD	Dean Martin
SEYMOUR	Jerry Lewis
YVONNE YVONNE	Corinne Calvet

JANE STACEY	....	Diana Lynn
SHARPIE	....	Lloyd Corrigan
MR. BRENT	....	Donald Porter
PETE	....	Harold Huber
SLIM	....	Joseph Vitale

In New York City, Irma and Jane learn that Jane's boyfriend, Steve, who still works at the orange juice stand with his partner Seymour, will be a featured singer on a television program that night. Steve is asked to sing a duet with the sexy French singer Yvonne Yvonne (Calvet). Steve is paid not by money but by being given twelve cans of spaghetti! This leads Jane to replace Irma's boyfriend Al as his manager. Jane finds a new manager, who turns out to be an imposter—but not before Irma, Al, Steve, Jane and Seymour board a train going to the west coast, paying their own fares—where they believe that a movie deal is waiting for Steve in Hollywood. This film was quickly put into production when it became apparent that the original film released nine months earlier was a huge box office success. Martin and Lewis have enhanced parts—and are even more of the focus in this sequel than they were in the original film.

A GIRL IN EVERY PORT
Released: January, 1952 (RKO)

CAST

BENNY LINN	....	Groucho Marx
JANE SWEET	....	Marie Wilson
TIM DUNNOVAN	....	William Bendix
BERT SEDGWICK	....	Don Defore
DOC GARVEY	....	Gene Lockhart
MILLICENT TEMPLE	....	Dee Hartford
NAVY LIEUTENANT	....	Hanley Stafford

This film is of chief interest because it is one of the few films to feature Groucho Marx away from the classic Marx Brothers. Groucho plays Benny, a conniving sailor whose buddy—the dimwitted Tim, inherits $1,450 and uses the money to buy a racehorse. Their superior officer gives Benny and Tim five days to clear up the matter (after all they can't have a race horse on a navy ship). Marie Wilson plays, Jane Sweet, who works as a carhop, and is the owner of the sister of the horse which Tim bought. She is as dimwitted as Tim, but attempts to "help" them get rid of the horse, but soon it is discovered that the horse is a potential winner, which changes everything. Leonard Maltin gives this film ** and writes that a "good cast is wasted."

NEVER WAVE AT A WAC
Released: January 28, 1953 (RKO)

CAST

JO MCBAIN	Rosalind Russell
ANDREW MCBAIN	Paul Douglas
CLARA SCHNEIDERMAN AKA "DANGER O'DOWD"	Marie Wilson
"SKY" FAIRCHILD	William Ching
SGT. TONI WAYNE	Arleen Whelan
SGT. NORBERT JACKSON	Leif Erickson
PHYLLIS TURNBULL	Hillary Brooke
GEN. NED PRAGER	Regis Toomey

Russell plays a Washington socialite, Jo McBain, the daughter of a Senator who learns that her boyfriend, Lt. Col. Schuyler "Sky" Fairchild, is being transferred to Paris to participate in SHAPE. It turns out Sky is being accompanied by Phyllis Turnbull, a flirtatious and beautiful blonde who may have designs on Sky. With this knowledge Jo announces she is going to Paris too. Eventually Jo joins the WACS so that she can be sent to Paris and protect her love interest. Jo enlists and is sent to basic training at Fort Lee, Virginia, where she befriends another WAC, a former show girl who was known as "Danger O' Dowd" (Wilson). Danger or Clara (her given name) is impressed by Jo's sophistication and wants to learn from her. Jo learns that strings were not pulled for her, and she will be treated no different than any other recruit. This movie could have inspired the 1980 Goldie Hawn hit *Private Benjamin*, which had a similar storyline about a spoiled rich woman who joins the service. Leonard Maltin gives this film **1/2 and writes that "Wilson as dumb comrade-at-arms is most diverting."

MARRY ME AGAIN
Released: October 22, 1953 (RKO)

CAST

BILL ANDERSON	Robert Cummings
DORIS DOOLITTLE	Marie Wilson
MAC	Ray Walker
JOAN PAXTON	Mary Costa
EDDIE JENKINS	Jess Barker
MR. TAYLOR	Lloyd Corrigan
COURTNEY	Moroni Olsen
DR. DAY	Frank Cady
BOB THOMAS	Himself

During the Korean War, Bill Anderson, a gas station attendant and legal secretary

Doris Doolittle are about to be married in a San Fernando, California chapel, Bill receives a summons from the Defense Department and must leave without completing the ceremony. Bill becomes a fighter pilot and is highly decorated. He returns home and is given a hero's welcome from the townspeople. Bill and Doris plan to hold the wedding, but without Bill's knowledge, Doris has inherited $1,000,000. Doris is afraid to tell Bill because he has always said he would be the sole breadwinner of his family. On the day of the wedding, by mistake, Bill finds out about Doris' windfall and when he arrives at the chapel—he calls off the wedding accusing her of making him out to be a fool. Eventually love conquers all and Bill and Doris do marry. This is one of Frank Tashlin's early directorial efforts. He later went on to direct Jerry Lewis in eight films. The Associate producer is Bob Fallon, who was married to Marie Wilson by this time.

THE STORY OF MANKIND
Released: November 9, 1957 (Warner Brothers)

CAST

SPIRIT OF MAN	Ronald Colman
JOAN OF ARC	Hedy Lamarr
PETER MINUIT	Groucho Marx
ISSAC NEWTON	Harpo Marx
MONK	Chico Marx
CLEOPATRA	Virginia Mayo
QUEEN ELIZABETH I	Agnes Moorehead
MR. SCRATCH	Vincent Price
NERO	Peter Lorre
HIPPOCRATES	Charles Coburn
HIGH JUDGE	Sir Cedric Hardwicke
SPANISH ENVOY	Cesar Romero
MARIE ANTOINETTE	Marie Wilson
KHUFU	John Carridine
SIR WALTER RALEIGH	Edward Everett Horton
WILLIAM SHAKESPEARE	Reginald Gardiner
NAPOLEON	Dennis Hopper
JOESPHINE	Marie Windsor

Excellent cast in an intriguing story about two angels, appearing as stars in the heavens, discuss how man has invented the super H-bomb sixty years ahead of schedule. A high tribunal of outer space is called into session to determine whether to prevent the bomb from detonating or allow it to go off. To present a defense is the Spirit of Man (Colman) and the prosecution is headed by Mr. Scratch (aka the Devil, played by Price) Both The Spirit of Man and Mr. Scratch present deeds of famous historical figures to support his case.

MR. HOBBS TAKES A VACATION
Released: June 15, 1962 (Twentieth Century Fox)

CAST

ROGER HOBBS	James Stewart
PEGGY HOBBS	Maureen O'Hara
JOE	Fabian
KATEY	Lauri Peters
JANIE	Lili Gentle
BYRON	John Saxton
MARTIN TURNER	John McGiver
EMILY TURNER	Marie Wilson
REGGIE McHUGH	Reginald Gardiner

Mr. Hobbs, a banker, who wants nothing more than a quiet vacation with his wife, who dashes those plans when she insists they take the entire family for "togetherness" to the seashore. From the beginning things go wrong, the seaside cottage is dilapidated, the cook leaves them, son wants to watch television rather than enjoy the ocean, and daughter is shy because of new braces on her teeth. The neighbors "The Turners" (McGiver and Wilson) are jolly alcoholics who live next door. Leonard Maltin gives this film **1/2 and calls it "Ultra-wholesome family fare." Wilson's last film. For many years Marie had a dog she named "Mr. Hobbs."

**Marie Wilson goes Hawaiian in an early publicity photograph, 1934.
(Courtesy of Andrew Pepoy)**

Marie in publicity pose from 1935. (Courtesy of Andrew Pepoy)

Marie showing in a cheesecake pose, circa 1935. (Courtesy of Andrew Pepoy)

Marie and fellow Warner Bros. contract player, Jane Wyman, circa 1936.
(Courtesy of Andrew Pepoy)

An exotic looking Marie, circa 1937. (Courtesy of Andrew Pepoy)

A pouty Marie in a publicity photograph for the film, *Virginia* (1941).
(Courtesy of Andrew Pepoy)

Marie in a publicity photograph for the film, *Harvard Here I Come* (1942). (Courtesy of Andrew Pepoy)

Marie as she appears in the 1942 film, *Broadway*. (Courtesy of Andrew Pepoy)

Marie reclining in a mid-'40s publicity photograph. (Courtesy of Andrew Pepoy)

Ohh-la-la. (Courtesy of Andrew Pepoy)

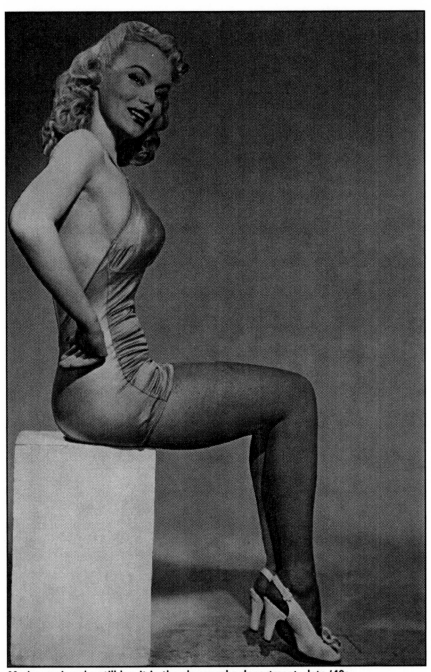

Marie proving she still has it in the cheesecake department—late '40s. (Courtesy of Andrew Pepoy)

Marie as the wide-eyed, lovable but dim-witted Irma. (Courtesy of Andrew Pepoy)

Irma and Jane (Cathy Lewis), late 1940s. (Courtesy of Andrew Pepoy)

Marie in a CBS publicity photograph, 1950. (Courtesy of Andrew Pepoy)

Marie with William Bendix and Groucho Marx in *A Girl in Every Port*, **1952.**
(Courtesy of Andrew Pepoy)

Two more publicity stills from *A Girl in Every Port*. (Courtesy of Andrew Pepoy)

Marie with her beloved dog, Hobbs (early '50s). (Courtesy of Andrew Pepoy)

Still a knockout—reunited with *The Blackouts* in the late '50s.
(Courtesy of Andrew Pepoy)

Nothing to hide—Marie with *The Blackouts*, late '50s. (Courtesy of Andrew Pepoy)

BIBLIOGRAPHY
SELECTED SOURCES

MAGAZINE ARTICLES

Colliers
"Little Miss Innocent," 2/23/46
"Oh, You Beautiful Blonde," 4/2/49

Coronet
"My Friend Irma Is Not so Dumb," November, 1950.

Dramatics
"My Friend Irma" by Si Mills, October, 1950.

Film Collectors Registry
"Marie Wilson" by Charles Stumpf, May, 1975.

Hollywood
"How to Live on Practically Nothing," by Joe Di Eddye, April, 1938.

Life
"Irma Is a Lady," 8/14/50.

The Philadelphia Inquirer Magazine
"Marie Wilson: Rich Little Dumb Girl," 9/11/49.

The Photoplayer
"Dizzy Blonde, But Not So Dumb," by Mary Powers, 9/3/49.

Photoplay
"Lovely Funny Face," June, 1936.
"The Marie Wilson Story," By Pauline Swanson, October, 1949.

Pictorial Review
"I Married Irma" by Robert Fallon (as told to John Maynard), 8/30/53.
"Home Is Sweet to Hollywood's Smartest Dumbell," by Louella Parsons, 1/30/55.

Radio Mirror
"Come and Visit Marie Wilson," By Viola Moore.

Screen Guide Magazine
"Maybe I'm Dumber Than I Think," by Marie Wilson, 1952.

Stage
"Susie to a T," by Douglas Churchill, October, 1938.

Time
"California Gold Mine," 2/12/45.
"Dizzy Blonde," 10/20/47.

TV Magazine
"Big Hearted Blonde," 8/1/54.

TV Star Parade
"Irma's Other Life," 9/52.

Variety
Vaudeville Tour Reviews, 8/30/39, 10/18/39, 11/8/38, 12/27/39, 1/31/40.
My Friend Irma radio show reviews, 9/1/48, 8/31/49, 9/19/51,12/9/52.
My Friend Irma television show reviews, 1/10/52, 10/8/52.
Skully's Scrapbook, 7/6/48.
Obituary, 11/29/72.

NEWSPAPER ARTICLES

Christian Science Monitor
"My Friend Irma to Introduce Radio Character to Screen," 3/25/49.

Los Angeles Herald Examiner
"Marie Wilson to Ask Divorce," 10/1/50
"Marie Wilson Protests: Vivisection 'All Wrong,'" 10/22/50.

Los Angeles Mirror
"Marie Wilson to Star in Three One-Acters," 9/24/50
"Circle Scores Thrice in 'Three Out of Four,'" 9/30/50.

"Marie Keeps Rollin' Along," 11/6/50.
"When They See Marie, Boys Will Talk," 7/13/51.
"Drape Shape," 1/4/56.

Los Angeles Times
"One-Track Mind Keeps Marie Wilson on the Job," 12/16/45.
"Secrets of Her Beauty Told by Marie Wilson," 10/1/50.
"Marie Wilson Chosen Police Department Sweetheart," 3/23/53.
Obituary, 11/24/72.

Newark Evening News
"Marie Wilson is a Hit," 7/12/61.

New York Daily Mirror
"Star To Go Under Knife," 3/6/37.
"Marie Wilson to Wed Director," 8/11/38.
"Tin Types," 8/24/38.

New York Daily News
"The Ayes . . . And Eyes . . . Have It," 12/15/51.
"Marie Explains Shape She's In — Doesn't Diet," 11/20/52.
"Marie Gives Baby Back to Mother," 10/8/57.

New York Herald Tribune
Radio Review, 3/22/48.
"How I Became a Star," 10/9/49.
"Marie Wilson Has Relapse," 5/16/51.
"My Friend Irma Review (TV-series), 2/1/52.
"Marie Wilson Adopts Baby," 12/1/55.
"Marie Wilson Giving Up Baby She Hoped to Adopt," 10/16/57.
"Ernestine Series May Be Out in '59," 8/27/58.
"Marie Wilson Puzzled Over Comeback Delay," 2/24/60.

New York Journal American
"Coed Sues Marie Wilson For Return of Her Baby," 10/16/57.

New York Post
Obituary, 11/24/72.
"Will Debbie Be a Bride Again?" 9/1/76

New York Times
"Marie Wilson Gets Leading role in *Boy Meets Girl*," 1/21/38.
"Marie Wilson To Be In 'Dulcy,'" 7/21/38.

"Marie Wilson Chosen for 'Horses, Horses, Horses,'" 11/19/38.
"Groucho, Marie Wilson, William Bendix appear in 'They Sell Sailors Elephants,'" 11/20/50.
"Marie Wilson Gets Divorce," 12/30/50
"Marie Wilson Improving," 5/16/51
"Marie Wilson to be Wed," 12/12/51
Review of *My Friend Irma* (TV), 1/11/52.
"Marie Wilson Adopts Child," 12/1/55
"Desilu Planning Six New Series," 11/12/56
Obituary, 11/24/72.

New York World Telegram
"Marie Wilson Wearies of Playing Dumb Blonde," 10/8/36.
"This Dumb Blonde Not So Dumb," 7/5/44.
"Marie Wilson in New Role," 1/27/53.
"Marie Wilson Stars as Preferred Blonde," 6/22/62.

PM
"Marie Wilson Tops 'Em All," 6/28/44.

BOOKS

Cagney by Cagney, by James Cagney, Doubleday, 1976.

Cagney, by Richard Schickel, Applause Books, 1999.

Dean and Me: A Love Story, by Jerry Lewis, Doubleday, 2005

Debbie, by Debbie Reynolds and David Patrick Columbia, Pocket Books, 1988.

Design for Living: Alfred Lunt & Lynn Fontanne, by Margot Peters, Knopf, 2003.

Fasten Your Seat Belts: The Passionate Life of Bette Davis, by Lawrence J. Quirk, William Morrow & Co., 1990.

Genius of the System: Hollywood Filmmaking in the Studio Era, by Thomas Schatz, Henry Holt & Co., 1988.

Jane Russell: My Path & My Detours, Franklin Watts, 1985.

Jane Wyman: A Biography, by Joe Morella & Edward Epstein, Delacorte Press, NY, 1985.

Judy Holliday: An Intimate Life Story, by Gary Carey, Putnum, 1984.

King of Comedy: The Life and Art of Jerry Lewis, by Shawn Levy, St Martin's Press, 1996.

Life on a Pogo Stick: The Autobiography of a Comedian, by Ken Murray, Holt, Rinehart & Winston, Inc., 1960.

Mother Goddam, by Whitney Stine with Bette Davis, Berkley Books, NY, 1974.

Movie and Video Guide, 1992, by Leonard Maltin, Plume, 1992.

On The Air: The Encyclopedia of Old Time Radio, by John Dunning, Oxford University Press, 1998.

Starmaker: The Autobiography of Hal Wallis, by Hal Wallis, MacMillan, 1980.

Those Crazy Wonderful Years When We Ran Warner Brothers, by Stuart Jerome, Lyle Stuart, 1983.

Warner Brothers Story, by Clive Hirschorn, Random House, 1987.

Wind at My Back: The Life and Times of Pat O'Brien, by Pat O'Brien, Doubleday, 1964.

INDEX

Breinigsville, PA USA
12 December 2009
229088BV00001B/57/A